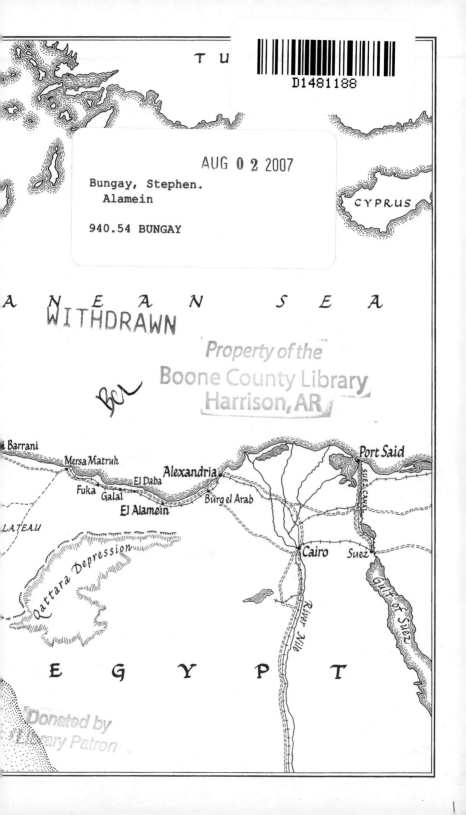

TU

D1481188

CYPRUS

A N E A N   S E A

Barrani
Mersa Matruh
El Daba   Alexandria
Fuka Galal   Burg el Arab   Port Said
   El Alamein   SUEZ CANAL
LATEAU
      Qattara Depression
   Qattara Depression   Cairo   Suez

                                                   Gulf of Suez
                                         River Nile

E   G   Y   P   T

ALAMEIN

ALA

ALAMEIN

STEPHEN BUNGAY

AURUM PRESS

First published in Great Britain
2002 by Aurum Press Ltd
25 Bedford Avenue, London WC1B 3AT

A catalogue record for this book is available from the British Library.

ISBN 1 85410 842 5

1 3 5 7 9 10 8 6 4 2
2002 2004 2006 2005 2003

Text design and table on p. 65 by Roger Hammond
Maps by Reginald Piggott
Typeset in 11/13.5pt Minion by YHT Ltd, London
Printed by MPG Books, Bodmin

CONTENTS

Maps

Table

List of illustrations

I

THE
STRATEGIC
WAR

THE MIDDLE EAST, JOURNALISTS SAY, is a powder keg. The Middle East, diplomats say, is strategically vital to every major power outside it. The Middle East, historians will tell you, has been fought over since men learned to bear arms. The first battle of recorded time took place at Megiddo in what is now Israel in 1469 BC. The losers suffered 83 casualties.[1] Despite this modest beginning, it became the scene of repeated belligerent encounters and is thought to be behind the name given in the Bible's Apocalypse to the final battle between good and evil: Armageddon.

To the north and east of this first battlefield, in what used to be called Asia Minor, Assyrians fought Babylonians, Hittites fought Egyptians, Persians fought Lydians and Trojans fought Greeks. Far to the west of it, across Spain and Italy and in what is now Tunisia, Romans fought Carthaginians for 150 years. In 1918 Megiddo became a battlefield once more. There, a British army under General Allenby, abetted by an Arab force under Colonel T. E. Lawrence, decisively defeated their Turkish opponents, in a campaign which resulted in control of Palestine moving from the Ottoman to the British Empire. But in between, one stretch of rocky, scrub-strewn sand was not stained with blood. It consisted of the northern coast of

Libya and the part of Egypt west of the Nile valley known as the Western Desert. It was not fought over because there was nothing to fight for, and armies could not live there.[2] There was no food and little water. There were no people. Just sand, rock and flies.

Until 1940. In the 3,400 years which had passed since the first battle at Megiddo, man's ingenuity had enabled him to live, for a time, in this wilderness. And where he could live, he could kill. From December 1940, for over two years, over a million men from ten far-away countries fought here, and more than 50,000 of them died.[3] Their deeds and sufferings captured the imagination of the world.

For two years it was the only theatre of World War II in which a British army was able to engage a German one. Its significance grew out of all proportion to its scale. On both sides, reporters flocked out to witness it. They were captivated by the haunting landscape and the fighting men of the desert, who flouted military conventions in their attitudes and their dress. In this little corner of an industrial war that consumed nameless millions, they found individuals and heroes, chivalry and romance. The fighting was personalised, and portrayed as a battle of wits between the commanders, whom the journalists turned into popular celebrities. The different nationalities of the soldiers put a colourful panoply of characters onto the stage in a variegated chorus around the heroes. National characteristics found gratifying affirmation. The reporters' copy was full of clever, methodical Germans, excitable, unsteady Italians, tough Australians and wiry New Zealanders, exotic Indians and gallant Free French. The British found their class system reflected in portraits of dour, long-suffering Tommies and their languid, fox-hunting officers. The desert war produced more household names and more legends than any other campaign.

This war was dominated by machines: by guns, trucks and, above all, by tanks. The fighting was more like war at sea than war on land. Possession of territory counted for little, with tanks manoeuvring like ships of the age of sail and loosing off their guns at each other across the desert's empty expanse. The pounding of heavy seas on planking and rigging was replaced by the grinding of rocks on tracks and grit on gears. Blinding salt spray on the faces of captains was replaced by clouds of dust in the eyes of commanders. Tank battles were interrupted by sand storms rather than gales. They were becalmed by lack of petrol rather than lack of wind. To abandon a vehicle in the open desert was to be adrift in the ocean. There had never been anything like it before.

As the fighting ebbed and flowed east and west across the desert the two sides seemed evenly matched. The tide finally eddied into a funnel of land in Egypt where it lapped up around a succession of rocky ridges and depressions running between the sea and an impassable depression some forty miles south. The end of that funnel was the only place in the desert where the southern flank could not be turned, forcing the armies to meet head-on. There, for four months, the two sides sallied out to fire broadsides at each other and retire, until, in October 1942, they fought the battle which finally decided the desert war.

This one was not like the other battles. There would be no squadrons of tanks scudding across open expanses. There was little manoeuvre. Infantry and gunners would dominate the action, while the desert ships fought at anchor. It was to be a battle of deliberate attrition, conducted in a way a veteran of World War I would have recognized. Its designer was a peculiar little man who had never commanded an army in battle before. It made him the desert's last great celebrity. It was not a very big battle by the standards of the war, but it was a battle he, his army and his country had to win. For the western Allies it would become a signpost in the history of the war, marking the point at which the path of defeat turned into the road to victory. The place where it was to be fought got its name from a sleepy little railway station near the coast. It was called El Alamein. What was it that brought all these people here?

It all began because two of the protagonists were already there. In 1912 Italy wrested possession of the north African colonies of Tripolitania and Cyrenaica from the Ottoman Empire, and merged them in 1934 to form its own colony of Libya. Britain had turned Egypt into a 'protectorate' during World War I to keep it out of the hands of the Turks and use it as a base for its operations in the Middle East. Technically Egypt was an independent state bound by agreements with Britain over the use of its territory for military bases. In practice, Egypt was a reluctant colony. When the European war broke out in 1939, the Egyptian government officially remained neutral.[4] Through Egypt flowed the waters of the Suez Canal, and beyond it, in Arabia, flowed oil.

On 10 June 1940, just after the German Army had ejected the British Army from continental Europe at Dunkirk and was in the process of finally defeating the remains of the French Army, the Italian leader Mussolini declared war on France and Britain.

Hitler had long admired Mussolini. Mussolini began his political career as a socialist, but the Italian Socialist Party expelled him in November 1914. In the turmoil of the 1920s, he became the first Fascist dictator to come to power in Europe. By dint of the violent activities of his black-shirted paramilitary gangs called *'fasci di combattimento'*, culminating in a march on Rome, he had forced the King to make him Prime Minister of Italy in 1922. In 1925 he imposed a dictatorship, calling himself 'Il Duce' – 'Leader'. On coming to power in 1933, Hitler adopted the same title – 'der Führer'. After both Germany and Italy had supported the Fascist General Franco in the Spanish Civil War, the two countries signed a secret protocol in Berlin on 21 October 1936. In a speech on 1 November, Mussolini referred to this agreement as forming an axis around which all the other European powers which desired peace and collaboration could work together. Italy and Germany thus became known as the 'Axis' powers. Despite his generals' misgivings about Italy's armed forces, Hitler wanted to make the Axis a military alliance. He got his way on 22 May 1939 when, at Mussolini's sudden instigation, the two countries signed the 'Pact of Steel', whereby the two 'high contracting parties' solemnly agreed to come to each others' assistance if either should suffer the misfortune of becoming embroiled in some sort of warlike complications.[5]

Mussolini never got as much blood on his hands as Hitler did, but his methods were brutal. In 1936, he sent a whole series of messages to his generals in Abyssinia demanding that they show more ruthlessness, and execute prisoners. His forces there were the only ones to employ mustard gas since World War I. He wanted war from the very beginning. His ambition was to turn Italy into a great power and a nation of warriors and he needed a war to toughen them up. While Hitler carried out his social revolution *before* embarking on hostilities, Mussolini saw a war as the only context in which his social revolution could be carried out. It would serve to sweep away his enemies in the Church, the monarchy and the comfort-loving bourgeoisie, all of whom could inhibit his plans for creating a modern Roman empire. The core of the empire was to be the

Mediterranean. He pursued these ambitions consistently within the constraints imposed by the Italian economy and the state of its armed forces. It was all a matter of timing.[6]

Mussolini knew that his army would not be trained or equipped to fight a European war before 1942, but Hitler was threatening to run off with all the prizes in 1940 and given the rate at which the Germans were going there was a good chance the Italian Army would not have to do much fighting anyway. But it had to do some, or the Berlin-Rome Axis would be too top-heavy. Whilst it was 'absurd and impossible', Mussolini opined, that Italy would stay out of the war, her entry had to be 'retarded as much as possible, consistent with honour and dignity' to give her time to prepare, so that her entry would be decisive.[7] As France collapsed, he felt he had to get off the fence. At 18:00 on 10 June 1940, speaking from the Palazzo Venezia, he told his countrymen that he had decided to fight 'the plutocratic and reactionary democracies of the West' in order to resolve the problems of Italy's maritime frontiers. The conflict, he said, would pitch 'young and prolific nations against sterile and declining ones'. It would be a war between 'two centuries and two ideas'.[8] He entered the war as much for internal as external reasons, for he never completely suppressed political opposition in Italy. A war would sweep away the 'revolting craven bourgeoisie' and others who just wanted a comfortable life.[9] Determined to shape the Italian people into his chosen image, he pushed them in at the deep end, forcing them to sink or swim. They sank.

At a meeting with Hitler at the Brenner Pass in the Alps in October 1940, Mussolini laid out his plans for an Italian empire spanning the Mediterranean, which he regarded as 'mare nostrum' ('our sea'). Those plans not only involved the young and prolific Germans giving him bits of French North Africa, but also the sterile and declining British allowing him to overrun Egypt.

The British decided not to do the latter and the Germans were cool about the former as well. The French had three colonies along the Mediterranean coastline: Tunisia and Algeria which abutted Libya, and Morocco, tantalizingly separated from the British naval base of Gibraltar by a strip of coastline belonging to Spain called Spanish Morocco. After the fall of France, the Germans set up a puppet government under the French World War I hero, General Pétain. It was based at the town of Vichy in central France, and the

Germans were quite content for the Vichy Government to rule all three of the French colonies.

The Italians had two armies in Libya, the Fifth in the west and the Tenth in the east, totalling about 236,000 men. On 13 September 1940, the Tenth Army, with about 135,000 men under the command of a reluctant Marshal Graziani, obeyed their Duce's orders and crossed the Libyan border into Egypt, where they ran into the 50,000 British, Indian and Australian troops of the Imperial Army of the Nile. The Army of the Nile was indeed imperial. In all the British Army's campaigns in Africa, more than half, and in these early stages, almost all of the infantry were provided by the Dominions and other countries of the British Empire. The armoured units were predominantly manned by troops from the mother country. Of the thirteen infantry divisions which fought at various times in the desert between 1940 and 1942, only four were British. Of the remaining nine, three were Indian (which contained some British battalions), three Australian, two South African and one from New Zealand. Two of the eight infantry divisions of Graziani's Tenth Army were Libyan.[10] The desert war began as a clash between two empires.

British forces in Egypt came under the Commander-in-Chief Middle East, General Sir Archibald Wavell, whose responsibilities encompassed the old commands of Sudan and Palestine as well. Wavell's demesne was not only vast but diverse and politically volatile. In June 1940, Wavell had instructed his commander in Egypt, General Wilson, to deal with the potential threat from the Italians by preparing for the invasion of Libya. Wilson put together two divisions, 7th Armoured and 4th Indian, (replaced after some days by 6th Australian) about 30,000 men, under General Richard O'Connor, and called it the 'Western Desert Force'. On 9 December, still wearing the Italian Silver Medal for Valour which he had won fighting alongside the Italians in 1918, O'Connor attacked on what was scheduled to be a five-day raid. O'Connor recalled that his instructions were 'very sketchy'. He did not object, however, as he did not mind being left on his own.[11]

Four days later Graziani's army re-crossed the Libyan frontier in the opposite direction, with O'Connor in hot pursuit. On 14 December, Graziani wrote a letter to Mussolini containing the following somewhat metaphysical appreciation of his position and intentions: 'Now, Duce, there is only one arbiter, destiny, to whose superior powers I cannot oppose anything but my own mortal ones which I continue to use to animate myself and all others up to the last moment. I am suffering the consequences of a state of affairs created not by my blindness or my will, but by those of all those who have miserably betrayed you, and with you, Italy.'[12] Whilst Graziani was thus engaged in updating Verdi librettos, the retiring Anglo-Irish gentleman Richard O'Connor joined his mortal hand with that of destiny and sent his forces round Graziani's southern flank.

By 6 February 1941, after a final action at Beda Fomm, the Italian Army had lost 130,000 men, the bulk of them prisoners, most of its equipment and half of Libya. It was to all intents and purposes destroyed. Wavell's liaison officer with the Western Desert Force, Brigadier Dorman-Smith, sent him a signal in clear, using a code they would all understand: 'Fox killed in the open.' O'Connor wanted to press on and sweep the Italians out of Africa completely. Wavell tentatively suggested this course in a signal to his boss, the Chief of the Imperial General Staff (CIGS), on 10 February, but on the 12 February the Prime Minister Winston Churchill replied, ordering Wavell to give priority to Greece. In doing so Churchill was merely confirming what had already been agreed by the Defence Committee and Wavell himself.[13]

As a second element in his plan to dominate the Mediterranean, Mussolini's troops had invaded Greece on the night of 27/28 October 1940, crossing the frontier from Albania, which the Italians had occupied in April 1939. The Greeks fought back fiercely. By the end of November, there were no Italians left in Greece and growing numbers of Greeks in Albania. The Greeks went on to the offensive in 1941, aided by British reinforcements. They were driving the Italians out of Albania when, on 6 April, the Germans arrived.

Wavell also had to deal with the third of Mussolini's imperial adventures, this time in East Africa. In 1936, Italian troops based in Italian East Africa, the present Somalia, had conquered Ethiopia. In 1940, there were 91,000 Italian and perhaps twice that number of African troops there, which in July tentatively advanced on the 9,000 British troops in the Sudan to the west, and the 8,500 in Kenya to the south. In August they occupied British Somaliland to the east. Wavell sent strong reinforcements of mainly African troops and, prodded by Churchill, launched offensives against the Italian possessions throughout the winter of 1940–41. They captured Mogadishu, the capital of Italian Somaliland, on 25 February, occupied Addis Ababa, the capital of Ethiopia on 6 April, and reinstalled Emperor Haile Selassie there on 5 May. To the north-west, British forces, led by 4th and 5th Indian Divisions, attacked Eritrea, and after a hard-fought campaign, captured it on 8 April.

The Italian army in East Africa finally surrendered on 19 May, leaving a total of 235,000 prisoners in British hands. In a few months, a small force detached from the Imperial Army of the Nile had destroyed Italian ambitions in North Africa, but its achievements have been forgotten. The origins of this historical amnesia can be traced to 12 February 1941, the day that Churchill confirmed that Wavell's major effort should be to aid Greece, and a junior German general arrived in Tripoli to take command of a small German mechanized corps which Hitler dubbed Deutsches Afrika Korps, or DAK for short. The original commander of this force and the first choice of the German General Staff had been General Freiherr von Funck. Von Funck had gone to Libya to assess the situation and told Hitler the force was too small. Thereupon, Hitler dismissed von Funck and appointed the man who had commanded his own bodyguard in 1939 and had led the 7th Panzer Division with startling brilliance in France, reaching the Channel coast before anyone else. Hitler distrusted Prussian generals, and wanted someone closer to his own heart, a man he described as 'the most daring commander of armoured forces in the whole of the German Army'.[14] His name was Erwin Rommel.

The Germans had got dragged reluctantly into Africa. Hitler could not allow the Italian military collapse to turn into a political one. He had covered the possibility of aiding the Italians in one of his high-level orders, Directive 18, which he issued on 12 November 1940, before O'Connor attacked. His provisions were restricted to air support, but he also ordered the army to reserve a Panzer division for possible use in North Africa. When he returned to the subject in Directive 22 of 11 January 1941, he explained that German help was needed for 'strategic, political and psychological reasons'. He envisioned the action needed to be entirely defensive: the DAK was conceived of as a 'blocking force' to defend Tripolitania against the incursions of British armoured units, and the Luftwaffe was to support Graziani by attacking British ports.[15]

There are two strange things about all of this. The first is that the

British gave the Germans the opportunity to intervene at all by failing to finish off the Italians when they could have done so. The second is that once they had intervened the Germans failed to finish off the British when they could have done so. Both of these failures resulted from the strategic direction set by the British War Cabinet and Chiefs-of-Staff Committee on the one hand and the German High Command on the other. Churchill and Hitler played major roles in both. In all else, their strategies and the views they took of the Mediterranean and the Middle East were diametrically opposed.

At the time, the German General Staff could not understand why the British did not press on and take Tripoli in February 1941 when there was nothing to stop them, and they are not alone.[16] As far as Wavell was concerned, the campaign in the horn of Africa, which was still going on, had always been more important than Libya. Italian East Africa was a threat to British supply routes through the Red Sea to Suez. O'Connor's original task in Libya had simply been to keep the Italians occupied, and the scale of his success came as a surprise. It opened up a strategic opportunity which was not taken.

There were some military reasons for halting O'Connor and diverting resources away from the desert to the Balkans. A successful defence of Greece was judged to be more important than the capture of Libya, for it would both sustain a small ally and protect the Middle East from any German threat from the north. Greece also had offensive potential, for the Ploesti oilfields in Rumania, upon which Germany heavily relied, could be reached from airfields there. But the main reasons for fighting alongside the Greeks were political. Britain had given Greece a guarantee in 1939, and Churchill was anxious to honour it. He believed that direct military support for Greece would impress Turkey, which he forlornly hoped to win over from neutrality, and he also hoped it would impress the Americans. Greece was the birthplace of democracy, and there were historic and emotional ties. Its fight for independence in the 1820s had caught the imagination of the British public. Lord Byron's less distinguished descendants in the British press ensured that its fight for independence in 1940 also became a popular cause. The Greeks were not so sure. They were dealing with the Italians very well by themselves, and feared that token British support would provoke a German attack without being strong enough to repel it. They were more or less right.

Once the Wehrmacht[17] arrived on the scene, it took them three weeks to defeat the Greek army and force the British and Commonwealth troops in Greece into another Dunkirk. They did not stop there but on 20 May 1941 launched a daring airborne invasion of Crete, which, though the battle turned on a knife edge, and cost the invaders terrible casualties, ended on 31 May with yet another ignominious British evacuation.

This defeat came hard on the heels of defeat in the desert. On 31 March 1941, Rommel had made his first sortie against O'Connor's forces, now bereft of their most experienced troops. As it was successful, he pressed on, despite the fact that he only had one motorized division, the 5th Light, available to him. A second, 15th Panzer Division, began to arrive during April, but Rommel was a man in a hurry. By 11 April, the British had been pushed back across the border into Egypt, leaving behind a garrison in the besieged town of Tobruk and O'Connor in a prisoner of war camp. Despite British attempts to counter-attack and relieve Tobruk, Rommel was still in Egypt at the end of May when Crete fell.

His presence was not altogether unwelcome to many Egyptians. Political power in Egypt was a delicate balance between King Farouk, a nationalist movement called the Wafd, and the British. The King and the Wafd manoeuvred against each other, and Egyptian opinion was split between those who wanted to help the British win the war in order to claim full independence afterwards as a reward, and those who wanted to help the Axis kick them out there and then. The Wafd tended to support the British so the King tended to support the Axis. The pro-Axis camp was further galled by the fact that following the Balfour Declaration of 1917 the British had been allowing Jews to settle in Palestine. In 1921 the Supreme Moslem Council appointed Mohammed Amin al-Husseini to the position of Mufti or senior judge of Jerusalem. He set about murdering Jews and moderate Arabs, and in 1937 a proposal to divide Palestine between the British the Arabs and the Jews provoked an Arab revolt which lasted for two years. In 1939, the British restricted Jewish immigration to placate the Arabs, but this led to Zionist terrorism. On becoming Prime Minister, Churchill wanted to arm the Jews in Palestine to free up the regular troops stationed there, but Wavell demurred, without thereby satisfying Arab nationalists. The German attitude to the Jews, as expressed in their propaganda, seemed to many of the radicalized

Arabs to be refreshingly robust. On 14 April 1941, King Farouk wrote to Hitler to say how much he admired him and expressed the hope that his country might soon be freed from the 'British yoke'.[18] The relationship between the young playboy King and the British authorities steadily deteriorated until a crisis was reached in February 1942. The British Ambassador, Sir Miles Lampson, demanded that Farouk appoint the pro-British Nahas Pasha as Prime Minister, which he did under duress on 4 February. The King's loss of face was observed with dismay by many Egyptians including two young officers called Abdul Nasser and Anwar Sadat. They did not forget it.[19]

Here then, was a golden opportunity for Hitler. The British were overstretched and in retreat. If Rommel were to be reinforced with just another couple of divisions, he could push on and take the Suez Canal to a hero's welcome. Small assault forces could deal with Gibraltar and Malta to secure his supply lines. There was some chance that gentle diplomatic pressure might even persuade Germany's old ally, Turkey, to join the Axis. The British Empire would be crippled, Churchill's political position imperilled, and the oilfields of Arabia open to German occupation.

On 2 May 1941, the newly installed Prime Minister Rashid Ali of Iraq, egged on by the Germans, ordered attacks on the British garrisons at Habbaniyah and Basra. Just outside Basra, at Abadan, the Anglo-Iranian Oil Company (later BP), had an enormous new refinery producing 3 million tons a year. When war broke out, 94 per cent of Britain's oil was imported and almost a third of those imports came from the eastern Mediterranean and the Gulf region. All the fuel needed by the Army, the Royal Navy and the RAF in the Middle East flowed through the pipelines running through Iraq and Syria to Haifa or was shipped to Port Said. Even when lack of tanker capacity led Britain to sign a 'shuttle' agreement with the Americans, the American ships loaded up in the Gulf.[20] Loss of this source would not only cripple all Britain's military effort in the region, it would seriously impair the capacity of the country as a whole to continue waging war at all.

Wavell sent a force from Palestine and the Arab Legion from Transjordan to occupy Baghdad and restore Ali's pro-British predecessor. The next month, Vichy French forces in Syria caused the British further trouble, only quelled in July. Between May and July, Wavell established control of the whole region, including Persia (present-day Iran), with three infantry divisions – one British, one Indian and one Australian. If the Axis powers could have conquered Egypt, a drive up through Palestine to Syria and Iraq would probably have met little opposition, and quite possibly been welcomed by the local leaders. These countries led to the most tempting prospect of all – more oil in the southern Caucasus, in the territory of the state Hitler was just about to invade: the Soviet Union.

This was Churchill's nightmare. He has written of early 1941 as the most stressful period of the war for him.[21] This period offered the Axis 'their best chance of challenging our dubious control of the eastern Mediterranean', he wrote. 'We could not tell they would not seize it.'[22] But they did not.

On 23 May 1941, Hitler issued Directive 30 expressing his desire to exploit the opportunity raised by the 'Arab freedom movement'. He sent some military advisors – who were under strict instructions to wear Iraqi uniforms – limited air support, a few weapons which were to go through the French authorities in Syria, and ordered propaganda activity. These measures were designed to strengthen the Iraqis' 'self-confidence and will to resistance'.[23] They were opportunistic and minimalist, and even as he issued the directive, Rashid Ali's rebellion was withering on the vine. Hitler was just a month away from launching the biggest land war in history. Even as Churchill saw the Middle East as central to his grand strategy, so Hitler saw it as a side-show, an annoying distraction. He did not reinforce Rommel or clear his back. He wanted the oil of the Caucasus, but he wanted to take it from the north, not the south. It may be that these were cardinal errors.

Why, then, was Rommel given only two Panzer divisions and one motorized division until mid-1942?[24] In October 1940, before any fighting had begun in the desert, General von Thoma was sent to North Africa to assess whether the Wehrmacht should assist the Italians in driving the British out of Egypt. He concluded that they should, and that the forces sent should consist of four Panzer divisions. This was twice the number actually sent in 1941, but still a very small force in absolute terms. Von Thoma considered this the minimum necessary to ensure success, but also the maximum which could be supplied. Desert armies on both sides would of necessity be small in comparison to European ones because of the problems in keeping them armed, fed and mobile – everything had to be brought in and moved over large distances under hostile conditions.[25] Given these limits on numbers, quality would be paramount, so he suggested that these armoured formations should replace Italian ones.[26]

This idea did not go down well with Mussolini, however, for he wanted to keep the glory of throwing the British out of Egypt to himself. When von Thoma put his idea to Hitler on 3 November 1940, the Führer told him that he could spare only one Panzer division. In any case he doubted the wisdom of sending troops across a sea they did not control whose security was the responsibility of a semi-committed ally.[27] He just wanted to offer the Italians a token force to show political solidarity. Von Thoma did not know it then, but Hitler's eyes were already on Russia. The High Command of the German Army, 'Oberkommando des Heeres', or OKH, headed by the Commander-in-Chief of the Army, Field Marshal von Brauchitsch, and the Chief of the General Staff, General Franz Halder, who knew all about the plans for Russia, shared Hitler's view that the Mediterranean was a strategic red-herring and warned against over-extending the Army. So nothing was done at all until the Italians had got themselves into deep trouble.[28] When, on 22 June 1941, Hitler invaded the Soviet Union, the German Army fielded some 3 million men in 146 divisions. German strength in the desert peaked at about 50,000 men in four divisions. The Wehrmacht committed less than 2 per cent of its strength to the desert war.[29] Had it committed 3 per cent at the right moment, it could have won.

As it was, Hitler could convince himself that he was not committing what he himself considered to be the fundamental error of Germany's leaders in World War I, that of fighting a war on two fronts. He did just enough to keep the British occupied. Otherwise, his strategy in the West was reactive. During the summer of 1940, he had even managed to convince himself that Britain's failure to make terms was because it had placed its hope in Russia and thus that by destroying the Soviet Union, he would bring the war with England to an end as well. Conquering Russia had always been his main war aim, and so he channelled the vast bulk of Germany's resources into doing so. It was a 'Russia first' policy. Britain, and Africa, could wait.

Hitler was in any case none too sure that the collapse of the British Empire, which would be brought nearer through the conquest of the Middle East, would in itself be a good thing. It would, he opined, merely benefit Japan and the United States. He had never wanted a war with Britain anyway, a country he saw as a natural ally of Germany. Even after they declared war on him in 1939, Hitler expected to make peace with the British, confidently expecting them to negotiate with him after the fall of France in 1940. He kept on talking about reaching a 'settlement' throughout 1941.[30] Even as, in 1942, Hitler decided to leave the vast industrial complex around Moscow intact and launch his summer offensive in the south to capture the grain and oil of the Caucasus, the oil of the Middle East did not lure him. As Allied generals watched the German thrust grow and saw the threat of Rommel linking up with it through Iraq and Iran, OKH and the Supreme Command of the German Armed Forces, ('Oberkommando der Wehrmacht' or OKW) kept their eyes on the single goal of defeating the Soviets. 'The great pincer movement against the Middle East, which your people imagined to be in progress,' von Thoma told Liddell Hart after the war, 'was never a serious plan. It was vaguely discussed in Hitler's entourage, but our General Staff never agreed with it, or regarded it as practicable.'[31]

On the contrary, Rommel's impetuous opportunism created serious concerns at OKH. Just a few weeks after Rommel's arrival in the desert, a German liaison officer in Libya submitted a critical report to OKH. Rommel's operational intentions needed to be based on a clearer recognition of fundamentals and what was possible, he said, particularly in terms of supply lines. A week later, OKH ordered Rommel to hold off his offensive until the whole of his forces had arrived. A week after that, staff officers at OKH reported that Rommel was making nonsensical requests, and all agreed that limits had to be placed on his 'boundless demands'. The invasion of Russia was to be the decisive operation of the war, had absolute priority and was not to be put at risk by romantic adventures in strategic backwaters. OKH even rejected Hitler's suggestion that Rommel be given another infantry regiment, as that would not get him anywhere. The only things that would help him were changing the supply situation and providing greatly increased air support, neither of which were on the cards. Rommel attacked anyway at the end of March 1941, and on 14 April was talking about taking Mersa Matruh and Suez. OKH told him his forces and supplies were inadequate and that he was to stop at Sollum on the Egyptian border and restrict himself to raids. The next day, Rommel reported that he was encountering strong resistance at Tobruk, and that his forces were too weak to take it. 'Far away as we are', Halder noted acidly in his diary, 'we have had that impression for quite a while.'[32] Things were getting out of hand. On 23 April, Halder decided that someone needed to take a closer look.

Halder had by then become seriously worried by the state of affairs in North Africa, and laid out all his concerns in a long entry to his diary. Rommel had not provided a single clear report on the situation and Halder smelled a rat. Reports from other officers down there suggested that Rommel was not up to his job. He tore about all day long among his widely dispersed units, sent out reconnaissance parties and dissipated his strength. No one had a clear overview of the state of his forces or what they were up to. By dividing up his tanks into small groups he had suffered heavy losses. His transport was breaking down and there were no spare parts. The Luftwaffe could not possibly meet all his silly demands for air transport. So Halder decided to send a trusted lieutenant, General Friedrich Paulus, on a mission to the desert to find out what was going on. He was to have authority to direct the Afrika Korps if he thought it necessary.

Paulus and Rommel were old friends. They had been together in Stuttgart in the late 1920s and Rommel had written a private letter to him in February just a fortnight after arriving in Libya. Rommel was full of the joys of spring, saying that he was working well with the Italians and welcoming any advice the chaps at OKH might have. Never mind the blocking force idea, he was out to conquer Egypt. Hitler pulled him up short in a conference in March, but he still did not understand why he was not reinforced. It was not until May that he learned about the plans for Russia.[33]

Paulus arrived in Libya on 27 April. That day, a report arrived in Berlin from the German military attaché in Rome, General von Rintelen, which suggested that OKH were not the only ones to be anxious about the activities of the loose cannon who had just arrived in the desert and was firing off in all directions. The Italian High Command were not very competent soldiers but they were not fools. They had a good appreciation of the capabilities of their forces, and were dedicated to prosecuting the war by doing as little as possible. Rommel was a serious threat to this strategy. The report, from the Italian Generals Guzzoni and Roatta, said that Rommel was planning to attack Tobruk in a few days' time and then head for Mersa Matruh. If the attack on Tobruk were to fail, they would have to withdraw. Whatever happened, they heartily disapproved of further forays into Egypt, as the Axis forces were not strong enough and could not be supplied anyway. No offensive action should take place before the autumn.[34]

Paulus interviewed Rommel, who told him that the Italians could not be relied upon and that he had to reduce Tobruk, or his position would be untenable. Paulus sanctioned the attack on the fortress town planned for 1 May. The attacks were beaten back with heavy losses, and in the evening as a sandstorm blew up, Rommel and Paulus broke them off. The Afrika Korps could not withdraw because of the negative propaganda which would result, so they created a defensive position where they were. Paulus then visited the rear areas, and concluded that Rommel's real need was not for men but for trucks and that both the Libyan ports and the convoys trying to get to them were chronically vulnerable to air attack. Paulus concluded that Rommel could not take Tobruk without 15th Panzer Division, air support and a proper logistical base. On 8 May, having told Rommel to restrict himself to limited offensive action against Tobruk and on no account to attack Egypt, he left.

In the meantime, Halder had been pondering. One of Paulus' officers reported back on 2 May, saying that things were not too bad but that the Italians were no use. The real problems went beyond Africa. As long as the British held Malta, he baldly stated, an offensive against Egypt would be impossible. This view was confirmed in another discussion on the 6 May, but the Italians thought that wresting Malta from the British was out of the question. On the 7 May, Halder finally laid his hands on a decent map and was horrified to discover that Rommel had thrown his troops all over the place and was completely disorganized. The next day, Paulus called in from Catania on his way back. The problem in Africa, he said, was not Tobruk or Sollum. It was all a question of supplies. On 11 May, Paulus reported in person. He was gloomy. By his insubordination, Rommel had created an insoluble supply problem. He was out of his depth. The only thing to do was to support von Rintelen in his efforts to get whatever supplies he could over to the desert. Otherwise, there was nothing anyone could do. So that was that.[35]

The Germans did not take the Mediterranean theatre seriously until the Allies forced them to do so. A larger force in the desert could have been supplied if control of the sea had been wrested from the

British by invading Gibraltar and Malta, putting sufficient U-boats into action to control the Royal Navy, and providing sufficient transport for Rommel's army. Though plans were developed for taking Gibraltar and Malta, none were carried out.

Churchill saw the Mediterranean as so significant that in 1940, facing an invasion threat from across the Channel, he sent tanks and troops to Egypt, relying on the RAF and the Royal Navy to defend Britain. In the event his faith in them was justified, but it looked like a terrible risk at the time. He saw Britain as part of an empire, and the Suez Canal as only marginally less important than the River Thames, as much for its political as for its economic significance. Continental historians still have difficulty in understanding this mentality, and some quote Churchill's actions in 1940 as evidence that he did not take the cross-Channel threat seriously.[36] He took it very seriously, though his assessment of its likelihood changed as events unfolded. However, even before the Battle of Britain he was convinced that it would fail, which is why he sent the tanks to Egypt.[37]

So it was that as both sides failed for various reasons, good and bad, to take the opportunities for a decisive early victory which the fortunes of war had thrown them, the war in the desert went on for nearly two years without a clear decision, until the two exhausted combatants faced each other at El Alamein.

II

THE TACTICAL WAR

THE DESERT WAR WAS FOUGHT over a strip of land just over 1,400 miles long between Tripoli in the west and Alexandria in the east. Tripoli was the capital of Tripolitania which formed western Libya, and Benghazi was the capital of Cyrenaica which formed eastern Libya and the border with Egypt. Both Tripoli and Benghazi were ports, and were the main destinations of the Axis convoys supplying the Italo-German desert army which on 31 July 1941 was named 'Panzerarmee Afrika', with Rommel as its official commander. Benghazi is on the western side of a large bulge of land curving out into the sea which ends in the east at a third port called Tobruk. When the British held Tobruk, they were able to land some supplies there, but their main supply base was Alexandria, the chief port of Egypt. Alexandria was also the main base of the Royal Navy in the eastern Mediterranean, and the largest station along a small railway line which ran westwards as far as Mersa Matruh, parallel to the only metalled road in the desert. Whilst Alexandria was a permanent logistical base, the Egyptian capital of Cairo was the permanent Headquarters of Middle East Command and the some-time headquarters of the desert army, which on 26 September 1941 changed its name from 'Western Desert Force' to 'Eighth Army'.

The North African coastal plain is largely flat, rocky scrubland interspersed with occasional hills and sand dunes, offering long, clear fields of fire for guns and ideal going for tanks. The bulge of Cyrenaica is rimmed by an area of rocky hills known as the Jebel Akhdar, and south of the coastal strip of Egypt run a series of hills known, paradoxically, as the Libyan Plateau. Beyond these two features, the hard, flat desert, which in fact forms the eastern edge of the Sahara, stretches far to the south before turning into the Great Sand Sea, so named because it consists of soft, undulating sand impassable to vehicles. To the south of the Libyan Plateau the land is open until it drops suddenly and precipitously into a dried-up salt lake called the Qattara Depression. Its lunar landscape forms an even more impenetrable barrier to movement than the Great Sand Sea. Running diagonally from south west to north east, the Qattara Depression creates a funnel which reaches its narrowest point some 40 miles from the sea marked by the small railway station of El Alamein. There is a ridge between the railway station and the sea called Tel el Alamein, the 'hill of twin cairns', which gives the station its name. Being about 50 miles from Alexandria, El Alamein was a convenient stopping place for people making the rail journey along the coast to the end of the line at Mersa Matruh. From the station they could make their way quite easily to the sea and bathe in its clear blue waters.

It was obvious that the defence of Egypt from the west depended on this position. Tel el Alamein afforded good observation. Seven or eight miles south of it the ground rose gently to form the Ruweisat Ridge, and a similar distance south-west of that rose the peak of Qaret el Abd. Between el Alamein and the Ruweisat Ridge towards the west the ground was dominated by the Miteirya Ridge. South of Ruweisat was a hard plateau ending at Bare Ridge and rising eastwards towards Alam el Halfa. None of these features rose more than a few hundred feet, but in the desert even gentle rises afforded a great improvement in view and an opportunity for cover. Between Bare Ridge and the Qattara Depression were a series of hills and escarpments making movement difficult, but offering a series of narrow passes. The whole position was ideal for defence and could not be turned to the south. In 1941, the British built defensive positions here which they believed could be held by two infantry and two armoured divisions. This line formed the eastern limit of the desert within which the tactical battle would be fought. Beyond lay the strategic prizes of the Suez Canal and, above all, oil.[1]

Having thrown the British out of Libya in his first dash, Rommel consolidated his front line, and in April and May 1941 made two unsuccessful attempts to take Tobruk. In mid-May and again in June, Wavell ordered two unsuccessful attempts to relieve it. The first more modest effort, under General Gott, was code-named 'Brevity' and succeeded in capturing some posts on the Libyan frontier until the appearance of German armour on the southern flank forced a withdrawal. The second, Operation 'Battleaxe', was on a larger scale involving 4th Indian and 7th Armoured Divisions under the command of General Beresford-Pierse. On the first day the British lost half their tanks to a combination of German anti-tank guns and mechanical breakdowns. Rommel spent the following day developing a thrust round the exposed southern flank, and by the third day this threat had grown so serious that Beresford-Pierce ordered a withdrawal. Inside Tobruk, 9th Australian Division, supplied from the sea, both resisted the siege and launched periodic counter-attacks, establishing a reputation among their enemies as the most formidable unit in the Eighth Army. As a result of political pressure in Australia, the Australians were withdrawn in a series of ferrying operations between August and October 1941, and replaced by the British 70th Division and a Polish brigade. They continued to hold out with equal determination. There was stalemate.

The stalemate could only be broken by one side building up overwhelming strength. For Rommel, the build-up was more organizational than real. The 5th Light Division was renamed 21st Panzer Division and he pulled together a few infantry battalions and some artillery to create a new unit called 90th Light Division. The Italians supplied three additional infantry divisions with obsolete equipment. On 22 June 1941, Hitler launched Operation 'Barbarossa', his invasion of the Soviet Union. As far as he was concerned that was the real war, and he left Rommel to muddle through. After all, all he really had to do was to keep the Italians out of trouble.

Churchill and the War Cabinet, on the other hand, were prepared to run considerable risks to achieve a decisive breakthrough. Throughout the summer of 1941 they sent convoys laden with tanks, planes and guns across the perilous seas. But Wavell had failed to deliver a second decisive victory after Rommel's arrival. They took the view that he was tired and overburdened with both theatre and operational commands. On 5 July 1941, following the failure of Battleaxe, Churchill swapped him with the Commander-in-Chief India, Sir Claude Auchinleck, as theatre commander in the Middle East.

Auchinleck was a big, burly man who wrapped his strong-willed pugnacity in the cloak of soft-spoken good manners worn by many English gentlemen of his generation and background. He had spent most of his career in the Indian Army and did not know many of the officers in his new command. One of them whose star seemed to be rising was Lieutenant-General Sir Alan Cunningham, the brother of Admiral Sir Andrew Cunningham. He had been knighted for his successful campaign in East Africa, and Auchinleck decided to appoint him as the operational commander of the army in the desert. Meanwhile, the various Axis factions were having a row about who should control what. OKW, OKH, the Italian Commando Supremo and Rommel were all struggling for influence until a compromise was reached on 15 August, leaving Rommel in control of what was now to be called the Panzerarmee Afrika. It included the Italian XXI Corps but the Italian XX Corps, containing their armour under General Bastico, reported separately to the Commando Supremo. It was a mess.[2]

On 18 November 1941, Cunningham attacked with over 700 tanks against 320 Axis tanks, half of which were obsolete Italian types of little value. Even as Rommel continued trying to break in to Tobruk, 70th Division played its part in the offensive by trying to break out. The offensive was code-named 'Crusader'.

Cunningham's plan was for one of his Corps to hold the Axis troops along the frontier whilst the other, containing the bulk of his armour, moved round their southern flank to destroy Rommel's armour in the desert south of Tobruk and then relieve the fortress itself. The result was a week of tank fighting during which British tank strength was heavily reduced, followed by an attempt by Rommel to cut through to the British rear, which ended with similar proportional losses to the Afrika Korps. The weakened forces on both sides then continued to hammer at each other around Tobruk until, on the night of 4 December, Rommel withdrew, staging holding actions and local counter-attacks. By the end of the year he was back at El Agheila.

The fighting was characterized throughout by sudden encounters and confusion. Cunningham's offensive opened with armoured columns of both sides blundering into each other, resulting in vicious gun fights, which, though small, involved very high casualty rates. There was no 'front'. Headquarters units and rear echelons collided with armoured units and went down, including the HQ of the Afrika Korps itself. Communications were disrupted and few people had any idea what was going on. The ignorant armies clashed by night and only discovered what had happened when day dawned. In all of this, Rommel himself led 21st Panzer Division on an offensive foray against the British rear, in what has become known as his 'dash to the wire', so-named as it aimed at the two-metre high tangle of wire the Italians had erected to mark the border between Libya and Egypt. This 'dash' aimed as much to paralyse the minds of the British commanders as to wipe out their support columns. Of doubtful material value, it was a psychological success, for Cunningham began to toy with retreat. But Auchinleck arrived from Cairo. He reckoned that Rommel was desperate, would not get very far and would soon run out of supplies if he tried to. So 'the Auk', as Auchinleck was known, resumed the offensive and replaced Cunningham with Major-General Neil Ritchie. The Auk was right, and when Rommel ordered a withdrawal, it caused a row with the Italians who rightly feared that their foot soldiers would get left behind and rounded up. They also less pertinently complained that Rommel was giving up the best territory in Libya.[3] Tobruk was relieved. By the end of 1941, Panzerarmee Afrika had pulled back round the bulge of Cyrenaica and stopped at El Agheila on the border of Tripolitania which was, as we have seen, back where he had started. The trapped garrison of Bardia surrendered on 2 January 1942 and the last frontier posts did so on 17 January. The Panzerarmee lost 20,000 Italian and 13,000 German troops and 340 tanks; the Eighth Army suffered 18,000 casualties and lost 440 tanks. Almost half the German and Italian losses were prisoners taken when their last strongholds fell. Auchinleck had saved the day and gained a victory – but not a decisive one.

Rommel got his first reinforcements on 19 December 1941, 30 tanks which had landed at Benghazi just before it was abandoned. On 5 January 1942, another Axis convoy with more tanks got in to Tripoli. A couple of weeks later, signalling his confidence in his 'boldest general', Hitler awarded Rommel Swords to add to the Oak Leaves already decorating his Knight's Cross. He was the first German general to be so honoured. On 21 January, Rommel struck back.

Meeting a newly arrived, inexperienced 1st Armoured Division, Rommel cut through it. The British retreated, and on 4 February 1942 stopped at Gazala, 30 miles west of Tobruk. Ritchie created a defensive line consisting of a series of 'boxes' designed for all-round defence and linked by minefields running south into the desert. Here he gathered his forces for another offensive. The Imperial force was fast becoming an international one, as Free French and Polish contingents arrived. The British now had about 635,000 troops in various parts of the Middle East, and Churchill urged Auchinleck to use them. Auchinleck wanted to give Ritchie time to prepare for a decisive encounter and planned to open an offensive in mid-June. Rommel forestalled him, and on the night of 26/27 May 1942 he attacked, starting what became known as the Battle of Gazala.

Panzerarmee Afrika had 330 German and 230 obsolete Italian tanks, 560 in all, against the 850 tanks of the Eighth Army, which also had a numerical superiority of 3:2 in guns. As was his habit, Rommel sent the DAK round the open southern flank and then tried to fight his way through to the sea. He was stopped by the British armour, now using some new Grant tanks from America, which had heavy 75mm guns. Trying to hammer a big enough hole in the defences to let him supply his leading tanks, Rommel withdrew into the British minefields, creating his own 'box', which he called, with more sense of drama, a 'Hexenkessel' or 'Witches' Cauldron'. He tried to eliminate part of the line held by 50th Division, whilst Ritchie, after dithering for four days, tried to eliminate him, with the Eighth Army attacking on the ground and the RAF bombing from the air. German and Italian troops tried to storm the southern-most 'box' held by the Free French at Bir Hacheim. It held out for ten days. Others managed to eliminate the 'box' in the Cauldron held by the 50th Division's 150 Brigade and then moved east, trapping and virtually destroying two British armoured brigades, and reducing the British box at 'Knightsbridge'. They thus threatened the British infantry still holding the Gazala line. On 14 June Ritchie abandoned it. The Eighth Army retreated eastwards in an operation the troops called the 'Gazala Gallop' to a defensive position at Mersa Matruh, leaving Tobruk behind, held by 2nd South African Division. Rommel laid siege to Tobruk once more, carried out an assault, and then, on 21 June 1942, in what for Churchill was the biggest shock of the desert war, took it. On 15 June, Auchinleck arrived at Ritchie's HQ and took over personal command of the Eighth Army.

The next day, Rommel attacked again. Shortly before dawn on 29 June, 90th Light Division entered Mersa Matruh, and the two adversaries raced each other eastwards towards the defences at El Alamein. Eighth Army reached them on 30 June. In Cairo, on a day to be known as 'Ash Wednesday', Headquarters staff were burning documents. At Alexandria the docks were mined for demolition as the fleet departed. That morning, Rommel wrote to his wife that his advanced units were only 200 kilometres from Alexandria. 'There are still some battles to be fought before we get to our goal', he wrote, 'But the worst is long over.'[4] By the evening he only had 60 miles to go. On 1 July 1942, the DAK attacked. The First Battle of El Alamein had begun.

This then, was the long, hard route which led the protagonists in the desert war to the one spot in the desert where there was no way round, and where, therefore, the decision both sides had failed to take before for strategic reasons had to be reached. By the standards of World War II, the fighting had been on a very small scale, but from a military point of view it was in many ways remarkable. In 1940 a tiny British army had defeated a far larger Italian one and from 1941 to 1942, an outnumbered and under-resourced Italo-German one had fairly consistently got the better of a British one. How had this happened?

The answers in each case were: equipment; the tactics and training of the armies; their acquisition and use of information; and generalship.

In the winter of 1940–41, O'Connor's Western Desert Force took 58 days to clear Cyrenaica and wipe out the eight divisions of the Italian Tenth Army, capturing 130,000 men and 845 guns and destroying 380 tanks. Though not in the end decisive, it was one of the British Army's biggest victories of the war. Its later victories over the Germans were gained as part of an Allied army in which the American contribution was larger. In 1944, British Commonwealth forces gained a more important victory against the Japanese in Burma, but the losses inflicted on the enemy were smaller. O'Connor's was a remarkable achievement, but it was not a miracle.

In the 1930s, Italy was a poor country still in the process of industrialization. In 1940, with a population of similar size to Britain's, Italy had only 25 per cent of its gross domestic product. Half of its population still worked on the land and about a third were illiterate or semi-literate. They were poorly adapted to fighting a technological war – it was hard even to find enough men who could drive trucks – and its industry was barely capable of equipping it to do so. Graziani's whole army only had 5,140 vehicles and 2,000 of them were in repair shops, leaving them with fewer than the standard complement of a British division. The bulk of his forces were marching infantry, whereas the Western Desert Force was fully motorized. During the 1930s, the Italian Army affirmed the primacy of numbers over mobility, summed up in the comment of one of their leading armoured warfare experts that 'the tank is a powerful tool, but let us not idolize it; let us reserve our reverence for the infantryman and the mule'.[5] The Italian infantry had a problem with their small arms. The Army was in the process of introducing a new rifle, and as a result there were two incompatible sets of ammunition, which led to confusion and shortages. Graziani had plenty of guns, but most of them were designed before World War I, many captured from the Austro-Hungarians in 1918. The result of this armaments disaster was that Italian divisions, which were in any case far smaller than those of most armies, lacked not only mobility but also firepower – the two cardinal factors in mechanized warfare.

The Italians' biggest hardware problem of all was tanks. A lot of the vehicles classified as tanks were in fact lighter than British reconnaissance vehicles. The most numerous tank, the M11, was a death trap which has been described as 'about the worst design of the period'.[6] All the British tanks were better armed, but the Matilda infantry tank, a machine which had caused great consternation to Rommel's 7th Panzer Division during the French campaign when it suddenly appeared at Arras in May 1940, was also invulnerable to Italian guns. When it first appeared in the desert on 9 December 1940, the Italian artillerymen facing it fought with great tenacity and died on their guns. But dying in their path did not stop the Matildas, as was observed by some of the survivors, and from then on the Matilda had a potent effect on Italian morale.

Poor equipment was not the end of it. Italian training, particularly of the infantry, was wretched. The generals did not believe in it. In

1937, one senior commander was sent off to Libya with the admonition not to do 'too much training'. There was a widespread belief, congenial to Mussolini, that intuition and valour were more important in battle.[7] What little there was consisted mainly of drill, with little live firing and almost no combined arms training. There was a gulf between officers and men, rations were poor and even proper uniforms were in short supply. By contrast, the units of the Western Desert Force had trained in desert conditions and 7th Armoured Division, which had been formed by the brilliant if eccentric tankman Percy Hobart, was probably the best trained in the British Army. O'Connor took things further by rehearsing his tactics in desert exercises before putting them into action.

During the 1940 campaign and thereafter, Italian troops often displayed bravery and determination. The few effective units they had, like the Folgore Parachute Division which had trained hard for eighteen months before entering the line at Alamein in 1942, earned the respect of the Germans and British alike. After all, the performance of their predecessors in World War I had been comparable to that of the other major European powers. They gave their Austro-Hungarian opponents such a hard time that the Germans were forced to send the 14th Army to help, which included one Oberleutnant Erwin Rommel, who won the highest German decoration, the *Pour le Mérite*, for his bold action at the bloody and hard fought battle of Caporetto in 1917. But between then and 1940, the Italian Army changed hardly at all. In modern battle, units which are poorly equipped and poorly trained usually disintegrate. Given its training and equipment, the Italian Army was bound to be ineffective in comparison both with its opponents and its allies.[8] When he followed O'Connor's victorious men into the fort of Nibeiwa, the journalist Alan Moorehead found a letter written home by an Italian officer which read: 'We are trying to fight this war as though it is a colonial war in Africa. But it is a European war in Africa fought with European weapons against a European enemy.'[9] Most of the soldiers did not understand why they were at war, and were ill-prepared for modern battle conditions. Time had passed them by. A report from an Italian Air Force officer in November 1940 stated that troops exaggerated enemy strength and called for air support if they saw one tank. Graziani panicked at the prospect of air attack. He ordered Benghazi to be evacuated after two minor raids.[10]

The great mass of hapless Italian foot-sloggers were inevitably out-manoeuvred by the mechanized units of the Western Desert Force. Once cut off, they could either surrender or starve, so they surrendered. But O'Connor rang rings round their leaders as well. He launched his first attack on the Italian camp at Nibeiwa, some twelve miles south of Sidi Barrani, just before dawn, and achieved total surprise. 4th Indian Division and 57 Matildas emerged out of the desert behind the Italian position, and caught them still half asleep. O'Connor consistently used speed and surprise, and exploited unexpected opportunities. He was prepared to use bluff, and had his enemies convinced that they were hopelessly outnumbered.

The command style of the Italian Army was designed for buck-passing. Responsibility was passed down as far as possible, with evidence collected on the way so that junior officers could be blamed in case of failure, which was the norm. However, junior officers were not trusted, so orders were very detailed and there was an inordinate amount of supervision. Showing initiative was positively dangerous.[11] O'Connor – unlike a lot of his colleagues – explained his intentions to his subordinates and then delegated authority to them. They could therefore make rapid decisions without referring back whilst at the same time being confident that it would all add up to what O'Connor wanted. He led from the front, which was also his downfall, for it allowed him to be captured in April 1941 by German troops whose commander was to exhibit precisely the same characteristics over the next 24 months. They served him and his cause as well as they had served O'Connor.[12]

During the course of 1941, the Italians improved the quality of their desert forces enormously, introducing two armoured and two motorized divisions which put them more on a par with their opponents. The M13 tank, which mounted a more effective gun than the M11, appeared in greater numbers. Even so, it was still easily the worst tank in the desert in 1942, slow and unreliable, and both the British and the Germans referred to them as 'steel coffins'. Going to war in them required considerable courage in itself. The Italians consistently fielded the larger part of the force which was to cause the British so many headaches over the following months. However, the most important factor in explaining the Axis successes was the arrival of the Afrika Korps.

The Germans brought with them modern artillery, proper

transport, and tanks which could match those of the Eighth Army. Their most numerous battle tank was the Panzer III, which mounted a 50mm gun with a performance comparable to that of the 2-pounder of the most numerous British tanks, the Valentine, Crusader and Matilda. They also had a number of the heavier Panzer IVs which carried a 75mm gun. The Valentine and Matilda were a lot slower than the Panzer III and Panzer IV, whereas the Crusader, while about as fast, was less well armoured. More seriously still, whereas the German tanks carried a dual-purpose gun capable of firing armour-piercing and high-explosive shells, the British 2-pounder could only use armour-piercing ammunition, which was of little use against anti-tank guns. The German tanks were reliable, but the hastily designed Crusader was notorious for breaking down. It was built around a pair of connected aero engines, chosen because they worked well in aircraft and there were a lot left over after the 1914–18 war. When put into a tank, however, the engines needed large cooling fans and these were driven off two water pumps on the end of a long chain. In the desert, the water pumps overheated and sand got into the chain, making it jump off the crankshaft driving sprocket. Repairing it took three days. In January 1942, there were 200 Crusaders in repair shops.[13] The Germans were also more careful to use the resources they had. When tanks were disabled in combat, the Germans stayed on the battlefield to recover them and get them to repair shops. The British left theirs where they were, perhaps because the repair shops were full anyway. A lot of the British tank losses were simply vehicles which had broken down and could not be moved.

During 1942, both sides improved their stock of tanks. The Germans shipped over a few Mk IV Specials, mounting a high-velocity, long-barrelled 75mm gun with considerably greater range and penetrating power. The British had greater difficulty in improving their own tanks. The suspensions were too weak to take much additional armour and the turrets too small to house larger guns, though some 6-pounders were squeezed into Crusaders. So they acquired a new type, the American Grant. The Grant had a dual-purpose 75mm gun, but it was mounted in a sponson on the side of the hull rather than in the turret on the top. This meant that to bring it to bear, the Grant had to expose its hull to return fire, whereas all the German tanks could fire from a less-exposed 'hull-down' position. By and large, however, despite contemporary British reports that German tanks were definitely superior, the differences were not decisive.[14]

The difference which often *was* tactically decisive, and which British reports confused with a difference in tank performance, was in anti-tank guns and the use to which they were put. The key weapon was the German 88mm flak gun. Designed by Krupp in Sweden in 1932 as an anti-aircraft weapon, it was discovered during the Spanish Civil War that it was also a very powerful anti-tank gun, and from 1938 it was provided with a shield to protect the crew and armour-piercing ammunition. In World War II it was Rommel's own 7th Panzer Division which first used it against tanks as the only means to deal with the Matildas which suddenly attacked them south of Arras in France in May 1940. They stopped the Matildas, the only gun they had which could do so. When firing on a flat trajectory, it sent the largest armour-piercing shell in use in the desert at a higher speed over a longer distance than any other tank or anti-tank gun, and did so with unerring accuracy. It could easily kill any British tank at 2,000 yards, twice the effective range of most British guns. At that range it could penetrate 83mm of armour, twice as much as the 75mm guns of the Grant, and more than carried by any British tank. The Afrika Korps used 88s for the first time during 'Battleaxe'. There were only a handful of them, but they did great execution.

Whilst the small number of Matildas the British used in 1940 drove the Italians to despair, the small number of 88s used by the DAK had a similar effect on the British. A psychiatrist investigating the effects of different weapons on troops discovered that men willing to charge the lethal MG 34 machine gun were terrified of the 88.[15] Every veteran soldier gets to know the distinctive sounds of different guns, and the 88 was described as having a 'crack'. Its shell travelled so fast that the 'crack' was often heard just after a tank was seen to be hit. Wherever it appeared, it dominated the battlefield. When it did not appear, the fear that it might led experienced British tank crews to exercise caution. Given its bulk and high profile, the 88 was vulnerable to air bursts from high-explosive shells and small arms. Lacking high-explosive ammunition, even if they were lucky enough to get within range, meant that British tanks facing 88s without artillery and infantry support were more or less helpless.

The standard British anti-tank gun, the 2-pounder, was designed for war in Europe, where ranges were not expected to exceed about 800 yards – which by and large was true there but not in the desert.[16]

It was also designed to take on other tanks, so it was only able to fire armour piercing shells rather than the high explosive ones needed to deal with anti-tank guns. It could penetrate 40mm of armour at 1,000 yards, which was at least as good as the standard German 37mm anti-tank gun or the 50mm gun fitted to most German tanks. It remained effective against any Italian tank, but the Germans had learned from their experiences in France and the Panzer III carried up to 60mm of frontal armour. Not until the 6-pounder anti-tank gun began to be supplied to the Eighth Army in the summer of 1942 could its frontal armour be penetrated at this range.[17] No one on either side had expected to fight in the flat, coverless desert, where targets could be identified at 2,000 yards. It just happened that the Germans were the only ones with a gun which could hit targets over a mile away. It was a lucky trump card.

The 88 wrought havoc on the battlefield throughout the desert war because the British were slow to learn. The pre-war British Army did not appreciate the extent to which a future war would be a battle between machines, and that technology was an essential element in tactics. In 1941, Auchinleck expanded the technical intelligence section of Middle East Command to two officers and a truck. The true performance of the key German weapons remained a mystery for a long time. When the 88 was tested, it was erroneously concluded that it could not penetrate the armour of a Matilda beyond 440 yards, so Matildas continued to be deployed against it, with disastrous results.[18] When the penny dropped, some attempts were made to employ the excellent 3.7-inch anti-aircraft gun as an anti-tank weapon like the 88. The 3.7 proved to be too sophisticated. It was designed to work with range data from radar, whereas the 88 had an optical sight which could be used on the ground, and the 3.7 weighed 9 tons as against the 2.5 tons of the 88, making it far too heavy to be moved about rapidly on the battlefield.[19] The 88 remained the queen of the desert.

The impact of the technical differences between just a few critical pieces of equipment was enormously magnified by how each army used them. In accordance with pre-war British Army doctrine, tanks were expected to perform two distinct roles and different machines were designed for each. There were heavy 'infantry tanks' (like the Matilda) to be used as support weapons for the infantry, and therefore distributed in small groups among them; and lighter 'cruiser tanks' (like the Crusader), grouped together but without infantry or artillery support. The cruisers were trained to fire on the move, which meant they could not hit anything, and to advance *en masse* in clanking twentieth century versions of the 'charge', which meant that any anti-tank gunners within range could hit them. The reason for this was the practical need to get within range and the lack of all-arms training, but it also appealed to the old cavalry regiments. When Hobart was training 7th Armoured Division in the desert, he gave up trying to co-operate with infantry and artillery because they lacked proper radio communications equipment and were too slow.[20] Throughout the desert war, the British Army organized some of its tanks into independent all-tank armoured brigades. Even within the armoured divisions which contained a balance of all arms, the tanks tended to operate independently. The British Army was for years locked into a sterile debate with itself between tank enthusiasts who saw tanks as a new independent weapon and the 'old school' who saw them as infantry support weapons. Both were wrong. Having framed the issue in the way it had, the Army could not possibly find a solution. The Germans had greater intellectual freedom, which they turned into greater effectiveness on the battlefield.

With the dissolution of the Imperial German Army in 1919, the German armed forces had to reinvent themselves. The Army took a good hard look at the implications of military mechanization, and formed an entirely new tank arm. It did not need to compromise with grooms and stabling, full-dress uniforms and balls at country estates, but got stuck in with oil and spanners, command and control systems and ballistics. The British also had a pure tank arm, the Royal Tank Corps, whose ethos was similarly bound up with grease and oil rather than grooms and hay. In April 1939, however, following a decision to create an entirely mechanized army, it was renamed the Royal Tank Regiment (RTR) and merged with the regular cavalry and territorial yeomanry regiments to form the Royal Armoured Corps. Not all of the cavalrymen gave up their horses willingly, and none of them gave up their traditions. They were socially much smarter than the Royal Tank Regiment, and British tank tactics were strongly influenced by inappropriate cavalry thinking. The cavalry regiments were usually equipped with cruisers and the RTR with infantry tanks. Rommel was an infantryman, but learned how to use tanks in the Guderian school, itself developed from the writings of the British tank theorists Fuller and Liddell Hart. Guderian massed tanks to create breakthroughs and then manoeuvre in the open, and created motorized infantry and towed anti-tank gun units with the same speed and mobility as the tanks to operate with them as part of a unified Panzer division. There was never any question of them either operating alone or merely as infantry support weapons. Tanks, guns and infantry always trained and fought together.[21]

The operating doctrines and training of the British and German Armies were based on common observations which led to opposite conclusions. Both had observed that modern war is chaotic. The German Army accepted that the chaos could not be controlled, but it still needed a command and control system. It adopted what it called 'Auftragstaktik' or 'mission command', developed from principles established by the German General Staff in the latter half of the nineteenth century, which themselves have their origins in the soul searching which followed the crushing defeat of the Prussian Army at Jena in 1806. The idea of mission command is that officers should understand their mission, but be left free to decide for themselves how best to accomplish it. A 'mission' consisted of a task and a purpose. Both were articulated in simple terms by the senior commander, but not specified in detail. Having understood the purpose behind their immediate task, the officers reporting to the commander were able to take decisions based on the situation as they found it but in line with their commander's overall intentions. This enabled them both to adapt to changing circumstances as the chaos of battle took hold and exploit unpredictable opportunities. They were under an obligation to show initiative, and even lieutenants were trained to command a formation up to the size of a battalion, so that units would not be paralysed in action if their commanding officers became casualties. Inaction was regarded as criminal. Training centred around field exercises so that tactical doctrine would be clearly understood and uniformly practised by officers throughout all arms of the army. This enabled them to react quickly, and co-operate with each other so as to improvise effectively in real crises.

British doctrine tried to avoid battlefield chaos by controlling it centrally through a 'masterplan'. Junior officers were only allowed to change their actions if circumstances changed, and needed author-ization to do so, which led to delay. Initiative was effectively banned. Training emphasized obedience, which was inculcated by drill. The modern battlefield was held to be so stressful that only autocratic control by senior officers and instinctive obedience to orders on the part of other ranks would avoid collapse. In all this, there were similarities to Italian doctrine, though for different reasons, but the effects were less drastic because of important differences in the way doctrine was applied. In line with what was taken to be a British instinct for improvization, the rigidity of the doctrine was loosened for senior officers. Orders became treated as suggestions or debating subjects for senior and middle-ranking officers who discussed the meaning of orders, and tried to improve on them before carrying them out. This liberal view was regarded as morally superior to rigid Prussian obedience. As tactical doctrine was not practised in exercises, there was no common understanding of it. The result was disastrous. The deadly combination of strict central control and the free expression of opinion in the middle ranks led to sluggish, unco-ordinated and unimaginative performance on the battlefield whilst the 'rigid Prussians' were fast, imaginative improvisers. Despite the crushing evidence of battlefield experience, British officers still believed that they had a talent for improvization and that German soldiers were methodical and unimaginative. This seems to have been rooted in some metaphysical beliefs about national characteristics, which many even claimed were innate. In fact, both armies did what they had been told to do in the way they had been trained to do it, which is hardly a great surprise.[22]

Whilst the British deluded themselves with fantasies about Germans rigidly obeying orders and planning everything down to the last detail (because of 'Teutonic thoroughness'), the Germans knew their enemy. The intelligence branch of OKH warned the men of the Afrika Korps leaving Germany that British officers could be expected to fight 'gallantly and devotedly', but that the higher level commanders would show 'reluctance to make swift decisions' and retain their 'laborious methods of issuing orders', whilst junior officers would demonstrate a 'lack of independence and inflexible methods'. The predictions were very accurate. As late as the Gazala battle, the intelligence branch of the Panzerarmee noted the behaviour of the Eighth Army with the bemusement of men to whom 'mission command' was a way of life: 'Their orders were schematic and went into the smallest detail. The middle and lower command were consequently allowed little freedom of movement ...

The British soldier generally gave a good account of himself ... His officers fought with gallantry and devotion; a certain shyness of independent action existed.'[23] On the other side of the hill, Alan Moorehead felt the effect of being in an army to which mission command was alien when he found himself caught up in a retreat which threatened to turn into panic: 'Rumour spread at every halt, no man had orders. Everyone had some theory and no one any plan beyond the frantic desire to reach his unit ... Had there been someone in authority to say, "Stand here, do this and that" – then half our fear would have vanished ... I badly wanted to receive orders. And so, I think, did the others.'[24]

These differences between the two armies were endemic. The methodical predictability of British tactics and the silo mentality of individual units were to dog the British Army in Normandy and north-west Europe. Similarly, the German Army often held on at points of crisis by throwing together a 'battle-group' of mixed arms, with its junior commanders routinely showing a flexibility, initiative and skill at improvization rarely matched by the Allies, except in the élite parachute divisions.[25] Of all the factors which can be cited to explain how the Germans beat the odds for so long, both in the desert and elsewhere, their use of a mission-based command system, and their opponents' lack of it, is the most important.

However, one German tactical innovation was peculiar to the desert war, and goes a long way towards explaining the very high tank losses suffered by Eighth Army in many engagements. They perfected the technique of using their anti-tank guns offensively as well as defensively. When German tank units met British armour, the German anti-tank guns would rapidly dig in, forming a screen behind their tanks. The German tanks would withdraw behind their guns, and the British tanks, much as their Anglo-Saxon forbears had done at the Battle of Hastings, would move forward in a charge, only to be cut down, not by Norman cavalry, but by German anti-tank guns. The guns were barely visible, and so their impact was often erroneously ascribed to the tanks, which were. When advancing, German tanks and anti-tank guns would leap-frog each other, moving forward and screening each other in turn. Used in this way, the Germans' most numerous anti-tank guns, the 50mm and even the 37mm, which were small and hard to see, were often as effective as the mighty 88s.

The final reason why the Panzerarmee beat the odds for so long can be summed up as the 'Rommel factor'. Rommel was an outstanding divisional and corps commander, on a par with many of his contemporaries in the Wehrmacht whose names are unknown in the west because they fought their war in Russia, and did not become darlings of Goebbels' Propaganda Ministry, as Rommel did. He had all the skills shown by O'Connor, plus charisma. He was a mercurial character, prone to depression and lacking the mental robustness demonstrated by the first rank of German generals such as Guderian or von Manstein. But when he was up, he was up. Given the size of his forces and the toughness of his opponents, he had to take calculated risks, but he had an extraordinary eye for the main chance. Often criticized for being in the front line rather than at head-quarters, where the overall shape of a battle could be controlled, his forward position was in line with Guderian's theory and practice: use speed to overcome superior numbers. Time and again, Rommel was the first decision-maker on either side to know what was going on at the critical point in a battle, and so exploit it. He used the confusion of battle as a weapon in itself. By the time his opponents reacted to the latest news they had, Rommel was already doing something else. According to the old adage coined by Confederate cavalry General Nathaniel Bedford Forrest, achieving victory is about getting there 'firstest with the mostest'.[26] Rommel generally got there first, but the British generally had the most, and so avoided decisive defeat.

None of this was magic, although to many soldiers in the Eighth Army it appeared to be. Rommel's ability to act faster than British generals, the frequent paralysis of British decision making and the sluggish way in which British units worked together all suggest the conclusion that German generals were clever and British generals were stupid. This conclusion is tempting, but wrong. The first reason for the difference in organizational performance is the Germans' use of mission command, which had the effect of a secret weapon. It was, after all, invisible. But the second reason is that British officers lost control over events simply because they could not talk to anyone. The barrier to flexibility was not just mental but physical as well – signals equipment and security systems.

Although a canny observer might have realized it from the campaign in France of May 1940, it was the desert war which showed clearly for the first time that technology had changed modern warfare fundamentally. It was still about getting there 'firstest with the mostest'. But knowing where '*there*' was and knowing *when* to get there, had become a major problem. War had a new element: information.

At the strategic level, the British enjoyed a major advantage because, in what was called 'Operation Ultra', the brilliant cryptographers at Bletchley Park had broken the codes of the German 'Enigma' machine, an encoding device which the Germans believed throughout the war to be unbreakable. Initially cracking the codes used by the Luftwaffe, the code-breakers later penetrated the secrets of the German Navy as well. They broke the Army codes in September 1941. The information gained was supplied to just a few people of the highest rank, and sometimes it was deliberately not exploited to the full in order to keep secret the fact that Enigma had been broken. It gave high level information about German force dispositions and intentions, including, for example, the invasions of Greece and Crete, though it could take some days to complete the decoding. False conclusions were sometimes drawn from Ultra sources. Rommel's communications with Germany were particularly tricky to interpret, as he sometimes lied to his superiors and often changed his mind about what to do at the last moment without telling anyone.[27] He also disobeyed orders. When Rommel first arrived in Africa, Bletchley Park intercepted OKW's signals to him ordering a limited defensive posture. As a result, his offensive took Wavell by surprise.[28] The quality of these conclusions improved after a brilliant and intense classics don on the intelligence staff in Cairo called Major Enoch Powell set up a committee which met every day to assess all the intelligence sources available.[29]

Nothing of comparable value was available to the Axis until in August 1941 the Italians succeeded in persuading a clerk in the US Embassy in Rome to let them discreetly make a copy of the secret code used by American military attachés. From the autumn of 1941, the often far from discreet messages sent to Washington by the American military attaché in Cairo, Colonel Fellers, were read by both the Italian and German intelligence services. They provided valuable insights into British strength and forthcoming intentions and were dubbed 'the Good Source'. The source was particularly valuable during offensive 'Crusader' before drying up at the end of June 1942. The British had become suspicious through their own reading of Enigma decrypts and finally traced the leak to the Good Source, who was promptly sent home.[30]

Ultra was a great coup. But Enigma was a brilliant invention and bears witness to the seriousness with which the Germans took battlefield communications. This extended to their use of radio. As part of their emphasis on mobile warfare, they developed radio communications rather than relying on the static land lines which had dominated World War I. Radio gives complete freedom of movement and flexibility, allowing a commander to control a battle from anywhere. However, it has one major disadvantage – it is very easy for an enemy to listen in. Radio signals require security, and the tighter the security, the slower and more cumbersome radio communications become. The more complex a code, the more training is required to use it, the greater the incidence of error and the slower the transmission rate. For example, in 1944 it was found that when using plain language Morse operators could transmit 300 language groups in ten minutes but took between one and two hours to do the same thing in code. A compromise must be reached. At the same time, there is high value to developing a good listening service, for it can reveal what the enemy is doing on the battlefield almost in real time.

The Wehrmacht developed a simple but high standard of radio security. This security system in turn made German officers confident enough to use radio communications a lot. They understood when speed mattered more than security and vice versa, and so used plain language and code flexibly. They realized that a lot of equipment would fail or be destroyed in battle, and so built in redundancy. They also realized that they could find out a lot about their enemies by listening to their radio traffic. One of the most important units in the Afrika Korps was the Third Company of Intelligence Unit 56, commanded by Oberleutnant Alfred Seebohm, which had operated from Le Havre in 1940 to listen in to British radio traffic. Seebohm was one of the leading specialists in his field and had already served under Rommel in the 7th Panzer Division.[31] His company joined an existing Italian interception unit commanded by an artillery officer and former journalist, Captain Guiglia. To preserve the security of Seebohm's own unit, it was renamed Long Range Reconnaissance Company 621 in April 1942. Its work, the results of which were immediately available even in the heat of battle, lay behind many of

Rommel's successes, for the British Army had a system which was uniquely vulnerable to the techniques of Blitzkrieg.

In the inter-war years, the British Army put little effort into signals. Equipment was in very short supply. Security was based on call signs which a unit like Seebohm's could crack quite easily with a bit of patience. As there was little training, people found the code system itself hard to use. One of those called upon to use it was the poet and writer Keith Douglas, who joined the Nottinghamshire Yeomanry, the Sherwood Foresters, in October 1941. He described the code as having been 'laid down by someone who had vague ideas of security and no idea of the mentality of mechanized (or non-mechanized) cavalrymen'. They supplemented it with 'veiled talk' of their own, a 'mysterious symbolic language in some ways like that of a wildly experimental school of poets' full of nicknames, allusions and references to horsemanship. The Germans quickly learned that 'I shall need a farrier, I've cast a shoe' meant that a tank had lost its track and would be an easy target. The British idiom was, Douglas wrote, 'quite insecure'.[32] In practice, aware that it was vulnerable, most British officers came to regard silence as the only form of security. They had the choice between silence and security – between not telling their friends what they were doing and giving the game away to the enemy. They did a lot of both. In the course of a mobile battle, their system would degrade faster than the German one, so in the end the choice was forced upon them: silence. When they did talk it was often without code, like the two brigade commanders who discussed with each other a 3,000 yard gap between their units. They agreed that neither of them could do anything about it. So a little later the Germans did.

Fighting the static Italians in 1940, these weaknesses did not count for much and encouraged the view that they did not matter. Defeating them was largely a matter of taking the stone forts they clung to. Against the Germans in 1941, the weaknesses were crippling. When a few wireless sets were knocked out, whole units disappeared from maps, paralysing higher unit commanders. Again and again, British units fought their desert battles alone, whilst Rommel was able to keep abreast of the overall shape of events, and so determine them, because, quite simply, he could talk to his people. In the desert, unlike Europe, territory counted for nothing. Victory depended on finding and destroying the other side's forces. The journalist Alan

Moorehead was one who saw that desert fighting was like war at sea, where men moved by compass. 'Each truck or tank,' he has written, 'was as individual as a destroyer, and each squadron of tanks or guns made great sweeps across the desert as a battle-squadron at sea will vanish over the horizon. One did not occupy the desert any more than one occupied the sea ... We hunted men, not land, as a warship will hunt another warship, and care nothing for the sea on which the action is fought.'[33] Maps were of little more use than charts of the oceans. The only way to find out where people were, let alone tell them what to do, was to talk to them.

But the British learned, and in 1942 enormous improvements were made, whilst increasing equipment shortages on the German side degraded their own system. As equipment supplies improved, the British were able to introduce some back-up to make their system more robust. They also began to adopt some German procedures. The culture of the British officer corps still blocked progress. Orders were debated, commands questioned and, conversely, authority was sought for decisions which needed to be taken and acted upon immediately. A lot of it was still done in the clear because they were not familiar enough with the cipher system. When the ciphers *were* used, Seebohm could do nothing. By July 1942, there was little to choose between the two armies' technical systems, and although the Germans still made better use of their equipment, the habits of British officers were also starting to change. The nature of the battles was changing as well. For as the two sides converged on the forty-mile line at El Alamein, the fighting ceased to be mobile, and became static. This was a necessary consequence of geography. It also neutralized one of the greatest single advantages enjoyed by the Afrika Korps.[34]

Much of Rommel's battlefield performance, and the effectiveness of the Afrika Korps as a weapon of mechanized warfare, can thus be explained. So can the failings of the Eighth Army. It was not so much out-fought as out-thought. What remains unique about Rommel is the reputation he had amongst his opponents. Ordinary British soldiers held him in such respect, bordering on affection, that they coined the phrase 'to do a Rommel' for anything clever which was well executed. In fact the performance of the Afrika Korps had far more to do with the doctrine and training of the German Army as a whole than the wiliness of the Desert Fox.[35]

It is a tribute to the gritty courage of the fighting men of the Eighth Army that they consistently fought so hard against someone to whom they ascribed almost magical powers. The hold he had over their men was a real problem for the British commanders. One joke doing the rounds had it that Hitler had sent a secret message to Churchill offering to remove Rommel from his command if Churchill agreed to retain all his generals in theirs.[36] It got so bad that Auchinleck issued a letter to all Eighth Army commanders on the subject of 'our friend Rommel', telling them to 'dispel the idea that Rommel represents something more than an ordinary German general', and to 'refer to the enemy as "the Germans" or "the Axis powers" or "the enemy" and not always keep harping on about Rommel'.[37] In November 1941, the British even sent a team of commandos to kill Rommel at his headquarters. He was not there and the raid was a complete failure. It leader, Lieutenant-Colonel Geoffrey Keyes, was himself killed and was awarded a posthumous VC. Hitler did not take kindly to these unsporting tactics, and the following year ordered that all captured commandos were to be shot. When Rommel received the order he was with General Westphal, and, as Westphal later testified at Nuremberg, he burned it on the spot.[38]

In the event, the Eighth Army showed such resilience, such an ability to take casualties, retreat, re-form and then attack again, that the tactical skill of the DAK and their commander were never enough to grant them a decisive victory. Decision, when it came, would have to be reached on the battlefield. But that decision would itself be determined by factors beyond the control of the desert soldiers and indeed their commanders. As General Walter Warlimont, Deputy Chief of Operations at OKW throughout most of the war, has pithily observed, the laws governing the Mediterranean theatre of war were ordained by the sea.[39]

THE
SUPPLY
WAR

THE GERMAN ARMY OF 1939–45 was arguably the most effective military force fielded by any European power since the Romans. Its battle-winning capability was unmatched in its day. In France in 1940 and Russia in 1941, it gained the largest and most spectacular land victories in the history of warfare. As the war went on, its enemies, in the west and the east, narrowed the gap in operational effectiveness, but never fully closed it. In the last three weeks of the war in Europe, during the Battle of Berlin, the battered remnants of the German Army inflicted over 300,000 casualties on the three Soviet Army groups which finally overcame them.[1] In a post-war analysis of Hitler's Wehrmacht, US Army Colonel Dupuy has concluded: 'On a man for man basis, the German ground soldier consistently inflicted casualties at about a 50 per cent higher rate than they incurred from the opposing British and American troops under all circumstances. This was true when they were attacking and when they were defending, when they had a local numerical superiority and when, as was usually the case, they were outnumbered, when they had air superiority and when they did not, when they won and when they lost.'[2]

In the end, of course, they lost. The most basic explanation for this

is that Hitler's hideous ideology gathered against him the overwhelming manpower resources and industrial strength of a 'Grand
Alliance' which included the two post-war super-powers, forging
links between ideological enemies which did not break until he was
dead. Needless to say, there is more to it than that.[3] The next
immediate explanation is that they won the wrong battles because of
a failure of overall strategy – that, in other words, they misallocated
their resources. The history of the German Army in World War II
therefore became a story of 'lost victories', as the autobiography of
one of its finest generals, Erich von Manstein, puts it.[4]

The Mediterranean war is no exception. Whilst Rommel and his
desert soldiers defied the odds to gain a string of battlefield successes,
these availed them nothing in the end because the desert itself was
only one front of the desert war. The outcome of the land fighting
was determined by a supply war, in which the main front was the
Mediterranean Sea. The supply war revolved around control of the
convoy routes over the sea, three main ports, and the supply lines in
the desert linking the ports to the front. Control of the convoy routes,
ports and supply lines on land required control of the air. Central to
the first two was the island of Malta. It was a war which the Axis
powers could have won, but which, at each critical point, they
conceded.

On land, supply depended on logistics. In order to live, men
needed water and food. In order to move, vehicles needed petrol and
oil. When they moved, vehicles broke down and needed spare parts.
The desert wore out mechanical parts faster than any other
environment. In Europe, without any fighting, tank engines lasted
for a maximum of about 1,600 miles. In the desert, the maximum was
about 900 miles. When fighting took place, damage was inflicted,
vehicles had to be recovered, ammunition had to be replenished, and
the wounded evacuated. Losses in men and equipment had to be
replaced, and reinforcements had to be brought up. Everything had
to be moved in trucks, which needed petrol themselves. The further
each army moved from its base, the more petrol the trucks used up in
getting to them, the longer it took for supplies to reach them and the
more vulnerable the transport columns were to air attack and
roaming columns of special forces. Each blow delivered into the
desert declined in strength the further from a supply base it carried.

The logistics were complex, for to be of any use, the right things had to be got to the right people in the right place, and the people were often on the move. There was a lot of loading, unloading and reloading. The German logistical system did as little as possible of this at the base, but at the front, corps supply units would unload supplies and reload them on to divisional transport columns which would then reload them into unit loads. It was a 'pull' system – demand was driven from the front. The Italians centralized everything in a 'push' system. Neither regiments, divisions nor even corps had logistical units of their own and demand was determined in the rear. There were few stocks at the front, for this 'Intendanza' offered its customers a daily service. Given the Italian Army's inability to provide its soldiers with regular field post, the system did not inspire a great deal of confidence. Units became rooted to the spot, afraid that any movement might interrupt the flow of ammunition, food and water. Even total immobility did not guarantee freedom from perdition through lack of food and water. Crippling its forces through the design of its logistical system alone was a unique achievement of the Italian High Command, emulated by no other army of the time.[5]

The British separated ammunition, fuel and rations at the unloading point, and the Royal Army Service Corps (RASC) took them to forward bases in divisional columns. At the bases, ordnance, ammunition and repair workshops were run by another organization, the Royal Army Ordnance Corps (RAOC). From July 1942, repairs became the responsibility of a new rear-echelon organization, the Royal Electrical and Mechanical Engineers (REME), which was officially established in October. The men in these organizations formed the growing 'tail' needed to keep the army fighting. Churchill was suspicious of its growth and frequently complained about its size.[6] Indeed this 'overhead' absorbed between two thirds and three quarters of the army's manpower, and grew faster than the number of fighting troops. It also introduced into the British Army in large numbers the sort of technically minded people it needed to fight a modern war.

Getting the supplies to logistical units in the first place involved a good deal of fighting, though not on the part of the armies. Every tank, shell, can of petrol, tin of food and cup of water had first to be brought to the desert before it could be moved over land. The only route most of these supplies could take was across the sea. And it was while it was on a ship that every one of these things was most vulnerable of all to enemy action. The British harnessed the local economies to provide what they could, but most equipment came from outside the Middle East. Supplies from Britain travelled by the Cape route, which meant circumventing the coast of Spain and the whole continent of Africa, but it was fairly secure. The Axis powers had a shorter route, for everything could start in Italy. But it was the only route they had. Everything had to cross the Mediterranean.

From the very beginning, the Panzerarmee Afrika faced an intractable problem, recognized by von Thoma in the report he made in 1940. In theory, a mobile infantry division at full strength needed about 350 tons of supplies a day, including water, i.e. about 10,000 tons a month. A Panzer division needed more, a marching infantry division less. In round terms, therefore, the ten divisions making up the Panzerarmee in 1942 required 100,000 tons of supplies a month in order to keep fighting, and that was the figure Rommel always used. He was exaggerating, as his divisions were never at full strength, and he got by quite well with about 60,000 tons a month. Nevertheless, even 60,000 tons needed a lot of transportation. The first question was where to land them.

Tripoli was the largest port in Libya, and being at the western end of the desert both it and the sea lanes to it were fairly secure from attack by the RAF. If the RAF left it alone and it worked at maximum efficiency, it could unload up to 80,000 tons a month, but in practice only about 45,000 tons a month could be relied upon. The German quartermaster general in Rome estimated that Benghazi could handle 60,000 tons per month, but the 'Benghazi mail-run' was a regular trip for Wellington bombers in Egypt, so he reckoned with 30,000 tons. The third significant port heading east was Tobruk, which could in theory take 40,000 tons, but in practice was again assumed to work at 50 per cent of capacity, giving about 20,000 tons a month.[7] Rommel really needed all three of these ports to supply his army. The fourth large port heading east was Alexandria, which was by far the largest and would solve all the problems, but it was firmly in British hands. As long as Rommel only had Tripoli and Benghazi, he could unload only just enough to keep his forces going, as long as he did not go too far.

The Italian High Command ensured that using these ports was as difficult as possible even if the British decided to do nothing but watch. Before the war, the Italian Navy decided that the Royal Navy would make it impossible to supply North Africa in wartime. So it did not build any specialized ships or convoy escort vessels and demanded that the Army build up stocks in Libya and look after itself. The Army was having trouble clothing and arming itself as it was, so it did nothing. When the war forced both the Navy and Army to do something, both retained their own logistical organizations and kept a careful watch on what the other one did wrong – just in case there were questions. When the Germans arrived, the level of complexity grew somewhat and the level of recrimination grew exponentially. The unloading of every ship was attended by careful and delicate negotiations between the various authorities involved. Eventually, the Chief of the Italian General Staff, General Cavallero, took personal control. Most of the 300 General Staff meetings in 1942 were devoted to discussing the movements of individual ships.[8]

Unloading supplies in a port was just the first step. Once unloaded, the supplies had to be got to the front in trucks. The normal rule of thumb is that fighting troops must be no more than 200 miles from their supply base. In the desert, this rule was stretched to 300 miles. To keep one division going 300 miles from its base required about 1,200 standard two-ton trucks running in continuous convoys. Keeping up the same flow of daily deliveries 600 miles from base would take more than twice as many. The trucks used up a ton of petrol themselves for every 10 tons delivered, and they would break down – usually about a third of them were out of commission at any one time. So as the supply lines lengthened, the effort required to sustain a given level of supplies to the fighting troops grew disproportionately. The threat of air attacks in itself could mean restricting driving to night, which effectively halved the maximum flow. Actual air attacks would reduce the truck fleet and destroy supplies themselves. The Panzerarmee never had enough trucks, and getting enough would have made their divisions the most logistically expensive in the whole of the Wehrmacht. The desert was uniquely difficult, its needs uniquely extravagant. Not even the vastness of Russia compared. The front at El Alamein was twice as far from Tripoli as Moscow was from the German-Polish border and there were no trains. At its extreme, the Axis logistical apparatus had to perform the equivalent of unloading the contents of a ship docked in London on to trucks which then had to drive to Athens to deliver them. In January 1942, Rommel asked for 8,000 more trucks to support the three divisions of the DAK. At that time, the four Panzer Armies in Russia with over ten times the number of mobile divisions had 14,000 trucks between them. OKH thought it was a bad joke.

For the British, geography rendered the problem less acute. Alexandria had plenty of capacity, it was 435 miles from Tobruk, and there was a railway as far as Mersa Matruh. Advancing westwards, if the British had Tobruk, Benghazi was only another 300 miles. The biggest problem was the 675 miles of winding road from Benghazi to Tripoli, but only O'Connor had got as far as contemplating that, and he never tried it. However, the British also made the problems they did have less acute still by giving them a high priority.

The British Army was used to fighting small colonial wars in big countries with primitive infrastructures. As a result, its doctrine emphasized logistics. The German Army expected to fight wars in Europe, where roads and railways would take care of all the problems, and its doctrine therefore emphasized operations. The skills of the two armies developed accordingly. Unlike the German Army, the bulk of whose infantry divisions relied on horse-drawn transport, the British Army decided in the 1920s to get rid of horses and replace them with trucks. As a result they had plenty of them. A standard British *infantry* division had an establishment of 3,745 vehicles. Rommel's Panzer divisions had an establishment of only 2,100, even including their tanks. In August 1942 all the German forces in the Panzerarmee Afrika actually had only 4,117 between them, some 1,500 below establishment.[9] Because they had more vehicles, British divisions also had a correspondingly longer 'tail' of drivers and mechanics to look after them, which annoyed Churchill but gave them a significant advantage. The rail line was extended west from Mersa Matruh so that by March 1942 it reached as far as Capuzzo on the Libyan frontier. Before the war, Hobart had developed a system of forward supply dumps in the desert called field maintenance centres, which were highly successful and later used in north west Europe.[10] Logistics by themselves do not win battles, but armies which do not pay attention to them cannot win wars either.

The reason why Rommel was only ever given two Panzer divisions is that that was the maximum number which could be supplied without reducing the size of the Italian contingent, which would have been politically very difficult. The reason why he was told to remain on the defensive and stay in Libya is that if he went further he would outrun his supply bases. In his first assault he recaptured Benghazi, 675 miles from Tripoli. Having got Benghazi he managed the next 300 miles to Tobruk. There was not enough coastal shipping to move supplies from Tripoli to Benghazi, so most still had to come to Tobruk from Tripoli, doing the 975 miles in trucks. He could not go on without capturing Tobruk, but it held out, so in the end he had to go back. By ignoring his orders and trying to kick the British out of Egypt, Rommel created a supply problem which in the context was insoluble. He was acutely aware of the problem, but regarded solving it as someone else's business. His attitude to the Commando Supremo in Rome and to OKH was 'give me the tools and I will finish the job'. The Commando Supremo could not. OKH would not, and wished Rommel would just do as he was told and stop making a fuss. The only solution Rommel had was to attack in the hope of capturing enough supplies to keep him going. Without the trucks he captured from the Eighth Army, his logistical infrastructure would have broken down completely. Living off the enemy was good, swashbuckling stuff, but the enemy could not provide 88mm shells, spare parts for Panzer IIIs and so on, even if the petrol and tinned peaches they did provide were more than welcome. The only way in which the Axis could have created a real solution would have been to change the context which made the problem insoluble. That meant tackling the overall strategic situation in the Mediterranean theatre.

To solve the supply problem for good, Rommel needed to get to Alexandria. In order to get there, another 435 miles beyond Tobruk, he needed Tobruk and a following wind, or he would be stopped by lack of trucks. However, Tobruk by itself was not enough, because convoys heading for Tobruk could be easily attacked from Malta. Convoys to Tripoli and Benghazi were also vulnerable, but by taking the shorter westerly route, they could be fairly well protected by the Axis air forces. As long as the British held Malta, however, convoys to Tobruk could be attacked from there as well as by aircraft in Egypt. Tobruk alone was useless. Only the combination of Tobruk and Malta would solve the problem and allow Rommel to fulfil his ambitions in Egypt. The second front of the supply war was the sea.[11]

British naval power in the Mediterranean was dependent on Gibraltar, which controlled the narrow straits out to the Atlantic, and so the supply route from that ocean. In the summer of 1940, faced with the daunting prospect of having to invade the British Isles themselves, OKW dallied with an indirect approach to bring the British to heel. Hitler approached Franco, hoping to lure him into the conflict by offering him Gibraltar. They met on 23 October, but Franco would have none of it. Spain needed peace to rebuild itself after its Civil War (which Franco had won with German and Italian help), and he had been disturbed by Hitler's attack on Catholic Poland. OKW toyed with the idea of a direct attack on the Rock, which was called Operation 'Felix', but rejected it.[12] Gibraltar was never seriously threatened throughout the course of the war. Churchill recognized, in a letter to the Chiefs-of-Staff Committee on 6 January 1941, that as long as Spain refused to co-operate with Germany, Gibraltar was safe, and he lost little sleep over it.[13] Hitler could have continued to cajole and bully Franco into letting him have a go. After all, Franco did later agree to send a division of volunteers to fight in Russia. But Hitler desisted. This was just as well, for the loss of Gibraltar would have been a strategic disaster for Britain.

The Royal Navy was therefore left in control of the Mediterranean, with one fleet, Force 'H' under Admiral-of-the-Fleet Sir James Somerville, at its western neck at Gibraltar, and another, the Mediterranean Fleet under Admiral-of-the-Fleet Sir Andrew Cunningham, at the eastern end at Alexandria. Both bases were secure, at least in the immediate future. The Navy's dominance depended, however, on retaining control of one small island in the very centre of the Mediterranean only about 60 miles south of Sicily – Malta.

Despite being somewhat smaller than the Isle of Wight, Malta is a nation in its own right. The proudly independent population, numbering about 250,000 in 1940, speaks a unique language derived from Semitic, the ancestor of modern Arabic and Hebrew. It has long been recognized that control of Malta meant control of the Mediterranean. In 1530, The Knights of St John, a crusading order, were offered Malta as a home by Emperor Charles V, and in 1565, they and the local population repelled a determined attempt by the Turkish Empire to win Malta for Islam in what became famous as the Great Siege of Malta. After the Turks' departure, the Grand Master of the Order of St John, La Valette, revived plans to build a fortified city on the tongue of land separating Malta's two great natural harbours, and the result was Valetta. The Knights stayed in Malta, bequeathing it the cross of their Order as a national emblem, until they were expelled by Napoleon when he was on his way to Egypt in 1798. The fiercely Catholic Maltese rebelled against the atheistic revolutionaries from France and after Nelson had destroyed Napoleon's fleet at the mouth of the Nile, the British helped them to get rid of the occupiers. 'Brave Maltese,' observed an English colonel who served with them, 'you have rendered yourselves interesting and conspicuous to the world.' But the Maltese still felt exposed and sought Britain's further protection, which she was at first strangely reluctant to give. Finally in 1814, Malta became a British possession, and remained so until 1964.[14]

The British soon became aware of the value of what they had been so freely given. Valetta has the only deep-water harbours in the Mediterranean between Italy, Gibraltar and Alexandria, and unlike the latter two, it is right in the middle. It quickly became the main centre for trade in the area as well as a naval base. Geologically, the island is an outcrop of yellowish-white sandstone, easy to quarry and easy to tunnel. Though somewhat powdery in texture, the rock develops a hard shell when exposed to the atmosphere. It is an ideal material for fortifications, as evidenced by the great walls of Valetta itself. Underneath those walls, the British built an underground control centre and the population created air raid shelters. Malta became the main base of the Royal Navy's Mediterranean Fleet.

In 1940, Malta sat in the middle of the Axis supply routes to Africa. It could therefore serve not only as a naval base, but as an unsinkable aircraft carrier. Aircraft and submarines operating from Malta could attack any Axis ship heading from Italy to Tunisia or Libya. If the Axis powers were to take Malta, they in turn could dominate the whole of the western Mediterranean and make life impossible for the Royal Navy and the British merchant fleet. If Mussolini wanted the Mediterranean to be Italian, he had to take the island.

For the Axis, the most obvious way to attack Malta was from the sea. The Royal Navy had to eliminate the threat posed both to Malta and to British convoys by the only other naval force in the area, the Italian Navy. The Italians had built the second largest navy in Europe. In June 1940 it included 113 submarines, the second largest submarine force in the world after Russia's.[15] It was the only part of the Italian armed forces to have modern equipment. Its weaknesses were its lack of radar, lack of experience and a shortage of oil, which it could only get from the Germans and a few oilfields in the Balkans.

The first ship-to-ship clashes around convoys ensued in the first few weeks after Italy declared war, but they were inconclusive. In November 1940, British intelligence revealed that all six Italian battleships were in harbour at the south Italian port of Taranto. On the night of 11 November, in an operation controlled from Malta, twenty-one Swordfish torpedo-bombers from the aircraft carrier *Illustrious* crippled three of the battleships as well as two cruisers. The British lost two aircraft. A little later, the Japanese naval attaché in Berlin, Lieutenant-Commander Naito, flew down to Taranto. In October 1941, he gave a lecture on his findings to the staff of the Imperial Japanese Navy and discussed with them the implications of substituting Taranto with Pearl Harbour.[16]

In the tradition of Nelson, the British admirals wanted a decisive action, something Mussolini equally wished to avoid. He wanted to keep his fleet in being and its operations were constrained by the lack of oil. Under German pressure, however, he did allow the Italian Navy to attack the British ships sending reinforcements to Greece. The British had cracked the Italian naval codes and on the morning of 28 March 1941, Admiral Cunningham's Mediterranean Fleet found the Italian task force off Cape Matapan.[17] In the first major fleet action since Jutland in 1916, Cunningham's ships sank three cruisers and two destroyers and seriously damaged the battleship *Vittorio Veneto*, the most modern and powerful in the Italian fleet. Thereafter, the main challenge to the Royal Navy's control of the sea was to come from the air.

The air threat to Malta was considered in London to be so severe that in the 1930s, as it became clear that Fascist Italy was becoming hostile, the Mediterranean Fleet abandoned it as its main base and moved to Alexandria. The Air Ministry believed that Malta could not be adequately defended, but nevertheless sent out some AA guns, a few searchlights and two mobile RDF (radar) sets. There was a plan to defend it with four squadrons of fighters, but in June 1940 there was just a fighter flight consisting of six Gloster Gladiator biplanes, backed up by another six kept in crates for use as spares.[18] They were Sea Gladiators belonging to the Fleet Air Arm, and the Admiralty in London issued indignant messages demanding to know why naval property had been handed over to the RAF.[19]

Mussolini announced his declaration of war on the evening of 10 June 1940 and at 04:30 the following morning, 55 bombers and 21 fighters of the Italian Air Force took off from their bases in southern Sicily to raid Malta. It was Italy's first aggressive action of the war. Three Gladiators intercepted them, slightly damaging one bomber. The Italian planes dropped 142 bombs around Malta's three airfields at Takali, Luqa and Hal Far, damaging some of the surrounding houses.[20] It was a small beginning for both sides.

The Italians continued with their raids whenever the weather allowed. On 22 June, a pair of Gladiators managed to score the RAF's first 'kill' over Malta by shooting down a lone Italian bomber engaged on a reconnaissance flight.[21] The main issue for the British, then and for the next two years, was how to get aircraft into Malta and keep them supplied. The supply war was itself a battle of supply – would Malta be able to cut the Axis supply lines to Africa or would the Germans and Italians cut Malta's first?

At first, a few Swordfish torpedo-bombers were flown in from French North Africa and Hurricanes were flown across France. The first five arrived on 13 June, and another eight – all that was left of the twelve which had left Britain – landed a week later.[22] Then France surrendered. The shortest route to Malta was now across the western Mediterranean from Gibraltar. On 2 August, twelve Hurricanes were successfully flown in from the aircraft carrier *Argus*. On 17 November, the same thing was tried again, but the Hurricanes, flown this time by relatively inexperienced pilots, were launched from too far away. Only four of the twelve arrived.[23] Some Wellingtons had arrived in late October to provide some offensive capability, but their mechanics were left behind, so they did not fly for long. The crews also discovered that the runway at Luqa was barely long enough for bombers, and several Wellingtons crashed taking off.[24]

In the meantime, the air raids continued. Legend has it that in these early days, Malta was defended by three Gladiators called 'Faith', 'Hope' and 'Charity'. In fact there were Hurricanes almost from the start. Of the six Gladiators which saw combat, only one was shot down, the others going out of commission through bomb damage and wear and tear. Four were still on strength at the end of 1940. The story of there being three probably stems from observers watching flights of three take off in the standard RAF 'vic' formation of the time. Most of the damage inflicted on the Italians was the work of Hurricanes. During 1940, Gladiator pilots claimed nine Italian aircraft shot down out of total RAF claims during 1940 of 31 destroyed, 11 probably destroyed and 20 damaged. Italian records show actual losses of 35 in total. No one is sure where the names 'Faith', 'Hope' and 'Charity' came from. They resonated with the Maltese. The reference is to St Paul's first letter to the Corinthians, and it was he who introduced Christianity to Malta when he was shipwrecked there on his way to Rome, and execution, in AD 60. One version attributes the names to Flying Officer John Waters. Some of his contemporaries deny any knowledge of these names being used at the time, and claim they were invented by a journalist later on. It certainly made a good story.[25]

Hurricanes continued to defend Malta throughout 1941. Some were flown in from carriers and others came via the arduous 3,697-mile route overland from Takoradi in Ghana, the main route taken by aircraft bound for the Middle East from England.[26] Aircrew passed by ship and submarine between Egypt and Malta in both directions, leading to some wry comments from RAF Headquarters in the Middle East that Malta was operating 'an extremely effective filter'. This was of course hotly denied.[27]

Important convoys got through to Malta in July and September, all subject to persistent air attacks. Following Rommel's first attack in March 1941, Churchill took a big risk and sent a large convoy, code-named 'Tiger', through the Straits of Gibraltar to reinforce Wavell. It passed south of Malta to reach Alexandria. The Royal Navy devoted almost all of its surface vessels to the convoy's defence. It docked in Alexandria on 12 May, with the loss of one ship, and unloaded 238 tanks.

From 10 January 1941, the attacks on Malta and the convoys were delivered by the Luftwaffe as well as the Italian Air Force. Fliegerkorps X was moved to Sicily with orders to attack the Royal Navy and British shipping lanes between the eastern and western Mediterranean.[28] The raids on the island built up in strength and frequency, initially centring around an attempt to sink the *Illustrious* which lay in Grand Harbour at Valetta after the Luftwaffe had crippled her while she was escorting a convoy. *Illustrious* slipped away to Alexandria on 23 January, but the raids continued. The Luftwaffe attained its peak strength of 243 aircraft in May, but at the same time the raids on Malta trailed off as Fliegerkorps X moved east to support the offensives in Greece and Crete There it stayed, with orders to defend the Balkans and support the Panzerarmee Afrika.[29]

Though the Luftwaffe withdrew, the Italian Navy took action. One specialized unit, the Tenth Light Flotilla, had been developing the techniques to use motor torpedo boats, midget submarines and manned torpedoes. On the night of 25 July 1941, they launched a desperately brave attack on the harbours at Valetta, which indeed turned out for most of them to be suicidal. The parent ship was picked up on radar, and the small craft were discovered by searchlights Every one was blown out of the water in a hail of gunfire. All the attackers were killed or captured, having succeeded only in blowing up the outer gates of the harbour. The Tenth Light Flotilla avenged this disaster later on when, on 19 December, its midget submarines successfully penetrated Alexandria harbour and crippled the battleships *Queen Elizabeth* and *Valiant*, putting them out of action for months. Coming after the sinking of the aircraft carrier *Ark Royal* and the battleship *Barham* by U-boats in November, this significantly altered the balance of naval power. The Axis never exploited the advantage gained by these dare-devil Italian special forces.[30]

So it was that ships, submarines and aircraft from Malta continued to attack Axis convoys. Details of Axis shipping movements were picked up from high-level Ultra decrypts, enabling the RAF and Royal Navy to be in the right place at the right time.[31] The commander of Fliegerkorps X, General Geisler, told Rommel that Malta had to be taken in order to protect his supply lines. Rommel wanted Geisler to use his aircraft to help him take Tobruk instead. On 29 August 1941, Mussolini met Hitler's Chief-of-Staff, Field Marshal Keitel, at the Brenner Pass. He told him that up to the end of July Italy had lost 74 per cent of the shipping capacity used to supply North Africa. Something had to be done. In mid-September, Hitler ordered U-boats into the Mediterranean. In November, a new force of British cruisers and destroyers called Force 'K' took up station in Malta and wiped out an Italian convoy. As a result, the Italians stopped all sailings to North Africa. So that month, in view of the fact that it was not really needed in Russia, Fliegerkorps II was transferred to Sicily. The commander of its parent airfleet, Field Marshal Albert Kesselring, was appointed Oberbefehlshaber Süd (Commander-in-Chief South), and he arrived in Rome on 28 November 1941 with instructions to establish air and naval superiority over the Axis supply routes, throttle the British ones, support Rommel and in particular to eliminate the threat from Malta.[32] To do so, Kesselring was given direct command of all German naval forces in the area as well as the 400 or more aircraft of Fliegerkorps II. The commander of Malta's air defences, Air Vice-Marshal Hugh Lloyd, only had 80 Hurricanes to defend it. So the job was quite easy.

Kesselring had heard this all before. In 1940, he had commanded the largest of the three German airfleets to take part in the Battle of Britain. His orders then had been to secure air superiority over south-east England in order to prepare for an invasion. Faced with the most formidable air-defence system in the world, Kesselring had unsurprisingly failed to deliver the goods.[33] He had his own views about how easy it was to neutralize an island purely from the air, especially when it was defended by the RAF, so he pressed for a combination of air assault and invasion. As theatre C-in-C he would control the whole exercise, so there would be none of the strategic confusion and arguments which had attended the planned invasion of Britain in 1940. When he first suggested this approach he was told to forget it, as there were no forces available.[34]

Kesselring built up his air force, directing it against convoys and the island, and persisted. He hatched an invasion plan called Operation 'Hercules'. Having lobbied the reluctant Italians he finally got to see Hitler at a stormy meeting in February 1942. Hitler ended the interview by grasping Kesselring's arm and confiding to him, in his thick Austrian accent: 'Keep your shirt on. I am going to do it!'[35] Italian troops were mustered and an invasion fleet prepared.

From 2 April 1942, the Luftwaffe subjected Malta to several weeks of the heaviest bombardment it had ever experienced. During that month, the Germans flew 8,788 sorties, twice as many as in March, which was itself twice as many as in each of the previous two months. Malta was subject to 283 air raids, an average of nine every day. The battle also took on a new and brutal character. Pilots who baled out were shot at, and crews floating in dinghies were strafed. Civilians, who had had enough after almost two years of bombing, were affected by the same emotions as the combatants. When one enraged mob got hold of a German airman who had parachuted down they cut his head off.[36] By 10 May, Kesselring felt he was ready to put an end to it all and launch Hercules.

Kesselring was ready, but the Italians were not. They did not agree with Kesselring that capturing the island would be easy. It called for a tricky combined sea and air operation. There were very few flat beaches, and those were heavily defended. Attacking other parts of the coast meant climbing sheer cliffs. Most of the islanders were farmers who marked out their smallholdings with stone walls, which precluded gliders from landing anywhere other than on the airfields. The main job would have to be done by paratroopers. The population of Malta was much larger than Crete and would be hostile. Despite having first attacked Malta from the air two years before, the Italian preparations were in much the same state the German's had been in after two months of planning the invasion of England in 1940. At a conference in Berchtesgaden on 29/30 April, the Italians persuaded their allies to attack Egypt first and carry on the softening-up of Malta for another three months.[37]

Thanks to the added air support, Axis convoy losses had moderated. Rommel was therefore able to launch his offensive at Gazala on 26 May 1942 with Malta still intact. This offensive forced the Luftwaffe to divert resources to lend direct support to Rommel and so gave the island a breathing space. 'We felt that our prayers had been answered,' a Maltese source is reported as saying. 'God had sent back the Italians.'[38] The Axis High Command had missed a golden opportunity, for despite the difficulties, Malta had been theirs for the taking.

Since the arrival in Sicily of Fliegerkorps II, Malta's Hurricanes had been having an increasingly rough time. In defending the island, they were now facing substantial numbers of Messerschmitt Bf 109Fs, arguably the finest version of Willy Messerschmitt's potent little fighter. The 109Es flown by the Luftwaffe during the Battle of Britain had been markedly superior to the RAF's Hurricanes in all but manoeuvrability, and the 109F increased the margin to a very dangerous level. On 15 January 1942, Air Vice-Marshal Lloyd sent a message to RAF HQ Middle East saying 'First problem here is fighter defence. Do not hold tools for job. Must stop day bombing ... Spitfire V only can make height in time to take on fighters.' He was promised fifteen in March. He said he wanted three squadrons. The Air Ministry in London had doubts about whether, in the tough conditions, Spitfires would operate as well as the more robust Hurricanes and pointed out that sending a new type would complicate the problem of supplying spares to keep them flying. They decided to gamble on it by infiltrating Spitfires before making a wholesale changeover. On 7 March the fifteen promised Spitfire Mk Vs were flown in from carriers.[39] They matched the performance of the Messerschmitts in almost every way.

However, one squadron of Spitfires did not a summer make – indeed they simply heralded a cruel spring. By mid-March there were only forty Hurricanes left and the bomber force had been more or less wiped out, leaving Rommel's convoys safe. There were indeed no spares for the Spitfires and precious few for the Hurricanes. On 26 March, Lloyd sent an excited message to RAF HQ Middle East observing that the previous night a Wellington had arrived carrying soap, toothpaste, razor blades and Brylcreem. He pointed out that four Hurricanes were grounded because of a lack of a certain type of rivet. 'We are fighting for our existence here,' he added, 'and Brylcreem is the last thing we need.' There was an embarrassed reply, recounting how the aircraft was changed at the last minute, how the nearest crate of supplies was slung on to fill the last bit of space, how there was no time to check its contents and so on. Such are the hazards of operating a supply chain.[40]

More Spitfires arrived on 21 and 27 March, but when the RAF's senior commander in the Middle East, Air Marshal Tedder, visited the island in mid-April, he found Malta's defences reduced to her AA guns and six serviceable aircraft. On 16 April 1942, as the bombing reached a crescendo, King George VI announced the unprecedented award of the George Cross, not to any individual, but to the island of Malta. That spring, its people endured 154 consecutive days and nights of bombing. Although the tonnage of bombs dropped on London during the 'Blitz' of 1940–41 had been higher, the 'Blitz' had only lasted for 57 consecutive nights.[41]

Desperate measures were needed. Churchill set to work, and on 20 April, by virtue of a personal arrangement between him and Roosevelt, 47 Spitfires arrived in Malta from the US carrier *Wasp*. The next day, as the Luftwaffe returned to bomb the new arrivals, an RAF reconnaissance flight over Sicily revealed the invasion preparations, including strips being built for gliders. That evening, after the day's bombing, only 17 Spitfires remained intact. No convoy had sailed for Malta in April. None could do so and survive in May either, unless more Spitfires got there first. Until they did, the island was naked.

They arrived on 9 May, 62 of them, flown in from *Wasp* again and

HMS *Eagle*. On 18 May another 17 arrived. The Luftwaffe's attentions were now directed towards North Africa. It had been a very near-run thing, but the opportunity for decision had passed. Between June and the end of October, 213 Spitfires joined Malta's defences, rendering them more formidable than they had ever been. Increasing numbers of bombers and torpedo-bombers joined them to re-establish its offensive strength. Though the direct threat had gone, these aircraft still needed fuel to fly and the population needed food to eat. In June the supply situation was still critical. Malta had to have a convoy.

In the second week of June 1942, two convoys set sail, one from Alexandria in the east and one from Gibraltar in the west. On 16 June, the one from the east, learning that two Italian battleships and four cruisers were heading to intercept it, returned to Alexandria. But on the same day, the two merchant ships which remained of the six which had set sail from Gibraltar berthed in Grand Harbour watched by a silent crowd.[42]

On 22 June, Rommel captured Tobruk along with 1,400 tons of fuel, 5,000 tons of supplies and, crucially, 2,000 intact vehicles. When he got the news, Hitler made Rommel a Field Marshal. The original plan had been to stop after this, and mount Operation 'Hercules' to secure Tobruk as a permanent base. This time, it was the Italians who wanted to stick to the plan and take Malta, and the Germans who argued against it. The situation in North Africa was unexpectedly favourable, and Rommel wanted to race on and take Egypt. In fact, as far as Hitler was concerned, 'Hercules' was already a dead duck.

In a meeting on 21 May, Hitler told his entourage that Hercules was too risky. He reckoned the Italian Navy would head for port the minute it sighted a British destroyer, the Italian Army had never even taken a bunker in the whole war, let alone an island and the memory of the heavy losses in Crete made him shy away from an airborne assault. He had visions of German paratroopers abandoned to their fate by their useless allies. The only way to deal with Malta was to starve it out. In any case, it was fine to let the British run convoys, as that gave the Germans the opportunity to destroy their shipping. When Admiral Raeder came to see him on 15 June he told Raeder the same thing.[43] The day Tobruk fell, the Führer needed no prompting from Rommel to send a telegram to Mussolini on telling him that a historical turning point had come. The Eighth Army was beaten, and Egypt was ripe for the taking. 'The Goddess of Fortune in Battle,' he wrote, 'approaches leaders but once. If they do not hold on to her tightly at that moment, she will often never return.'[44] How right he was. She had been fluttering over the skies of Malta from mid-April until the Spitfires from *Wasp* and *Eagle* shooed her away on 9 May.

That was not how Hitler saw it. After the fall of Singapore in February, the fall of Tobruk knocked aside another of the shaky pillars propping up the British Empire. The entry of Japan into the war in December 1941 had given him the opportunity to split the power of his enemies. He had declared war on the USA after Pearl Harbor in order to prevent her from concentrating on Japan and overcoming her quickly. Since the beginning of the year, he had watched Churchill's political position deteriorate as Britain took blow after blow. That old drunkard's government of plutocrats would never survive the loss of Egypt. With Rommel in Cairo, the British would finally come to some arrangement and he could get them off his back at last. It all made perfect sense: they could deal with the Japanese and he would deal with the Bolsheviks. Of course it was risky, but Rommel had the right stuff. He had proper National Socialist fire in his belly. Look at his record. He could do anything.

On 26 June, there was a conference of Axis commanders at Sidi Barrani. 'Cavallero and Rintelen are coming today', Rommel wrote home, 'no doubt to put the brakes on again as much as they can. Those two are always whistling the same old tune!!'[45] Now speaking with the authority of a Field Marshal, Rommel announced to the sceptical Italian commanders and a frustrated Kesselring that with the booty from Tobruk he could be in Cairo in ten days, and that Malta did not matter any more. In his mind, time was running out and this was his last chance. He had noted the arrival of American tanks as a sign of things to come. He guessed he would soon face an Allied army whose material superiority would be overwhelming. It was now or never. He was also telling his colleagues what Hitler wanted to hear, and that won him the debate with Kesselring. It also lost him the battle of El Alamein. Capturing Tobruk had been a brilliant tactical success, but it was a strategic trap. Capturing Crete in May 1941 had also been a major German success, but Crete's defenders had won a hidden victory in their defeat, for the price they exacted of their victors helped to persuade Hitler not to invade Malta.[46]

Kesselring was furious. Hitler told him to mind his own business. Kesselring's relationship with Rommel deteriorated from this time on. Mussolini consoled him with the notion that his forces would be ready to take Malta in August – or if not, perhaps in the spring. At all events, the Luftwaffe should get back to bombing it again. In the meantime, Mussolini himself was going to Africa. He arrived on 29 June to get ready for his triumphal entry to Cairo. After all, he needed a bit of time to practice – triumphal entries had been a bit thin on the ground of late. The story goes that he took a white horse with him for the occasion, though a black limousine was the more usual fashion.

From late May, aircraft from Malta had begun to ravage the Axis convoys again. But the real turning point came in July. Up to then, Malta had survived. From then on, it conquered.

On 14 July 1942, a Sunderland flying boat arrived over Malta during an air raid. It circled for about a quarter of an hour, until the senior officer on board ordered the pilot to go in and land because everybody was cold and hungry. When the officer got out, he was upbraided by Lloyd for taking unnecessary risks. The officer took the dressing down in good humour because he had arrived to replace Lloyd. His name was Air Vice-Marshal Keith Park. He was the man the Germans had dubbed 'the defender of London'. The hitherto defender of Malta showed the defender of London around the bomb-damaged areas, which was most of the island, stressing that, like London, Malta could take it. Park thought he was dumb. 'Why don't you stop the bombing?' he asked. It was not a joke. Within three weeks, Park had done just that.[47]

Lloyd had led Malta's air defences with great courage and tenacity throughout the worst year in its history, but he was a bomber man. He had been a strange choice for the Malta job, for he was wont to express contempt for Fighter Command and had a deep dislike of the Royal Navy.[48] His successor was the most experienced and successful fighter commander anywhere in the world. Throughout the summer of 1940, this tough, wiry New Zealander had been in charge of 11 Group, the largest group in Fighter Command, which covered south-east England and London. He had frustrated Kesselring's every move and thwarted the Luftwaffe with a brilliance which put him in a class of his own. After the war, Tedder, then Chief of the Air Staff, once observed that 'if ever any one man won the Battle of Britain, he did'. He was about to demonstrate his quality for a second time.[49]

Fliegerkorps II's attacks on Malta had peaked in April. The 8,788 sorties they flew in that month fell to 2,476 in May, and dropped again to 956 in June because of the needs of the desert itself. But in July, bombers from France and fighters from Russia arrived in Sicily. That month, with 150 aircraft, Fliegerkorps II flew 1,819 sorties against the island.[50] They were given a beating.

Park spent the first few days after his arrival assessing the situation. He later wrote down what he discovered. Malta's three airfields were being bombed three or four times a day, inflicting losses on aircraft and personnel. 'The tactics in vogue,' he wrote, 'were to dispatch our fighters to the rear of Malta whilst they assembled and climbed in big formations, and then to come in and attack after the bombs had been dropped and the enemy was diving away in full retreat under cover of its fighter escort. These tactics were being employed by the Commander of the Fighters, who had been station commander at Duxford in No. 12 Group which originated the Big Wings led by Bader in 1940. I immediately sent this officer back to England, and changed the tactics to what I called a forward interception plan used in No. 11 Group. I sent the fighter squadrons forward, climbing to meet the enemy bombers head on, and to intercept well before they reached Malta, when the bombers were in tight formation, heavily laden and unable to take evading action.'[51]

The officer concerned was Group Captain Woodhall, who had come to Malta in February 1942, having been the senior controller at Duxford during the Battle of Britain. There had been at the time a famous controversy between the commander of 12 Group, Trafford Leigh-Mallory, and the Deputy Chief of the Air Staff Sholto Douglas on the one hand, and Park and the Commander-in-Chief of Fighter Command, Sir Hugh Dowding, on the other. Leigh-Mallory and Sholto Douglas believed that it did not matter whether enemy aircraft were intercepted before or after they bombed as long as lots of them were shot down, and that the way to do that was to form wings of at least three squadrons and attack them in strength all at once. Park and Dowding believed that enemy bombers should be intercepted before they inflicted any damage on the ground, and that the way to do that was to send up fighters in squadrons or pairs of squadrons without forming them into wings. Park and Dowding won the Battle of Britain that way, but Leigh-Mallory and Sholto Douglas won the argument at the Air Ministry, and so took over their jobs, with Leigh-Mallory inheriting 11 Group from Park and Sholto Douglas inheriting Fighter Command from Dowding.[52]

Park issued his 'Fighter Interception Plan' on 25 July. He generously suggested that past tactics had been forced on the defenders by lack of fighters, but that they now had sufficient numbers to stop daylight bombing. Squadrons were from now on to follow instructions from the controllers, who were to put one squadron up-sun to attack the German top cover, one to attack the close escorts and a third to deliver a head-on attack on the heavily laden bombers to break them up and force them to jettison their bomb-loads. He tightened up radio discipline and controlling and demanded take-off from 'standby' in two minutes. Park's four-page document gave a full account of the purpose and method of the new policy, and was to be read by every fighter pilot in Malta so that everybody knew exactly what they and everyone else were to do and why.

The effect was immediate. On 10 August, Park issued a second set of instructions in which he reported the results of the new tactics. During the first half of July, 34 British aircraft had been destroyed or damaged on the ground. In the latter half of July, the comparable figure had been four.[53] Whilst 380 tons of bombs had fallen on Malta during the first two weeks, after Park took over the figure dropped to 160 tons.[54] During July, the Luftwaffe suffered a loss rate of 5.8 per cent,[55] even higher than the 5.1 per cent loss rate suffered by the US Air Force in the disastrous Schweinfurt-Regensburg raid of August 1943, which almost persuaded them to abandon the daylight bombing of Germany. Unlike the Americans, the Luftwaffe was truly persuaded. Having flown 1,819 sorties against Malta in July, they reduced their activity to 862 sorties in August and reduced it further to a mere 391 in September.[56] As in the closing stages of the Battle of Britain, they switched from bombing raids to fighter sweeps. Park had stopped the bombing, saved his aircraft and airfields, and defeated the Luftwaffe in the air.

However, he had not yet saved Malta itself. The island was still under siege. It needed food, petrol and ammunition. On 17 July, three days after his arrival, Park had told London that his stocks of aviation fuel would last just seven weeks.[57] No further ships had arrived since the two which had struggled in in June. Another convoy had to get through.

Accordingly, on 10 August, the fourteen merchantmen of Convoy 'Pedestal', escorted by four aircraft carriers, two battleships, seven cruisers and twenty four destroyers, sailed from Gibraltar in what might well be termed a 'maximum effort' on the part of the Royal Navy. There followed the fiercest convoy battle ever witnessed in the Mediterranean. The two Axis air forces between them had 540 serviceable aircraft to pit against 'Pedestal'. After the main British battle-fleet had been forced to leave the convoy, the Italians sent out a force of cruisers to attack it as well. Park fooled them into believing they were about to be attacked by a non-existent force of bombers and they turned back, only to have two of their number torpedoed by a submarine on their return journey.[58] At 18:00 on 13 August, after an extraordinary four-day battle, four merchantmen docked at Grand Harbour. Two days later, a final ship, the tanker *Ohio*, without whose cargo of fuel Park's Spitfires would have been grounded by the end of the month, crept painfully into Valetta lashed between two destroyers to prevent her from sinking. She bore a macabre memento of her struggle for life. On her foredeck was the wreck of an Italian Stuka which had hit the sea alongside and bounced up on to the ship. As soon as she docked, surrounded by jubilant crowds, her fuel was pumped off. As water flowing through the many holes in her sides replaced her load, she settled slowly on the bottom. Her master was awarded the George Cross, and Park, casting rationing regulations aside, held a slap-up dinner for the crews of all the ships. 'Pedestal' had cost nine merchant ships, two cruisers and the carrier *Eagle*. It was, however, a strategic victory, for 'Pedestal' was the last Malta convoy whose passage was seriously challenged.[59]

Park now had sufficient fuel to increase the amount of flying and intensify his offensive. The information provided by Ultra, both about Axis shipping and the impact of sinking it, had improved further.[60] To preserve the secret of Ultra, Park sent reconnaissance aircraft to where he knew the targets to be and only launched strikes after the ships had seen the spotter planes, so disguising the real source of his knowledge.[61]

Having captured Tobruk in June, the Axis started to land supplies there directly. Of the 18,400 tons of supplies sent from Italy to Africa for the DAK in July, half went to Tobruk. They also used coastal shipping to get supplies from Tripoli and Benghazi to Tobruk and in August it turned over 25,000 tons. However, only 5,000 tons of that arrived directly from Italy. In August, with Malta now on the offensive, the RAF sank over 20,000 tonnes of Axis shipping, the highest total since October 1941. British submarines found Valetta a quieter berth than before, and were able to sink another 35,000 tonnes. In the whole of August, 24 per cent of the Axis shipping capacity used to supply North Africa went to the bottom.[62] In September, the Axis convoys went back to using Tripoli and Benghazi where they had better air cover. They landed nearly 60,000 tons and shipping losses declined. However, those 60,000 tons spent the following weeks sitting in the dockyards or on trucks, plying the 1,350 miles from Tripoli to the front. In the month of August, Axis trucks drove a total of 3.3 million kilometres to bring 12,000 tons of supplies from Benghazi via Tobruk to Mersa Matruh.[63] Park had rendered Tobruk unusable as a main supply port.

The siege of Malta had still not been lifted, however. On 25 September, Park reported that at the current consumption rate of 230 tons per week he had enough high-octane fuel to last until the second week of November. If air activity were to intensify, stocks would run out before that.[64] Food was also a problem. Working men in Malta were on rations giving them 1,690 calories a day. Women and children got 1,500 a day. Rationing in the UK never fell below a rate of 2,800 calories a day throughout the war.[65] The Air Ministry in London wrote to the Governor of Malta advising him that one vessel would slip through to bring food in October and another to bring fuel in November. In the meantime, slaughtering 'all livestock other than draught animals' ought to 'postpone the exhaustion date of the population by about one week'.[66]

In September, the Italian Chief-of-Staff, Marshal Cavallero, described the 'neutralization' of Malta as 'a matter of life and death'.[67] Once again, something had to be done. Kesselring had told his colleagues, including Rommel, that they were going to dig themselves into a hole by abandoning 'Hercules'. Now that they were in it, they naturally blamed him and told him to dig them out.

On 11 October, Kesselring launched a last, forlorn attempt to 'neutralize' Malta. The Luftwaffe flew 2,842 sorties. Kesselring kept going until 16 October, then called it off. His bombers had suffered a loss rate of 7.5 per cent.[68] It was all over. The ships the Air Ministry had promised got through, together with a barely molested convoy in November, and in December the first convoy to sail to Malta since 1941 without being attacked docked at Grand Harbour.

Like everything else in the Mediterranean, the Battle of Malta was on a fairly small scale. Over two years, it cost the Luftwaffe 357 aircraft, over three quarters of them in 1942. In Russia that year, it lost about the same number of aircraft every *month*.[69] The Italians lost 175 aircraft in all, taking the Axis total to 532. The RAF lost 287 Hurricanes and Spitfires destroyed, and at least another 82 written off as a result of air fighting. At least 64 fighters were destroyed on the ground. Malta's AA defences were very good, so it is not possible to say what the balance of the air fighting was, but it is clear that the Hurricanes and Spitfires inflicted more damage than they incurred. Nevertheless, the overall material damage suffered by attackers and defenders, taking into account aircraft lost in ferrying, accidents and bombing, is probably similar. The exact figures are not known.[70] Many more aircraft than this were lost operating offensively from Malta against shipping, ports and other targets.

However, the aircraft losses were not the decisive factor. What was decisive was Malta's ability to supply itself. Between June 1940 and October 1942, 349 Hurricanes and 367 Spitfires flew in to Malta, and of those 716 aircraft, 566 stayed there to defend it, the others flying on to take part in the desert war.[71] Those lost were replaced. The aircraft lost by the Luftwaffe added to the burden of attrition which was wearing it down at the periphery and soon spread to its heart. The RAF's losses over and around Malta made a desert victory possible. The Luftwaffe's achieved nothing.

What the Battle of Malta achieved can be seen from the table on page 65.[72] It shows monthly Axis shipping volume to Libya and the losses it suffered, from all causes. The losses correlate inversely with the amount of attention the Luftwaffe paid to the island. During the periods of intense air attacks, they go down, reaching their lowest level when Kesselring launched his maximum effort in the spring of 1942, but the minute Malta is left alone, they go up again. The overall volumes also show a pattern. They peak with Germany's entry into North Africa in 1941, when Malta's offensive capability was limited, and show a declining overall trend, punctuated by isolated efforts, as shipping capacity is destroyed. They rise during the siege of Tobruk in the summer of 1941 as both sides tried to strengthen their forces, and again during the build-up to the Gazala offensive in the spring of 1942, but without ever achieving the earlier levels. From July 1942, Park steadily put paid to them, and Kesselring's final effort in October hardly affected Malta's offensive operations. With attacks

AXIS CONVOY TONNAGE AND LOSSES

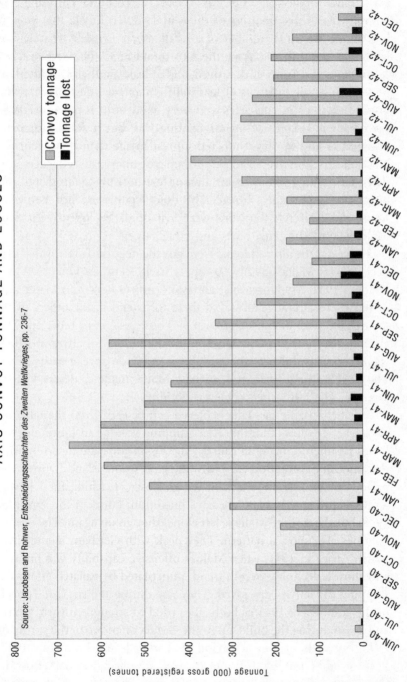

Source: Jacobsen and Rohwer, *Entscheidungsschlachten des Zweiten Weltkrieges*, pp. 236-7

being made on almost every Axis convoy, the volumes reaching Libya withered away. Between June 1940 and the end of 1942, the Italians lost 72 per cent of their merchant fleet in the Mediterranean. The Germans added more ships of their own and they built new ones, but not enough to make up the difference. The overall size of the Axis merchant fleet declined by 23 per cent.[73] That was not a catastrophe, but it was bad enough. However, by effectively forcing the Axis convoys to stick to their westernmost ports, Park rendered Rommel's triumph at Tobruk valueless, and stopped him from solving his truck problem.

In November, just 103 sorties were flown against Malta. There was little point in any case. The Axis commanders had messed about for too long and time had run out. For by then, things in the desert had taken a new turn.

IV

THE SOLDIERS' WAR

BEFORE THE SOLDIERS CAME, THE human population of the desert was very small. According to the 1939 census, the whole population of Libya numbered only about 918,000, including 100,000 Europeans, mainly Italians. In Egypt, beyond some 30,000 inhabitants of the towns along the coast, the desert itself was home only to a few nomadic Bedouin and the 5,000 inhabitants of the Siwa oasis.[1] In 1940, the British interned about 8,000 Italians who lived in Egypt and evacuated most of the Arabs who lived along the coast.[2] The nomadic Bedouin were left largely to themselves, but in June 1942, a few of them who had set up camp near El Alamein were evacuated to a refugee camp near Alexandria.[3] The desert was a natural sanctuary for wildlife.

However, the animals were rarely seen. There were herds of small gazelle in the area south of the appropriately named Gazala, which provided the soldiers with a bit of excitement and some food when hunting parties were organized. But the creatures were shy and fleet of foot, and the hunts could be hazardous, with trucks driven at break-neck speeds across rock-strewn ground. Arachnids, especially scorpions, were more numerous and inherently more dangerous, but once caught they provided safer sport. Soldiers used to dig out a ring of sand, pour in some petrol, light it, and put a pair of scorpions inside the ring to fight it out. The practice knew no distinctions of rank, as evidenced by Auchinleck's account of fights between his own scorpion and his chief engineer's tarantula, which took place in a tin after dinner.[4]

The main role of other animals in the lives of men was to provide them with names. *Vulpes zerda*, the fennec, was a shy, nocturnal species of fox, no more than 40 centimetres long, with large ears and a habit of burrowing very quickly into sand if disturbed. As a result it was rarely seen. It was perhaps its fast reactions together with this talent for disappearing which led to its identification with Rommel. Around the time of the first attempts to relieve Tobruk in the 'Brevity' and 'Battleaxe' operations of 1941 the British started to refer to him as 'The Desert Fox'. The Germans also took it on, though it gained more currency after the war than during its course. Rommel did not mind. He liked foxes and had kept one as a pet when he was in France in 1915.[5]

The Australians also adopted as an honorific a title bestowed upon them by their enemy, though it was not meant to flatter. During the siege, the German propaganda broadcaster William Joyce, known as Lord Haw-Haw, referred to them as 'the rats of Tobruk'. Rats were plentiful in the town, big, bold and unfriendly. The wounded tried not to fall asleep unless someone was on watch, for otherwise rats would come and gnaw at their wounds. The Australians were quite pleased to think of themselves as big, bold and unfriendly, and the 'Rats of Tobruk Association' is still in existence.

In February 1940, 7th Armoured Division adopted *rodentia dipodidae*, the jerboa, a more benign creature than *rodentia rattus*, as its official emblem. The jerboa was a small jumping rodent with long, spindly hind legs, popularly known as the desert rat. The wife of the then commanding officer designed their insignia after studying a jerboa at Cairo Zoo.[6] Given all the rodents around in Tobruk and in the desert, journalists, who were not particular about the rights of 9th Australian or 7th Armoured Divisions to their specific titles, started to refer to the Eighth Army as a whole as the 'Desert Rats', and the name has stuck.

However, by far the most common and companionable of all the forms of wildlife was *diptera*. Though one of the most ubiquitous creatures on the planet, before 1940, its numbers in the desert had been limited. When the armies came, that all changed. For with the armies came food. Apart from the food they consumed themselves, the soldiers brought plentiful quantities of further nourishment, the products of their bodies: sweat and faeces. When they started fighting each other, the soldiers provided the greatest bonus of all: their bodies themselves. Soon the desert was filled with millions and millions of flies.

The flies grew fat and bloated, but this only seemed to make them insatiable. The desert species, *musca sorbens*, is more aggressive than the European housefly *musca domestica*. They came in vast and inseparable swarms just after sunrise and, like Egypt's biblical plague of locusts, they seemed a punishment from God, sent to destroy men's souls. They settled on faces, concentrating around the edges of eyes and mouths. If men shut their eyes, the flies settled around the lids, creating the sensation that they were trying to prise them open. When men were eating, they were not so much an irritation as a serious competitor. Food had to be consumed under cover. Drinking a mug of tea took two hands, one to hold the mug and the other to cover the rim to prevent the flies from landing on it. Death had no sting for them, for they were ready to drown in tea and to follow morsels of food into the depths of men's gullets.[7]

The flies were a serious health hazard. Together with the action of sand, they turned any lesion of the skin into a 'desert sore' which would not heal. They moved promiscuously from food to sweat to faeces to rotting flesh and back again, spreading disease. Campaigns to slaughter them were eventually stopped as their burst bodies released their malodorous and malignant contents, increasing the risk of infection. In quiet times, anti-fly squads trapped them in nets, and killed and burned them in bin-loads, but it seemed to make little difference to their numbers. In the end, they just had to be tolerated, along with those other diminutive and faithful companions of the front line soldier in every theatre, lice, a problem the Germans never really coped with.

All the soldiers had really come to the desert to kill each other, but they spent most of their time learning to live there, in what the Eighth Army called 'up the blue'. It was not easy.

The environment was unfriendly. In the summer, which lasted from May to October, daytime temperatures ranged from 20–60°C. It was often over 40°C in the shade, the highest temperatures being reached in the late afternoon. During the other seasons, it usually reached over 20°C, and got very cold soon after the sun set, which it did rapidly. Nights were very dark, making it easy to get lost without moonlight. To the south were rolling sand dunes, but vehicles could not use them, so the fighting area was confined to the 40 to 50 miles of land next to the coast where the going was hard. It was rock covered by a layer of grey-brown grit and stones. Most of it was flat, giving considerable importance to the low ridges or depressions which were the only features on the map, but when viewed up close there were usually shallow depressions which formed dead ground for infantrymen to shelter in. The grit, sand and dust got everywhere. Dust halved the life of engines, which also suffered from the constant use of low gears forced on them by the rough going. When on the move, every vehicle blew up a great cloud of dust making concealment impossible. Grit and dust became embedded in clothing and irritated the skin. Desert veterans could be recognized from their red eye-rims as well their brown knees.

The first serious problem was water. Rain only fell in the winter, when it came in sudden torrents, scouring out watercourses called *wadis* and then disappearing. The *wadis* remained as steep-sided ditches. Every morning there was heavy dew, but little was collected. The men relied on water rations laboriously brought up by the supply columns. In the Panzerarmee, the official ration was 4–5 litres per head, but they rarely got that much. In the Eighth Army, each man was issued with four to six pints a day, half of which went to the cookhouse. It was chlorinated and usually too foul to drink, so it was turned into tea. The most welcome mug of the day (there were no cups in the front line) was the first, brewed by lighting tins of sand soaked in petrol. It was rated by its strength, perhaps because the stronger it was the better it disguised the taste of the water. Best of all was 'sergeant-major tea', which when mixed with tinned condensed milk was cappuccino brown. In 1942 the British government presciently bought up the world's annual stock of tea. This was a wise move, for tea kept the army going and was crucial for morale. Brewing it was a ritual performed three or four times a day, and nothing was allowed to interfere with it. Tankmen learned to brew tea on the move and crews of disabled tanks were observed to get out and brew up behind their vehicle in the middle of a battle.[8]

The remaining water went through a complex cycle. It first

entered a soldier's mouth while he washed his teeth with it. It was then spat into a mug and used as shaving water. Then, in what was called a 'cat's lick', it went on a brief journey around various body cavities, featuring armpits, genitals, the anal crack and the face, though the order was a matter of personal discretion. After this, what was left went into the radiator of a truck. Cleanliness was important, so if there was no water, washing was done with a sand-rub, though like as not, this just encouraged desert sores to fester.

Washing day was a luxury largely reserved for troops out of the front line. A German doctor has estimated that troops in the line got to wash their clothing twice every eight weeks. They used petrol, which was less valuable than water. It evaporated quickly in the sun, and left no smell. In the early days, the Eighth Army lost a lot of petrol from their flimsy standard issue cans, which had been designed to buckle and leak after a few journeys in the back of a truck and to cut into the hands of anyone carrying them. They were soon replaced by a straight copy of the robust but simple German design, which was therefore known for ever afterwards as a 'Jerry-can', and has hardly been improved on since. The Germans, on the other hand, coveted their enemies' clothing. The olive-green uniforms of the Afrika Korps, designed by the Tropical Institute of Hamburg University in 1940, were the wrong colour, too stiff and soaked up water. At first, the soldiers were issued with topees. Steel helmets had to be sent over in a hurry and splashed with sand-coloured paint. Italian uniforms were better, but in short supply, so the Germans used what they could find of the woollen clothes of the British, which were more comfortable and warmer at night. The most valued item of clothing they had was a silk scarf which prevented their collars from chafing their necks and was a godsend in a sandstorm.[9]

Food was usually the same every day for every meal. In the Eighth Army there were tins of M&V (meat and vegetable) stew and 'bully beef', usually mixed with crumbled biscuit. British biscuits were inedible in themselves, but could also be soaked overnight and mixed with condensed milk, sugar or jam to make a porridge called 'biscuit burgoo'. The men grew to hate bully beef. When the Germans captured stocks of it at Tobruk, they loved it. They had to live off something labelled 'AM', the precise nature of which was indeterminate. It stood for *'Alimento Militare'*, but the Germans called it 'Alter Mann' – 'Old Man' – and the Italians called it 'Asinus Mussolini' –

'Mussolini's Anus'. Australian bully beef was sent back to Germany as a luxury, reserved for the most precious loved ones.[10] The Italians would have coped quite well with pasta, more practical a staple than bread or potatoes, easier both to transport and store. However, it had to be cooked. The Italian Army's mobile kitchens, dating from 1907–9, were fuelled by wood. In the treeless desert, supplies of wood were not prodigious. So unless they improvised a method of boiling water, the Italians in the front-line, like the Germans, lived off AM and hardtack. It was the worst diet in the desert, seriously deficient in vitamins, above all vitamin C, which was not helped by an order forbidding the consumption of fresh fruit or vegetables for fear of infection. The men had to get by with an occasional lemon. As a result of the diet, skin diseases and diarrhoea were almost universal. The Eighth Army provided some canned fruit, most commonly peaches from Australia or South Africa, and when they captured any of those, the Germans fell upon them.[11]

The waste products of this food had then to be disposed of. The rear echelon troops did not have to worry about this too much. These 'base wallahs' as the front-line troops called them, who got the supplies to the front, were widely believed to keep the best for themselves. Combat soldiers were inventive in finding ways to express their contempt for those who did not share their dangers. As one front-line poet put it:

'And every time they pulled the chain
Went three days' rations down the drain.'[12]

In forward areas, however, there were no chains to pull. This was a serious matter. In most wars before the twentieth century, more casualties, including deaths, were caused by disease than by combat. The simple business of bringing together large numbers of men in field armies was almost invariably more dangerous than fighting. Medical advances meant that in World War II the rate of fatalities from disease drastically declined, but the ratio of battle to non-battle medical cases did not.[13] In the Middle East in 1942, for every 1,000 men on its ration strength, the British Army suffered 48 battle casualties and 506 non-battle injuries and cases of sickness. In other words, in the course of the year every other man would report sick or injured. One of the commonest causes of accidents was the ubiquitous 'desert stove'. The incidence of domestic to combat burns, even in periods of heavy fighting, ran at 2 or 3:1.[14] Though fatalities were few, accidents and illness were a drain on resources and took men out of action for a time. Desert sores were usually started by brushing against camel thorn, which was hard to avoid. The sores could end up as big as a fist, and took about four weeks to heal properly, which a lot of them never did. The most common medical conditions were to do with the digestive system, dysentery being the most prolific and most serious single ailment, followed by skin diseases. All of these were directly attributable to diet, desert conditions and flies. The story was worse on the other side. In September 1941, 11,000 out of 48,000 German servicemen in the desert were on the sick list. During the course of 1942, German medical records show 68,879 men reporting sick at some time, 28,488 of whom were in such a bad state that they were evacuated to Europe. Given that the average strength of German troops in Africa in 1942 was 44,000, this means that on average each man went sick every 7–8 months, and that two thirds of the troops were invalided home because of illness. These figures imply a sickness rate three times that of the Eighth Army, which had better medical facilities, better supplies and a better diet. The most distinguished German victim of intestinal troubles was Rommel himself. Hygiene mattered.[15]

The best thing to do when the ground was soft was to dig latrines. Every morning the sanitary squad would pour petrol over the contents and burn them off. If the ground was rocky, you had to use a thunder-box, if you had one and the snipers let you. The Germans used tin-cans, but found that with the amount of diarrhoea about, few of them were big enough.[16] If there was no thunder-box, you had to 'take a shovel for a walk'. That was the only time when men were alone, and so it offered the opportunity for 'a crafty wank' as well – again assuming that there were no snipers.

A 'crafty wank' was the only form of sex available to heterosexuals. Although the Italians provided some mobile whorehouses, the other armies restricted sex to periods of leave, when men would make up for lost time, despite the dangers of VD. Catching it led to a loss of pay, but that was a risk many were prepared to take. It might be their last chance before dying. Egyptian boys earned some welcome pocket money by touting girls they claimed to be their sisters with the surprising news that they were 'all pink inside like white lady', or if

that were too risky, offering themselves instead.[17] Egypt was known
as the land of the four S's: Sun, Sand, Sin and Syphilis. Some lobby
groups in England tried to prevent men from having access to sex,
but the Army just tried to prevent them from catching a disease when
they sought comfort from a local girl, known as a 'bint'. Faced with
the same problem later on, the American authorities explained to
civilians that the condoms issued to troops were to prevent moisture
from getting in to machine gun barrels. All these efforts enjoyed only
moderate success. Throughout the desert war, the incidence of VD
was comparable to the rate of combat casualties.[18]

Most Eighth Army soldiers with leave passes went to Alexandria or
Cairo for bonks with 'bints', booze with each other and brawls with
the RAF. They mixed very little with the local male population, whom
most of them regarded as being on the make. To the average soldier
they were 'Wogs', a term dating from the late nineteenth century,
possibly derived from 'Working on Government Service'. It was taken
to stand for 'Wily Oriental Gentleman' or worse.[19] Its use did not
further the cause of Anglo-Egyptian relations. Most of the Egyptian
population were detached from the war. Some were pro-British,
others were not, and made their feelings felt when the Eighth Army's
fortunes were low and Cairo seemed to be threatened. When the
Italians retreated in 1940, a lot of local Arabs turned on them and
Italian settlers in Libya sought the protection of British troops.[20]
Mussolini had treated the local tribes with brutality in the 1930s and
his people paid the price. The Germans had little contact with any
Arabs. Home leave was unknown. On the Axis side, the Germans
tried to stick to tours of duty of twelve months, but the Italians had
to keep going for thirty-four. Despite being nearest to their homes of
all the nations involved, the Italians got the least home leave. By 1942,
some of the men in the front line had not seen their homes, be they in
Germany, Italy, Britain, Australia or India, for two years.[21]

Cairo was an unreal world, hardly touched by the war. For those
based there, life was far better than in Britain. Though it was airless
and oppressive in summer, in the winter the climate was idyllic.
There was no rationing and it was never bombed. People could eat as
much as they liked, drive as much as they liked and were safe. With a
population swollen to almost two million, its luxurious restaurants
and numerous bars and night clubs were always full. It was an old
imperial city, radiating the mystique of effortless superiority which

the British cultivated across the Empire. Polo was played and officers relaxed in the Turf Club or Shepheard's Hotel. Shepheard's had been built in 1841 and one visitor compared it to living in the British Museum. Women were not allowed in the Long Bar so that men could talk freely, and that they did. The Swiss barman, Joe, was one of the best-informed people in Cairo, and anyone in need of information about British military plans only needed to spend a few hours at the bar over a whisky.[22] Beneath the gloss, Cairo was seedy and dirty. 'If towns have gender,' Moorehead wrote, 'Cairo is a lady ... Its mood was gay, rather flashily romantic in the evening, shrill and ugly in the morning. By instinct, I am afraid, the lady was a prostitute.'[23] Those who consorted with her on a regular basis were despised by the men in the front line.

Like most soldiers, the men in the desert spent the bulk of their time living in a harsh, uncomfortable environment and learning to cope with deprivation. Surviving without fighting was enough of a challenge. The heat was intense, but not unhealthy, and most men got used to it. No one got used to the seasonal sandstorms which blew up sometimes for days, especially in the spring, which the Egyptians called *khamseen*, and the Libyans called *qibli*. Arabs both sides of the border said they justified murder. But after a while, getting used to everything was the greatest problem. In the featureless landscape, some found the monotony, what one man has called the 'unbroken succession of empty, ugly, insipid days', the hardest thing to bear, and it resulted in a form of depression known as 'desert weariness'. The desert induced a mental torpor which if unchecked became total apathy, and morale and fighting efficiency declined.[24]

To make life bearable rather than out of any concern with their efficiency, they made the most of the small comforts they had. They played football when things were quiet. They did not sing much, as soldiers had in World War I, but if they had access to a wireless they listened to whatever was on. It was in the desert that 'Lili Marlene', the song which became the universal theme tune of the war in the west, first became popular on both sides. The words were written by a young German soldier called Hans Leip in 1917 to express his longing for two girls, Lili and Marlene, whom his imagination fused into one. His wistful poem was set to music in 1937 by Norbert Schulze, who was to earn his keep later on with such hit numbers as 'Bomben auf Engelland', 'Panzer Rollen in Afrika Vor' and 'Führer Befiehl'. The resulting song was recorded in 1939 by Lale Andersen, a German girl with a Danish father, and quickly forgotten. When the Germans set up a radio station in Belgrade to broadcast to the Afrika Korps, they had no music, so a soldier was sent off to get some. He found a copy of the recording amongst a few others in a Viennese cellar and Radio Belgrade broadcast it for the first time on 18 August 1941. So many soldiers wrote in asking for it to be repeated that the station adopted it as a signing off signature tune and played it at 9:55 every night. Goebbels did not like the sentiment of the song – his taste for Schulze was more in the line of 'Panzer Rollen in Afrika Vor' – the British did not approve of it because it was German, and the Americans tried to ban it because they thought that Lili was a prostitute and the immoral lyrics would corrupt their clean young GIs. Goebbels managed to find one master copy and destroy it, but there was another in London and soon there were other recordings as well, and many variants on the lyrics. When Lale was unwise enough to correspond with the Jewish director Rolf Liebermann, with whom she had worked in the 1930s, the SS threatened her with a concentration camp, and she attempted suicide. When the BBC told the world that she had died in a concentration camp, Goebbels changed his mind and got her back to show what liars the BBC were. The estimated 1,000,000 letters Lale received from German soldiers might also have influenced him. It is possibly the most popular German song ever written, and knew no borders.[25] The Eighth Army men listened in to the German broadcasts from Radio Belgrade and the song's resigned melancholy captured the mood of the emotionally deprived fighting men. German medical staff played it to their patients as the only available form of psychological therapy.[26]

Fighting filled but a small part of the soldiers' time – for most of them, probably less than 5 per cent. But it was the whole purpose of their being where they were. That purpose dominated their lives and when it was fulfilled, it was overwhelming.

Throughout most of recorded time, the maximum amount of violence which could be released on a battlefield has been limited by the strength of man's arm as it wielded a sword or drew a bow-string. At first this was augmented by the harnessing of the strength of animals, most usually horses, to add their bulk and speed to the violence of impact. The use of machines which combined the power of many men was long restricted to siege engines, and the size and speed of the larger missiles some of them used was still limited by the human labour involved in loading, winding up and firing them. This began to change with the use of gunpowder, but it took centuries for muskets to surpass the effectiveness of bows and arrows. Not until the nineteenth century did cannon become much more destructive than medieval sling-shots. But with the invention of rifling and explosive shells, destructiveness suddenly increased exponentially. By the mid-twentieth century, the battlefield had become dominated by artillery, machine guns and tanks. The amount of violence which could be dispensed at one place at one time was limited only by the ingenuity with which the designers of weapons could exploit the laws of physics to destructive purpose and the ability of industrial economies to produce the results of their deliberations. Human beings on a battlefield had to confront the laws of nature which their fellows had harnessed merely in order to destroy them faster, more efficiently and in greater numbers than ever before.

The greatest risk most of us today run to experiencing anything like battle is being involved in a road accident. Then too, the laws of physics governing the behaviour of machines made of metal collide with the biology of an animal whose evolution has not equipped it to deal with such things. The aftermath of a motorway pile-up is a bit like the aftermath of being shelled. The speed of events and the magnitude of violence produced by a collision overwhelms the human nervous system, producing a state of shock. Some people are temporarily paralysed. Those who are not walk about dazed. Just prior to a collision, people experience a loss of control over events, and just after it they are also unable to do much for the injured. The injured themselves are often completely helpless. When moving at quite low speeds, even metal designed not to injure tears, crushes and lacerates the human body in fearful ways. Most people in a car will suffer from concussion, even if they are not injured. Some damage, such as crushed limbs, cuts and bruising is immediate. Other damage, such as internal bleeding, loss of blood from external injuries and collapse of the nervous system, can take effect after a short delay. Pain is often delayed, but when it comes will last for a long time unless treatment if given. The worst effects are from fire, a danger whenever a machine using hydrocarbons is involved.

Battle is far worse, for shells are actually designed to kill and incapacitate, and added to shells comes gunfire aimed with aggressive intent. Shells and bullets travel much, much faster than cars, and shells contain explosive. Explosive caused the greatest amount of damage. In World War II, 75 per cent of British battle wounds were caused by shells, bombs, mortars or grenades. Bullets caused only 10 per cent of wounds, though they were rather more lethal, with about 25 per cent of men hit by bullets dying, as against about 20 per cent of those hit by shellfire. Taking the two sets of figures together, it appears that in broad terms, 80 per cent of deaths were caused by high-explosive weapons. The big killer was artillery.[27]

In World War I, doctors had coined the term 'shell shock' to designate the extreme psychological effects of battle. In World War II, the British army called it 'combat exhaustion'. It had many cumulative causes, but the original term identified the main one: the 'powerless waiting for an impersonal death'.[28] Troops under shellfire were confronted by the weapon delivering the most concentrated degree of mechanical violence on the battlefield. The only protection was digging a hole and getting into it. If, as in many places down the Alamein line, the ground was rocky, digging was impossible, and positions had to be blasted out with explosives. If they were advancing across open ground, men were impotent in the face of the arbitrary course of pieces of hot, jagged metal moving at the speed of sound. In most theatres of war, shells often hit trees and burst in the air, but in the desert they hit the rocky ground, usually setting off sparks and adding pieces of rock to the metal shrapnel. These fragments caused terrible wounds and being hit or not was a matter of complete chance. Men very close to the centre of an explosion would disintegrate, leaving behind just fragments of body extremity such as a foot, or sometimes nothing at all. Observers found it hard to comprehend.

Shells always arrived suddenly and often without any warning. Men clung to the ground, holding their breath, and trying to make themselves as small as possible by contracting every part of their bodies, including their bowels. Prolonged shelling led to constipation. After a few hours, the nervous system gave way and men broke down, either giving way to sudden, passing panic or becoming long-term psychiatric cases. How long men could take it depended on how intense it was and how well protected they were. During World War I, soldiers in trench systems with dug-outs withstood sporadic shelling for weeks. Sustained fire would incapacitate some within a day. Most men outside shell-proof dug-outs could only take a barrage for two to four hours. The desert offered scant protection.

Bombing had a similar effect. A survey of British wounded in the desert found that 83 per cent feared shelling and bombing more than small-arms fire. Although it was the most vulnerable aircraft on either side, the Stuka dive-bomber was the most potent psychological weapon in the sky because of the impression it gave that it was aiming directly for anyone who lifted his head to look at it. The shout of 'Stuka!' could reduce a group of soldiers to paralysis. Whilst the fear of high explosives was fully justified by their actual effects, the stress imposed by them was further heightened by the victims' complete lack of control. At least a fire-fight gave them something to do, and let them feel like soldiers rather than 'cannon-fodder'.[29] This may be the reason why the incidence of breakdown in the desert war was highest among support troops. An unarmed man driving a truck for long hours in the desert, alone in his cab, being periodically dive-bombed, broke down sooner than a man in an infantry platoon attacking an enemy position under shell fire.[30]

Though running a long way behind on the 'most hated' list, mines were usually next. At least there was time to discover them and their whereabouts were usually known. Only about 3 per cent of the mines in the Axis defences at Alamein were anti-personnel mines, but they greatly inhibited mine-clearance. The 'S-Mine' shot a small charge into the air designed to explode at about groin height, which produced particular revulsion. Mine-detection techniques were known and therefore countered, with some mines in layers and others booby-trapped. A lot of them are still there.

'Jimmy' James, one of the first psychiatrists sent to the desert in 1942, found his worst cases among the Royal Engineers who had to clear minefields. Their work required intense concentration and was done under fire. Those with mine-detectors had to stand upright listening carefully for a whine in their head-phones which indicated a buried mine. The job of lifting the mines was even worse because of all the booby-traps. The strain was so intense that the Engineers worked in half-hour shifts. After completing a shift most of the men instantly fell asleep. James treated one sapper who had seen his best friend blown up by a mine. He collapsed and went dumb. He was evacuated to Cairo 'tremulous, dazed, tearful' and easily startled. Within ten days, his symptoms had disappeared. Within two months, he returned to the Army and went on to fight in Sicily and Italy. Most of what he had needed in order to recover had been a rest. The balance of what he had needed was never made up. When James visited him after the war, his wife reported that he was quite normal except that he was 'inclined to rush out of doors when the children are noisy'.[31]

Whilst trying to get through a minefield, perhaps under sporadic shellfire, infantry would face bullets, first from heavy machine guns and then from light machine guns and rifles. Men going forward could make use of cover, but there was not much of that in the desert. Advances would usually have to be made across open ground, which was one reason why the Eighth Army launched so many attacks in the hours of darkness. The only defences were speed, agility and luck. At some point, every front-line infantryman had to get up, expose himself to enemy fire and run forward. In the end, it all came down to the last few yards.

In the desert, for a lot of the tanks it often came down to the last few yards as well. For men actually going to war in machines, the dangers they faced were to a large extent a function of the technical capabilities of the machines themselves. If the enemy had tanks with more powerful guns and better armour than you did, you either had to trick him or were faced with the tank equivalent of an infantry attack over open ground, except that you could not dodge or take cover. You were entirely dependent on the machine. If it broke down during a battle, you were helpless. Stony ground could be enough to throw a track. At the best of times, the inside of any tank was cramped and very hot. If the going was rough, there was a lot of protruding metal to hit your head against. In action, the men in the small turrets had to avoid the recoil of the gun, and breathing became difficult because even machine gun fumes were toxic and built up inside the confined space. The noise of the engine and the guns made communication within the tank difficult, and drowned out the noise of gunfire outside. However, if a shell landed nearby, the hull of a tank acted like a drum, with results so drastic they could result in concussion. In action, even shouting was useless and all the crew had to rely on radio. It was hard to see much outside. The driver had a slit visor and the gunner had a sight. Many tank commanders opened the top hatch and exposed their head and shoulders in order to be able to see what was going on, even in action. Half deaf and half blind, tank crews were slow to detect danger and their machines were ponderous in reacting to it. They offered protection from bullets and firepower which the infantry lacked, but in order to be effective they needed the eyes, ears and agility of infantrymen up with them.

Working in these conditions, fatigue was a chronic problem even when the crew were not in action, and in battle it became acute. Everyone's mental and nervous energy was sapped by the task of simply operating the machine on the move. Drivers had to wrestle with two clutches and sluggish controls. The rest of the crew had to cope with the constant noise and chronic boredom. A lot of crews kept a stock of Penguin books in the turret so that they could read to keep their minds occupied. 'Those who had nothing to read,' observed Keith Douglas, 'slept uneasily, huddled up like birds'. Night driving, when attempted, was a particular strain. After dark, refuelling, loading and general maintenance had to be carried out, which took 1½ to 2 hours. It was usually at this time that replacement tanks arrived. They were never ready for action and often had faults. Getting them ready kept men up for hours after nightfall. A report written in July 1942 concluded that it was rare for the men to get more than three hours sleep a night. Dawn and dusk were the commonest times of battle, so crews had to be up before sunrise to endure several hours of tension. 'There is no knowing what thoughts may come during these approach marches', Keith Douglas has written. 'They are the only moments when it is hard to avoid reveries, and they take place during the last and most depressing hours before dawn.'[32] These hours have left scars on many memories. 'There is no cold like the cold of a desert dawn. It is a long, slow strangulation of sinew, blood and bone ... You get up and you hug whatever you have in the way of covering around and over you. You see monstrous shapes moving slowly in the strange, suffused light and hear muttered cursing, and you begin to see the flickering flames of sand burning inside a score of cans ... Generals do not choose to make their attacks at dawn simply because of its deceptive visibility. They do so because men of war discovered long ago that this is the time when man is most susceptible to the terrors of his imagination.'[33]

Few infantrymen envied the tankers. Tank crews had lower casualty rates than the infantry, but there were horrors to compensate for that. As one infantryman has remarked, 'It might feel safer inside so long as nothing happens, but you couldn't hope for a pleasant death if anything did happen'.

In the tanks, the sounds of catastrophe were not the sobs of youths crying for their mothers which were so familiar to the infantry, and the sights were not of gushing blood, trails of intestine and smashed body parts. They were more eerie. When a tank was hit, the others in the troop would just hear a 'click' over the R/T, and then see the puffs of smoke as it brewed up. Shermans, which always caught fire, produced distinctive rings through the turret hatch, like a monstrous cigar. If their own tank was hit by a glancing shell, the crew would have to dodge shards of metal which flaked off the inside of the armour that was supposed to protect them as it glowed white-hot at the point of impact. If the shot penetrated, there was terror. Statistically, the odds on survival were about even. If the tank was disabled, the crew immediately tried to exit, for the shot would invariably be followed by a second, lethal one. Crews trying to leave a tank were regarded by both sides as fair game for machine gunners, but that was a risk they had to take. Rather a bullet than fire. Once fuel had ignited, the crew had 90 seconds at most to scramble through the turret hatch or a trapdoor in the hull. It could take half that time to open an escape way, leaving three or four men ten seconds each to get out. If the escape routes were jammed, they died. If they were lucky, the ammunition would explode, caking their remains to the inside of the tank in a black, sticky paste. If they were unlucky, they would remain alive for the first ten minutes or so of the twenty it took most tanks to burn. Some tankmen can recall hearing trapped crews screaming even through the din of battle. As one of them has explained, 'You would sit, read *Good Housekeeping*, and die like a dog.' Not many dogs are roasted to death, though. There are reports of tanks being found after battle with puddles of fat underneath them, covered with flies and slowly congealing as it cooled. Inside were blackened dolls about two feet high.[34]

In most theatres of war, gunners suffered lower casualty rates than the infantry or the tankmen because they were behind the front line. In the mobile battles in the desert, however, they were often as close to the killing zone as the other two arms. Between the end of May and mid-July, one regiment of the Royal Horse Artillery lost 463 men killed, wounded and taken prisoner out of a complement of 670, a casualty rate of 70 per cent. Even when not in the front line, life was not cushy. They lived like the infantry, but serving the guns was hard labour, and often resulted in partial deafness. Death usually came to them from their own kind – firing gave away your position and invited counter-battery fire or air attack. In the front line, anti-tank gunners and men serving the light and medium field pieces such as the British 25-pounders would find themselves engaged in nerve-wracking duels with other guns and tanks. They went on until one side or other retired or ran out of ammunition, or there was nobody left.[35]

The dead still played a role in the lives of the living. Bodies had to be buried after recovering their identity discs. Enemy dead were searched for any information they might be carrying. It was not a pleasant task. Bodies turned black in the heat and the gases inside them expanded rapidly. They were known to move as the temperature rose and fell, expanding in the day and contracting in the evening. After about a week, limbs came off it they were tugged on. 'There was no dignity in death,', one soldier has written, 'only masses of flies and maggots, black swollen flesh and the body seeming to move, either because of the gases within it or else the thousands of maggots at work.'[36] The armies fought along the Alamein line for four months, so there the corpses accumulated. The battlefield developed a smell of its own, a mixture of petrol, excrement and the odour of buried and unburied corpses, described by all who have experienced it as 'sickly-sweet'.[37]

In World War II about twice as many men were wounded as were killed. Though the battlefield had grown more deadly over time, the fate of the wounded was one previous generations of soldiers would have envied. Their survival rate was vastly improved by hygiene, blood transfusions and penicillin, albeit that in the desert supplies were limited. In the American Civil War in the mid-nineteenth century, 13.3 per cent of the wounded died soon afterwards. In World War II, the corresponding figure for the US Army was 4.5 per cent. In World War I, the mortality rate from chest wounds was 54 per cent. In the second it was 5.7 per cent.[38]

One of the other reasons for these improvements was rapid evacuation, but getting to a point of treatment was no picnic. Each man had a field dressing to apply to himself or a comrade if he could, and the wounded man then had to get to a regimental aid post, either by himself or on a stretcher. If the wound were serious, he would be sent to a dressing post behind the line for a blood transfusion. From there, the route led to a casualty clearing station and thence to a hospital well behind the lines. Even if the facilities had been there, flies made operations in forward areas very difficult. The longer the lines of communication the higher was the incidence of DOAs – 'Dead On Arrival's. In an effort to shorten the lines, dressing stations were moved forward, and, especially when the fighting was fluid, could actually be on the battlefield. Sometimes, they were captured and the medical staff carried on their work under different management. Both sides treated patients of all nationalities in any case. Many conscientious objectors worked in the Medical Corps, and so numbers of them became casualties themselves. However, the dressing stations were usually in the rear, especially if the army was advancing. That meant a long drive back along the bumpy desert roads, a torment for a seriously wounded man. The rail link was a blessing, though the journey could be 200 miles or more. The atmosphere at the casualty clearing stations where the men were unloaded was quiet, but not peaceful. There was a grim silence, leaving the moans of pain audible, punctuated only by the cries of men who had become delirious. The only regular sounds were of orders to stretcher-bearers and the scrape of boots on the platforms. There was time for all to contemplate the consequences of mechanized warfare.[39]

Apart from a very few abnormal individuals, everyone faced with combat was afraid. Sometimes, especially with inexperienced troops, it was hard to distinguish the fear from excitement, but prolonged exposure to battle produced tension and anxiety. Men returning directly from battle could be identified through their clenched jaws, which just sagged open when released, making them look stupid. The commonest symptoms of fear, registered by a majority of men entering combat, were a pounding heart, trembling, feeling sick – including actual vomiting – cold sweating and feelings of faintness. Significant numbers wet themselves or defecated involuntarily. Thinking often slowed.[40] In battle, all the senses are assaulted. Explosions are deafening, the ground shakes to heavy shells, sight is obscured by smoke, taste is affected as the mouth goes dry, and the nostrils are soon filled with the smell of cordite or worse. How were men induced to go through with it?

Some were not. For those deciding, for whatever reason, that the war was not for them, the desert was a good place to desert. Between 1941 and 1942, the British Army had over 20,000 deserters, and in May 1942, Auchinleck cabled London suggesting the re-introduction of the death penalty which had been applied in World War I and since abolished. The suggestion was rejected.[41] The German Army in contrast shot an estimated 15,000 of its own men during the war, many in its latter stages, which probably goes some way towards explaining its tenacity. During World War I it shot 58, and in 1918, desertion was rife.[42] There is no evidence that the Afrika Korps participated in this stark form of coercion, but discipline does appear to have been tighter than on the other side. There it was well known that groups of men 'dropped out' and went 'on the trot'. They were known as 'Trotters' Union'.[43] Officers would sometimes come across them camping somewhere out in the blue, and ask the way. They were usually perfectly friendly and it often only occurred to people later on that they had probably deserted.[44]

Among those who stayed in the ranks, few men were natural born killers. Moreover, most of the combatants were from Christian countries and knew the commandment: 'Thou shalt not kill'. Few of the men fighting in 1942 had been professional soldiers before the war and suddenly killing was not only their main job, but their duty. Montgomery was a devout Christian, and he knew the issue very well. In a letter to Brooke in November 1942 he observed with characteristic directness: 'The trouble with our British lads is that they are not killers by nature; they have got to be so inspired that they will want to kill, and that is what I have tried to do with this Army of mine.'[45] Montgomery saw his core task as motivating his men to fight. Everything he did, including some of his more aberrant behaviour, was directed towards that end, and he stressed it in everything he subsequently wrote. He rated the human factor more highly that strategy and tactics. He has described military command itself as 'a great human problem' and asserted that a commander must be 'a student of human nature'.[46] Montgomery had his work cut out.

To most of us now, World War I is seen through the dark glass held up by Owen and Sassoon, Remarque and Trakl, as a pointless, bitter slaughter, the massacred soldiery its pitiful victims. The rights and wrongs are unclear and as time goes on it seems more and more like a tragedy with many misguided authors, a folly rather than a crime. World War II, on the other hand, was a clash of ideologies which seems like a more clear-cut case of right versus wrong, a war more vast and terrible still, but necessary in order to extirpate the evil of its progenitor, whose criminal responsibility is very clear.

Yet these views were not common amongst the respective protagonists. Soldiers of World War I, on both sides, were for the most part convinced that their cause was just, and were motivated by an unquestioning patriotism. Pride in their nation and a willingness to die for Kaiser or King and country was usually enough to see them through. They were proud men doing their duty, not victims. God, of course, fought on both sides. During World War II the answer to the question, 'Why are we fighting?' came less readily.

Few Germans had welcomed Hitler's war, but with their thoughts circumscribed and emotions manipulated by a totalitarian régime, they were for the most part highly motivated. Not many of them questioned what they were doing. The men in the desert had not volunteered. All the German units had been thrown together in a hurry. The units making up the original 5th Light (which became 21st Panzer), the bulk of which came from 3rd Panzer Division, had not even had time to train together. The 15th Panzer Division was put together from the 10th Panzer Division's 8th Panzer Regiment and Grenadiers from the 33rd Infantry Division. The only special qualification was to pass a medical examination designed to ensure that a man's circulation was robust enough to withstand the desert climate and his dentition good enough to deal with the unpalatable rations. In 15th Panzer Division, 78 per cent passed. They were ordinary German soldiers with strong hearts and good teeth.[47]

One of their Italian allies observed some differences amongst them. 'The Germany of the Panzergrenadiers,' he wrote in his diary after a dinner with some men of the Afrika Korps, 'is certainly warlike, but it preserves a basis of humanity, something of that romantic, sentimental, Goethe-like quality which no one can deny is a fundamental characteristic of the country. The Germany of the paratroopers on the other hand is 100 per cent Wagnerian – disquieting, grandiose and full of a sense of impending disaster.'[48] Associating romanticism and sentimentality with Goethe betrays that the writer was not a student of German literature. That aside, he is clearly trying to express a sense that these strange north Europeans were animated by some sort of idealism, some of which he could sympathize with, some of which he felt to be corrupt. Relations between ordinary Italian soldiers and their allies were not warm. They were resentful of what they saw as arrogance and of being used as scapegoats for anything which went wrong.[49] The Germans resented having been dragged in to get a lot of incompetents out of a mess of their own making. Some of this attitude went right to the top.

The Italians fought because Mussolini told them they had to. His public support was partial and fickle. Unlike Hitler he had brought his people no great successes to secure himself politically. Before he declared war, his informers had told him that the majority of the public, while resentful of the arrogance with which the British asserted their control of the Mediterranean, were 'in the majority anti-German'. After all, only twenty years before, Germany had been the enemy. Public opinion was summed up as 'May God save Italy from a war for which no one sees the necessity'. The German victories in northern Europe in 1940 swung opinion round to the view that Italy had to do something, but the Army remained reluctant. Mussolini had no illusions. He was out to do some social engineering, to 'harden the Italians through travail and sacrifice', taking the view that even setbacks would have the desirable effects of 'improving the race'.[50] How many Italian soldiers in the desert realized that they were there to harden up their race it is hard to say. The sense of Italian national identity was limited in a country which was only unified as a kingdom in 1861. Men from different regions spoke mutually incomprehensible dialects and the culture was dominated by 'campanilismo' – loyalty to what can be seen from the local church tower. Its culture has been described as 'amoral familism', the distrust of outsiders and especially the state. It was one in which the man who supplied the troops with cardboard shoes could be considered some sort of hero. The vast, impenetrable state and army bureaucracies were designed to prevent corruption. They effectively restricted active corruption to the bureaucrats, leaving the rest of the population the solace of minor acts of vengeance such as tax avoidance. The Italians were mystified by what to them was the irrationality of the Germans' respect for the law, obedience to authority – except for that of the Church – and loyalty to the state. To most of them, the war had been somebody else's crazy idea. British propaganda portrayed Italians' limited enthusiasm for dying for their country as the result of cowardice. In many ways their attitude actually showed unusual perspicacity. In most cases, despite their broadly accurate reading of what had got them into trouble in the first place, Italian soldiers endured their lot with stubborn fatalism.[51]

The Allies also confronted an ideological vacuum. Though it was clear to most that Nazism was an unpleasant phenomenon, its true horrors were only revealed towards the end of the war. Few soldiers felt like crusaders for democracy, or had much positive idea why they were fighting. As one man put it in a letter home: 'We know what we are fighting against – but what are we fighting for?'[52] The advent of war only twenty years after the first conflagration was seen by most as a catastrophe, and the old promises rang hollow. The 'War to end Wars' had proven to be nothing of the kind. Old certainties had been ruptured and faith in the institutions of society and its leaders had been shaken. But once the old business started again, there was nothing to do but to fight it and get it over with.

The Commonwealth troops were volunteers, but were animated more by a sense of duty than by ideological zeal. The Australian official history describes the recruits as being of the type who are unable to resist when a call is made.[53] Alan Moorehead, an Australian himself, writing in July 1942, described a race of young Greek gods: 'Australians swarmed everywhere and they looked magnificent. None of us had seen such troops before. They had adopted a new uniform during the long months when they were fattening and working in the sun behind the lines. It consisted of a pair of boots, short woollen socks, a pair of khaki drill pants, a piece of string holding two identification discs round the neck, and a wide-brimmed hat turned down all the way round. Their bare backs and shoulders fascinated me. They were burnt brownish-black by the sun. Under the shining skin the muscles bulged like tennis balls ... They were the Rats of Tobruk ... They wanted to fight. They were delighted to be in the desert.'[54] Their hosts did not share that delight. When Commonwealth troops began to arrive in the Middle East in 1940, the Egyptian government, with memories of how Australian soldiers celebrated in Cairo when World War I ended, insisted that no Australians be billeted in Egypt. The British authorities kept them in Palestine for a while to show willing.[55]

Moorehead discerned less sensuality in the New Zealanders, whom he watched advancing along a Tunisian road, well after the Alamein battles: 'They were too gaunt and lean to be handsome, too hard and sinewy to be graceful, too youthful and physical to be complete.' He did not mean to be unflattering, however. They were, he wrote 'the finest troops of their kind in the world ... if ever you wished to see the most resilient and practised fighter of the Anglo-Saxon armies this was he'.[56]

In the 1930s, Australia and New Zealand were culturally very English, with many families which were only first or second generation immigrants. Both countries followed Britain very quickly in declaring war on Germany in 1939, and neither decision was controversial. To some of their young men, war still seemed to offer the chance of adventure. It also offered the opportunity to assert their national identity, which was still forming. In World War I, the Australian and New Zealand armed forces were regarded as having defined the virtues and characteristics of their new nations in a way that those of the European powers did not. The story of the ANZACS at Gallipoli had become a formative national myth in something of the way that Homer's story of the siege of Troy had been for the ancient Greeks. The 'Diggers' of the Australian Imperial Force and the New Zealanders who joined 'the Div', as 2nd New Zealand Division was known back home, wanted to be part of that.[57] They were playing a role in creating a history for their nations in way that the British were not.

South Africa was less of one mind about the war, but under Smuts' leadership also followed Britain into the fray. With a few exceptions, only whites were recruited as fighting soldiers, which posed severe manpower restrictions on the size of the South African army. In 1941, there were about 60,000 South African soldiers in Egypt, 75 per cent of them white Europeans, the remaining 25 per cent being mainly what they termed 'coloureds' of Asian origin, who served mostly in the rear echelons. When 2nd South African Division was captured at Tobruk in June 1942, half the South African Army went into captivity. It was a national disaster which the 1st Division felt it had to avenge.[58]

The Indian soldiers were also volunteers, recruited from what were regarded as the 'martial races' of the sub-continent, such as Sikhs, Rajputs, Dogras, Pathans and Jats. That restricted their numbers, which were not increased in part because India could not spare large numbers of men from the land and in part because of concerns about the reliability of the Indian Army. Indian Army officers, including Wavell and Auchinleck, thought this was nonsense. The few instances of mutiny which did occur were over local grievances, and letters home revealed no groundswell of political feeling to the censors. The most common concern was about the family at home. On the one hand there were expressions of a desire to gain honour for them, and on the other hand worries about their ability to survive on the soldiers' pay, and conditions in India. The prospect of famine loomed in 1943. British newsreels stressed Indian loyalty and the high morale of the troops, and Axis attempts to recruit Indian prisoners to their cause were abject failures. The men were more used to hardship than Europeans and patriotism and honour ranked more highly in their value system. For Hindus, cowardice was the ultimate disgrace. Nevertheless, they wanted the whole business to end as soon as possible so that they could get home.[59]

Montgomery's personal message to his troops of 23 October includes the lines: 'The sooner we win this battle, which will be the turning point of this war, the sooner we shall all get back home to our families.' That succinctly articulates what was probably the most universal and immediate motivator amongst the Allied fighting men, the Italians and some of the Germans as well. As one man put it, 'Soldiers don't fight for something. War was something which caught them up.'[60]

There was little hatred or even animosity between the soldiers on the two sides. The authorities had to engage the help of propaganda and some clergymen to work up a desire to fight. One purpose of training was to draw out deep-seated aggressive and predatory urges in nice young men, and turn them into killers. There was a lot of emphasis on the least-used weapon, the bayonet, for this returned war to a human form. It was man against man rather than man against shards of metal, and restored a measure of control to the protagonists. In practice it rarely happened, though when it did, it was mostly in conditions such as those which Montgomery had created at Alamein. In 1942, the BBC carried a talk by a young colonel about a new 'battle school' in which he described the methods of the new 'hate-training'. It produced outrage from others in the Church and the army, including Montgomery. One army psychiatrist said that hate just produced guilt, whereas what was needed was a positive cause to fight for.[61] The will to kill came in any case once

ABOVE: The tiny station on the line from Alexandria to Mersa Matruh which gave its name to the position where two of the three battles were fought between July and November 1942. This is the first train to pass through after the troops moved on. IWM E19087.

BELOW: Sandstorms rolled unpredictably out of the desert, advancing walls of dust and grit, turning an unfriendly environment into a laceratingly hostile one. One temporarily covered the Axis advance on Alam el Halfa on 31 August 1942. IWM E17599

ABOVE: Rommel after some typically hard driving in his Horch staff car in November 1941 during his withdrawal after the British 'Crusader' offensive. His captured goggles and scarf were invaluable desert equipment, but they also provided the media with invaluable visual symbols for the 'Desert Fox'. Hulton Getty

BELOW: Auchinleck, 'the lonely soldier', standing on the scrubby sand by the coast road at the end of June 1942, watching his retreating army move into positions on the 'Alamein line'. Auchinleck's self-effacing style and ill-fitting uniforms made him a tough media proposition. E13881

BELOW: Marshal Graziani, commander of the Italian army defeated by O'Connor in 1940, after his capture in Italy in 1945. IWM NA24746

ABOVE: An Italian soldier killed south of El Alamein. There was no dignity in death. Bodies were turned black by the sun, and slowly moved as the gases inside them expanded during the day and contracted at night. At the time this picture was censored. IWM E14630

BELOW: Images of endless lines of Italian prisoners escorted by just a few British troops came to symbolise the first campaign in the desert. This one was taken by Geoffrey Keating on 16 December 1940, one week into O'Connor's 'raid'. IWM E1379

ABOVE: Two of the leading allied war reporters, Alexander Clifford and Alan Moorehead (standing), preparing to move on after a night in the desert. Moorehead published three volumes about his North African experiences during the war. Reprinted many times, his vivid *African Trilogy* is still in print. IWM E13368

ABOVE: Invulnerable to Italian anti-tank guns, the Matilda infantry tank helped the British to dominate the Italians psychologically as well as physically. The only gun which could stop it was the German 88, which in turn dominated British tank crews psychologically as well as physically. IWM E1416

RIGHT: Air Vice-Marshal Keith Park pictured in January 1943 in the Barracca Gardens overlooking Valetta Harbour in Malta, enjoying the peace he had done so much to establish. Having arrived on the island in July 1942, he stopped the bombing in three weeks. IWM GM2550

BELOW: The aircraft that gave Park the means of victory. A Spitfire V, modified with a tropical filter to protect the engine from dust and sand, in a blast pen behind some local admirers. IWM CM3226

LEFT: The crippled tanker *Ohio*, lashed between two destroyers and accompanied by minesweepers and tugs, approaching Valetta Harbour on the evening of 15 August 1942. The last ship of convoy 'Pedestal' to arrive in Malta, her cargo of fuel kept the Spitfires in the air. IWM A11261

RIGHT: A Sea Gladiator, said to be the aircraft christened *Faith*. Legend has it that three Gladiators – *Faith, Hope* and *Charity* - were for a time the only fighters defending Malta. Though untrue, the story helped to fortify the defenders in days when faith was sorely needed. TRH Pictures

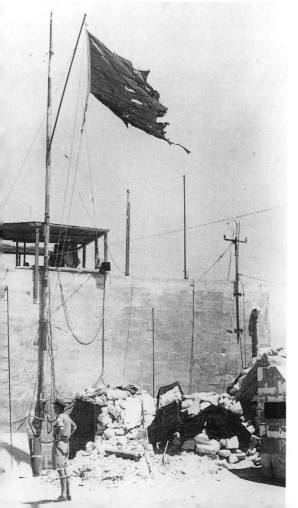

LEFT: The battered and much-used red flag which was hoisted in Malta to warn of air raids. Between 1 January and 24 July 1942, when Park's tactics started to take effect, there was only one 24-hour period in which Malta was not raided. IWM CM3219

ABOVE: Rommel and Field Marshal 'Smiling' Albert Kesselring of the Luftwaffe, who on 28 November 1941 was appointed theatre commander in the Mediterranean. He was supposed to win the supply war and support Rommel, a difficult enough job which Rommel made no easier. Hulton Getty

RIGHT: Top fighter ace Hans-Joachim Marseille, the 'Star of Africa', and at twenty-two the youngest Hauptmann in the Luftwaffe. The Nazis turned him into a heroic superman, but he really just wanted to fly fast aeroplanes and lark about with his chums, as he does here.
DIZ-Süddeutsche Verlag

battle was joined through the rising, if temporary, hatred of those firing at you and killing your mates, and the urge to get back at your tormentors. To men advancing under heavy fire, close combat could come as a relief, an escape from the impotence so often imposed by modern weapons and an opportunity to wield power oneself – to be a man again.[62]

The truth seems to be that if men are given weapons, trained to use them and then put into a situation in which killing starts, they will keep the killing going. They do so partly so as not to feel helpless, partly in self-defence and partly to help their comrades. Real purposive aggression was only present in a minority of individuals. Small unit cohesion, the loyalty of men to each other, was the glue which kept armies together and inspired most acts of courage. When one of your mates was hit you wanted to stop that from happening again and the only way to do that was to get the person or machine doing it. Soldiers always defended themselves. What was more difficult was to initiate the process, to make them go forward. No more than about 10 per cent of most infantrymen showed a strong desire to close with the enemy. Getting the rest to do so was the main task of the officer corps.

Before the war, the British Army had some fixed ideas about what made leaders of men. The right stuff was produced by breeding and moulded by public schools. In 1939, 85 per cent of Sandhurst entrants had been to public schools and of those, 40 per cent were the sons of officers. In some ways, these ideas were right. These young men expected to be leaders and took naturally to such a role in the Army. They routinely displayed incredible bravery in the nonchalant manner associated with their background. They had, as one observer of them put it, 'been bred and conditioned to bust themselves for the house' and commonly possessed a charm which allowed them to relate to and be accepted by anyone. They were the ones who got men off the ground and out from cover and led them forward. They paid the inevitable price of their boyish courage with casualty rates which were on average about ten percentage points higher than those of other ranks. By the middle of the war, the Army had to change its fixed ideas because it was simply running out of public schoolboys. In 1942, the War Office set up selection boards using psychological tests. Competence supplemented bravery as a criterion, and passing out grades rose by 12 per cent. Applications for commissions rose by 25 per cent. As the aristocratic officers literally died out, so did the ideas which had gone with them, with immense consequences for post-war society. The gulf between officers and men, which many army regulations deliberately widened, was bridged in combat, and that changed ideas as well. In the rear areas, they remained rigid, but in the heat of combat, they softened or even melted away.[63]

Relationships between officers and men went a good way towards explaining battlefield effectiveness. In the Italian Army the social distance between officers and other ranks was comparable to that in the British Army in the nineteenth century. Many of the soldiers were illiterate peasants. The officers, whilst often scarcely more technically versed or better trained, treated them as another caste. The suggestion made during the war that rations for officers and men be made the same was greeted with horror by the officer corps and withered on the vine. Significantly, the best infantry division in the Italian Army, the Folgore, was the only one in which officers and men shared hardships, including parachute training.[64] In the Wehrmacht, the Nazis had carried out a social revolution, and officers were largely created on merit. Thanks to the Wehrmacht's tactical doctrine, men were expected to understand their unit's objectives and carry on without officers if necessary. The British soldier was far more dependent on officer leadership, a result of doctrine and training as much as, or more than, social distinctions. The Commonwealth forces were more like the German in the officer–other ranks relationship. The New Zealand troops regarded officers as equals, senior rather than superior, and were on Christian name terms. As in the Afrika Korps, men were expected to lead if the officers became casualties. The Australians had the most relaxed relationship of all, and were regarded by the British as highly undisciplined when off duty. Some thought their battle discipline was also faulty, leading to higher casualties than necessary, but many regarded them as the best assault troops of all. Their performance at Tobruk and Alamein certainly gave grounds for such a view. The key, as usual, was not so much personal courage, though they had plenty of that, but individual initiative. They were not hampered by the assumptions of the British Army's Field Service Regulations. The men were told their objectives and pursued them with or without further orders. There were always tensions at the top between the Commonwealth commanders and their British superiors. The Commonwealth generals were given to a large amount of 'belly-aching', strengthened by the fact that many were senior in rank to the men issuing their orders and that they had the right to refer back to their own governments. Amongst the fighting men of the Eighth Army, however, there seems to have been mutual respect between the nations, and relationships were generally very friendly. The 51st Highland and 9th Australian Divisions trained together and developed a high regard for each other. Tensions only ran high between the infantry and the armour, regardless of nationality.[65]

A soldier's expectations were low. He expected few comforts, and little of life after the war. He hoped to survive, but as time went on he realized that the odds were against him. In the meantime, his main wish was for recognition. In late 1941, the acronym for 'Middle East Force' was said to stand for 'Men England Forgot'. Montgomery certainly changed all that, and it meant a great deal to them. He put them on the map. Once he had done so, they guarded their identity as will any group of men who have gone through a hard, long and harrowing experience together, finding a reward in the sharing of that experience itself. They were jealous of that experience and outsiders were not admitted to the group. When they met the First Army in Tunisia, they referred to them as 'those bloody Inglese'.[66] Their attitude did not go unnoticed by one soldier poet in First Army, who wrote:

'His blood flows just as steady
His sharp wound cut as deep
The sand soaked just as crimson
By booted, shattered feet.

But Praise's voice is muted,
Seek no record of his fame –
The poor boy died at Medjez
And not at Alamein.'[67]

The similarities between the experiences of the combat soldier in the different theatres of World War II were greater than their differences. Nevertheless, whereas the Eighth Army had enjoyed very low levels of psychological casualties during and immediately after the period of Alamein, they began to increase during the subsequent fighting in

Tunisia.[68] The terrain there was tougher, the weather worse and mobile warfare was replaced by weeks of grinding attrition. The desert offered baking heat and chilly nights, but it did not offer weeks of rain, steaming jungle or months of snow and ice. It offered flies and dysentery, not mosquitoes and malaria, desert sores not trenchfoot or frostbite. There was less sniping and mortaring than in other theatres. The landscape was open, so death did not constantly lurk round the next hedge or behind the next tree. Quarter was usually given, and prisoners were not massacred. In a global conflict unprecedented in its comprehensive awfulness, the desert was the nice bit of the war.

V

EL ALAMEIN – ROUND ONE

O N THE LAST TWO DAYS of June 1942, Claude Auchinleck, 'the Auk', now in direct command of the Eighth Army, went out on to the coast road beyond El Alamein to take stock of the state of his forces as they streamed back from Mersa Matruh. Standing by the roadside he was an imposing figure. Tall, good-looking, and strongly-built, he looked ten years younger than his fifty-eight. Moorehead recalls his 'friendly eyes, thick reddish hair, a strong vigorous face with the usual faint military moustache'.[1] He wore the same type of shorts and shirt that were worn throughout the army, his rank apparent only from his shoulder tabs. This was no sybaritic staff officer, no red-faced gin tippler from the cricket lawns of Delhi. It was a battlefield commander, come to rally his men and to view for himself the battlefield he had already chosen, the battlefield on which he meant to defeat his enemy.

'The troops were bewildered,' he wrote later, 'but completely unconcerned. There were no signs of panic, such as people trying to pass each other. The spectacle was encouraging from the point of view of morale, but there was terrible disorganization, and I could see the army would need refitting.' Auchinleck set up headquarters behind the Ruweisat Ridge and issued an order of the day: 'The enemy is stretching to his limit and thinks we are a broken army ... He hopes to take Egypt by bluff. Show him where he gets off.'[2]

Such sentiments would have been scorned by most armies which had suffered 80,000 casualties and were retreating in disarray after having been roundly beaten. But Auchinleck's words caught the right tone. They also showed his awareness of the laws of logistics which ruled the desert war, and a good instinct about his enemy. It was indeed a bluff. The DAK had 1,500 infantry and 60 tanks, the Italians about 5,000 infantry and 30 tanks.

The authorities in Middle East Headquarters were taking no chances. The fleet left Alexandria. The 'Gabardine swine', as the headquarters staff in Cairo were known to the front-line troops, were busy feeding bonfires with their paperwork on what became known as 'Ash Wednesday', or simply 'the Flap'. Whilst they were thus occupied, the soldiers of the Eighth Army were drilling weapon pits in the rock and siting their guns. They took some satisfaction in the reports of panic behind them. As one tank commander remarked, 'we were unpatriotically delighted at the thought of generals and staff officers fleeing for Alexandria or wetting themselves in slit trenches'. General Tuker, the commander of 4th Indian Division, expressed his sympathy for them. 'After all,' he observed, 'up front all a man has to lose is his life, while way behind a man can easily lose his luggage. That prospect can be most worrying.'[3] Churchill later described the soldiers as 'very cheerful ... but bewildered at having been baulked of victory'.[4] Amazingly, despite their bafflement, they were still ready to slog it out with the Desert Fox.

Auchinleck was not baffled. He had worked out what he was going to do if Rommel broke out of his 'Cauldron' and reduced the 'Knightsbridge' box two weeks before. He had explained his intentions to a group of journalists on 13 June. Auchinleck had no intention of trying to hold the Egyptian frontier, but was going to draw Rommel on to the position at El Alamein, whether or not Tobruk was invested. This would shorten his lines of communication and lengthen Rommel's. As one of the journalists put it, the idea was to 'stretch Rommel and break him on ground of our own choosing, bring him on to our anvil and use the sledgehammer'.[5]

As tired troops came back from the west, so fresh ones arrived from the east. Auchinleck organized them into brigade groups, putting lorry-borne infantry together with towed artillery. He wanted mobile units which combined the different arms. For the first time in the desert, he concentrated the heavy guns together under Eighth Army control. The position was often called 'the Alamein line', but the defences were not continuous as the trench lines were in World War I. They consisted of a series of four fixed strong points, still called 'boxes', though Auchinleck disliked the term, with mobile brigades between them. As they arrived, the troops filled them. Running from north to south, 3rd South African Brigade occupied the Alamein box, the fresh 18th Indian Brigade created a second just in front of the Ruweisat Ridge at Deir el Shein, 6th New Zealand Brigade moved to a third at Bab el Qattara (Qaret el Abd) and 9th Indian Brigade set up the southernmost box at Naqb Abu Dweis. Auchinleck organized his Army into two Corps whose command infrastructures were already in being. XXX Corps under Norrie held the north, with 1st South African and 10th Indian Divisions, soon reinforced by 9th Australian from Iraq. XIII Corps under Gott held the southern sector, with 1st and 7th Armoured Divisions and 2nd New Zealand and 5th Indian Divisions. He held 50th Division and two armoured brigades in Army reserve.

The retreat from Mersa Matruh had been so rapid that their pursuers had lost track of where the British were. Colonel Fellers' usually informative messages to Washington stopped on 29 June, a time when they would have been of special value. Panzerarmee intelligence thought the 50th Division was at El Alamein, and had no idea that the South Africans were in the line at all. They also made false assumptions about the positions of the Indians and New Zealanders.[6]

On 1 July, Rommel took a running leap straight at Deir el Shein, and ran into the box held by 18th Indian Brigade, which he did not know was there. Though he took it with 15th and 21st Panzer Divisions, it stopped him. As 90th Light tried to rush the Alamein box, Auchinleck's artillery pinned them down. They broke and ran under the terrible fire, and although they rallied, not even Rommel himself was able to get his men to move forward. They were exhausted. That evening, as the RAF bombed the German positions, the Auk held a conference. He ordered Gott to attack the DAK the next day, taking it in the southern flank with his armour. His Acting Chief-of-Staff, Major General Dorman-Smith noted in his diary for 1 July: 'Battle of El Alamein.'

It lasted for the rest of the month. There was no one decisive engagement. The main locus of the fighting moved up and down the line, first as Rommel tried to break through in different places, and then as Auchinleck tried to throw him back. There was an assault, then a pause, then another, until both sides were exhausted. There was no manoeuvring over empty desert spaces as there had been in the previous weeks. It settled into positional warfare, a presage of what was to come. To the men on the ground it seemed like stalemate. But the battle was not a draw. It had a very clear victor.

On 2 July, Rommel attacked along the Ruweisat Ridge, trying to envelop the Alamein box. He was held up for most of the day by the 25-pounders of 11th Field Regiment, Royal Artillery and a battalion of the Essex Regiment, who fought a sacrificial action while the tanks were moving up. When the British armour arrived, it met the DAK head-on instead of from the flank, and the result was just further attrition on both sides. The day after that, Rommel had another go with the DAK and sent the Ariete Armoured Division south. The Italians ran into the New Zealanders, who gave them a bloody nose. The DAK was now down to 26 tanks. On 4 July, Rommel called it off and wrote a depressed letter home. 'Dearest Lu', he wrote to his wife Lucie, 'I'm afraid that things here are not going our way. The opposition is too strong, our own force is worn out. Hopefully we'll still manage to find a way to reach our goal. I'm feeling a bit tired and run-down.'[7] The chance of a quick dash to the Delta was gone.

Auchinleck sensed his opponent's state of mind, and knew from Ultra the state of his army. He ordered Gott to attack from the south with XIII Corps once more and drive for the sea. But Gott, his officers, and his men were as exhausted as their enemy, and Seebohm's radio intercept unit overheard them chatting to each other. All that came on 5 July was pressure, not a drive, but it forced Rommel to lie low for four days, during which he extricated his armour and replaced it with Italian infantry.

Then on 10 July Auchinleck struck a real blow, this time with XXX Corps. Having replaced Norrie with Ramsden on 7 July, he launched the South Africans and the fresh 9th Australian Division against the Italians in the north. The Australians advanced out of the defensive box, broke a newly arrived Italian division, the Sabratha, and took the hill of Tel el Eisa to the west of El Alamein. They also did something far more important. Seebohm, now a Hauptmann, had located his

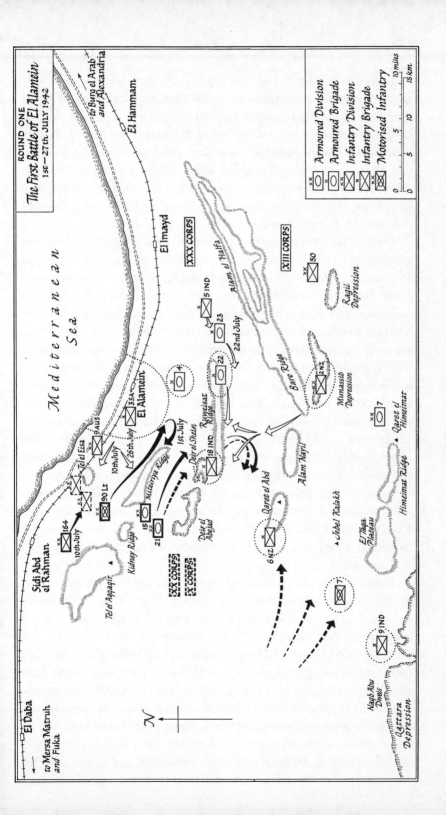

radio-interception unit in a very exposed position between Tel el Eisa and the coast. A reinforced Australian Brigade supported by tanks drove round behind Seebohm's unit, cut it off and destroyed it, killing a lot of his men and capturing all the rest, together with their code books. Seebohm himself was captured with severe leg wounds, and died in a field hospital in Alexandria a few days later. His methods were now revealed and the only source of radio intelligence left to the Panzerarmee was Guiglia's unit. The Germans treated information from Italian sources with scepticism.

It seems that the radio interception unit had always been the main target. On 4 July, Auchinleck had received a mass of very detailed information from Ultra, over 100 signals, giving information about units and their whereabouts in great detail. Seebohm was an ambitious man and wanted to get the best possible results. The area he had chosen provided excellent reception but it was very far forward. His decision may have been influenced by what he took to be the insulting reprimand he had had from a senior officer a few weeks before who told him he had evacuated his position too early. He wanted to prove he was no coward. It was a reckless thing to do, and not even the number of RAF aircraft overflying his position with all its radio masts on display could get him to move. Only a few senior Australian officers knew the true purpose of their attack, which was conducted with great stealth, the men wrapping their boots in cloth. Coming just a couple of weeks after Fellers had fallen silent, this attack struck Rommel a crippling blow. Never again would he be able to identify and exploit the Eighth Army's weaknesses on the battlefield with the apparently miraculous accuracy he had displayed before.[8]

Rommel was forced to move back 15th Panzer Division to stop the rot, which they did, but at heavy cost. The line was stiffened by the arrival of his first German reinforcements, 164th Light Division from Crete. 'Not a day here passes without a major crisis', Rommel wrote to Lucie. 'You just can't depend on the Italians in a fight ... they need German support everywhere. It's enough to make you weep! I hope things get better soon.'[9] The next day, Auchinleck launched the Australians at Tel el Eisa again, this time mauling the Trieste Division, and taking the whole feature. Again the DAK had to move north. They counter-attacked on 12 July but the Australians beat them back. Rommel had lost ground in the north and his southern thrust was over. He wrote to his wife that the British commander was showing 'considerable enterprise and audacity'. This was something new and worrying.

But Rommel was not finished yet. He had one last try, this time in the north, for that was where his main forces now were. On 13 July, 21st Panzer Division launched an assault on the Alamein box, but it was broken up by massed artillery. It was a bitter disappointment, Rommel told Lucie. 'We'll have to put up with it and gather our courage for new operations.'[10] On the night of 14 July, Auchinleck hit back in the centre along the Ruweisat Ridge and in the darkness, despite the momentarily successful intervention of German tanks, the New Zealanders and an Indian brigade swept two Italian divisions off it in confused fighting. During the night, Captain Charles Upham of 4th New Zealand Brigade led his company in a manner that led to his being awarded a second Victoria Cross to add to the one he had earned in Crete in May 1941. He remains one of only three men ever to have won it twice. 21st Panzer had to come back down to plug the gap, and in the afternoon counter-attacked 4th New Zealand Brigade. The New Zealanders were supposed to be supported by 22nd Armoured Brigade, but it sat around waiting for an opportune moment to strike, thinking the infantry could hold the attack whilst 4th New Zealand Brigade, and its HQ were overrun. Upham was wounded in the elbow and legs, and he and most of his men were taken prisoner.[11] The New Zealanders were not amused. With the bulk of his depleted forces now around Deir el Shein, Rommel tried to exploit this local success and push on there, but suddenly the Australians attacked again along the coast road in the north, scattering the Trieste Division and threatening his whole position. Once again, the DAK had to be moved out and used as a fire brigade to push the Australians back.

On 17 July, there was a pause. Kesselring and the Italian Chief-of-Staff, Marshal Cavallero, visited Rommel who told Kesselring that he had better do something about his supplies. The RAF had been bombing Mersa Matruh and Tobruk. What was the Luftwaffe up to?

On 20 July, having spent three weeks kicking his heels waiting to enter Cairo, Mussolini flew back to Rome. Whether he took his white horse with him is unrecorded. Rommel had been too busy to see him, which did nothing to sweeten his mood. The whole business was taking far too long. Meanwhile, Auchinleck prepared his next moves.

He was determined to keep up the pressure.

His next move came in the centre on 22 July, but it went badly wrong. While the Australians and South Africans applied pressure in the north, the New Zealanders and Indians attacked along Ruweisat Ridge again, aiming now not at Italian infantry but at the DAK itself. The tanks of 22nd Armoured Brigade decided that they could not move at night, so the infantry were given a hammering by the tanks of 15th Panzer Division, which could. Another New Zealand Brigade, the 6th, was overrun while British tanks sat about waiting. The 22nd Armoured Brigade finally got wind of what was happening and moved forward, but ran into a minefield and anti-tank guns. In a planned follow-up attack by 23rd Armoured Brigade, which was fresh from England, radio communications broke down as usual, and acting like cavalrymen, they charged the Desert Fox as if they were following hounds. It was, as the New Zealanders observed, 'a real Balaclava charge', with similar results. The 23rd Armoured Brigade lost 86 out of 97 tanks. In the north, the Australians were active again, but failed to rendezvous with their tanks. This time, the tanks were in the lead, and lost 23 of their number waiting for the infantry, who were somewhere else. British tank losses for the day were 132. The DAK lost three.

While this action made it obvious that the old problems had not been solved, Auchinleck knew from Ultra intercepts that Rommel was stretched and that his own forces were stronger, so he delivered another blow to the north. This also went wrong, and once again it was a tank–infantry problem. General Morshead, commander of 9th Australian Division, had had enough, and objected to his orders, saying that he had no confidence in the armour. Auchinleck persuaded him. On the night of 26 July, the Australians attacked and gained the eastern end of Miteiriya Ridge. The armour supposed to support them got stuck in minefields. The engineers had not cleared them as expected, so there was a delay. By the time they got through, the DAK had cut off the Australians, and being without armour, they were overrun. The attack was called off. The Battle of El Alamein was over.

Rommel, of course, had called off his attacks long before. He had been forced on to the defensive. 'Militarily, this is the most difficult period I have ever been through,' he wrote to his wife. 'As you know, I'm always an optimist. Still, there are times when everything looks black. I expect it will pass.' He was relieved when the attacks stopped. 'Holding on to this position we've established at Alamein has been the toughest fight in all my time in Africa', he wrote a few days later.[12] He did not manage to use the one word which summed it up: defeat.

At a cost of about 200 tanks – over half of them in 23rd Armoured Brigade's single foray – and some 13,000 casualties, Auchinleck had put paid to Rommel's ambitions and dented his self-confidence. Auchinleck played the battle like a game of tennis: he returned Rommel's first balls, then broke his serve, then had him rushing around at the back of the court returning volleys which came with unpredictable violence. Of course, the Auk knew exactly what he was doing in a way Rommel never imagined. He had set up a Special Liaison Unit in Egypt to show him Ultra signals as soon as they arrived. The unit accompanied him in the desert. He could thus send balls over the net which were calculated to get Rommel off-balance. Rommel played them brilliantly, but only by using the DAK defensively, which stopped him from using it to break through. Auchinleck had rattled him. Rommel commented that his opponent's handling of the battle had been cool and skilful and that although the British had suffered higher casualties, they had stopped him – which is all that mattered. Rommel's judgement was endorsed by his colleagues.[13] For all the operational ineptitude the Eighth Army still displayed in handling tank–infantry actions, its units had been very cleverly deployed.[14]

Auchinleck had enjoyed another significant advantage besides Ultra: command of the air.

The RAF had begun to build up its strength in the desert just after the Battle of Britain, and just in time for O'Connor's first offensive in December 1940. When it opened, the RAF had about 220 aircraft, mostly bombers and Army Co-Operation Lysanders, with just two full squadrons of Hurricanes, hardly enough to establish air superiority. However, after Wellingtons from Malta and Egypt had attacked their bases, the Italian Air Force had been reduced to 140 bombers and 191 fighters and ground attack machines actually fit to fly. Despite the Hurricane's superiority over the Italian CR42 biplane, the Italians could have caused the RAF a lot of trouble, but they hardly intervened as O'Connor's advance pushed them from airfield to airfield. By the end of the campaign, the Italians had lost 58 aircraft in air combat, 91 captured intact on airfields and a staggering 1,100 more reported captured damaged or simply unserviceable on the ground.[15] RAF losses from all causes were 26.

The RAF was then compelled to dissipate its forces in Greece and East Africa in the same way as the army, so when Rommel arrived, there were only four squadrons to oppose him. He himself came with only 50 Stuka dive-bombers and a handful of twin-engined fighters, so during his first offensive, air-power had little impact, except to convince the soldiers on both sides that the other side dominated the air.

Rommel had little time for the Luftwaffe and none for its desert commander, the *Fliegerführer Afrika*, Generalmajor Stefan Fröhlich, who felt the same about him. In March 1942, Fröhlich went to Russia and was replaced by General Hoffman von Waldau. It quickly became apparent that he was no doormat either. Waldau did not like planning his operations on guesswork and then being taken to task when his air support was not where Rommel wanted it to be.

It was different on the other side. In mid-1941, the RAF's newly-appointed AOC-in-C Middle East, Air Chief Marshal Arthur Tedder, sat down with the newly arrived Auchinleck, to work out how the RAF and the Army should work together to defeat a common enemy. The RAF would bomb ports to disrupt supply lines and attack lines of communication behind the battlefield in what is now called interdiction. Moreover, it would also support the Army directly on the battlefield. This cast pre-war RAF doctrine aside. To fulfil the vision, Tedder reorganized his Command, turning his forward group into Air Headquarters, Western Desert, which soon became known as the Desert Air Force. In July, the Desert Air Force also got a new commander, in the form of the New Zealander Air Vice-Marshal Arthur Coningham, who was known as 'Mary', a corruption of 'Maori'.

When the Eighth Army opened Operation 'Crusader' on 18 November 1941, it was supported by 650 aircraft: three reconnais-sance squadrons, eight squadrons of bombers, two squadrons of long-range fighters and fourteen of short-range fighters: Hurricanes and American P-40s.[16] The Luftwaffe started with 170 aircraft and the Italians had 420, of which only about a third were in flying condition. The RAF went for communications and infrastructure, then Luftwaffe airfields, and then moved to battlefield support. Each Corps and armoured division had an Air Support Control unit, staffed by Army and RAF officers, with radio links direct to the squadrons. The Desert Air Force dominated the air over the area of the fighting, but its interventions declined in effectiveness as the Army's radios went off the air and ground units lost their way, for they were called up less and less often and they could not find their targets when they were. When 'Crusader' was broken off in January 1942, the RAF had lost an estimated 440 aircraft against 260 for the Luftwaffe and about 200 for the Italians. In the air, it was more or less a draw.

However, though the interventions of the Desert Air Force had not saved 'Crusader', they had been more effective than those of their opponents. Most of their bombers got through, and they started using Hurricanes as fighter-bombers, adding to the misery of Axis supply columns. Their losses were high for two reasons: German light flak was plentiful and very good indeed, and the recently introduced Messerschmitt Bf 109F fighters out-classed the Hurricanes and P-40s, especially at altitude. They were flown by the Battle of Britain veterans of JG27 (Jagdgeschwader or Fighter Group 27), who were joined by part of JG53 from Russia, whereas the ranks of the Desert Air Force were full of novices who did tours of duty which meant that just as they had got the hang of things they left for home. A large number of squadrons were not RAF but SAAF – South African Air Force – units, which had had no prior combat experience. In fighter combat, more than any other form of warfare, effectiveness and the chances of survival are defined by aircraft performance and pilot experience. There are hunters and hunted. The old hands of JG27 were the hunters and the novice Allied pilots in their inferior machines provided them with game.

This led the Luftwaffe into a trap. Instead of attacking the British bombers doing the damage to the Afrika Korps or getting down on the deck and doing some damage themselves, the German fighters flew at high altitude and bounced the inferior RAF and SAAF fighters in aerial ambushes which got them some very high personal scores. These tactics placed them at relatively little risk, but equally had little impact on the land battles. German bombers attacking British ground troops, on the other hand, could expect to be challenged by Hurricanes or P-40s. Luftwaffe fighter units operating over the desert filed about 1,400 claims. Of these, roughly 170, or about 12 per cent, were for bombers. RAF fighter units filed slightly fewer claims, about

1,200. Of these, however, 570, or 48 per cent, were for bombers.[17] Part of the reason for this is that the German fighters concentrated on escorting their own bombers, and would meet British fighters trying to intercept them. But part of it was choice. One leading German ace commented after the war: 'Perhaps we could have shot down more bombers, but it is possible that we were not too interested – they had tail gunners.'[18]

The top Luftwaffe aces fought a private war and honed their skills to a remarkable degree, like master duellists from the age of chivalry. Goebbels' propaganda machine could not get enough of these Aryan warrior-heroes, who showed just what his master-race could do. It cost the master-race a lot of lives amongst bombed soldiers, but the number of kills was impressive and the young aces were very photogenic. The Luftwaffe did not have a Keith Park to sort out all this nonsense.

The answer to the British fighter losses was the same as in Malta: Spitfires. They did not arrive because other, quite different, preconceived ideas about air warfare held sway within the RAF as well. As Park has acidly observed: 'Early in 1942 Sholto Douglas and Leigh-Mallory had 75 fighter squadrons in England, carrying out massive sweeps over France, as compared with only 52 Squadrons when the Luftwaffe was at its full strength during the Battle of Britain. When the C-in-C Middle East asked for Spitfires for Malta, Fighter Command refused ... when as few as five Spitfire Squadrons could have saved Malta from the terrible blitz of spring 1942. This all arose from the mania of Sholto Douglas and Leigh-Mallory for Big Fighter Wings.'[19]

Park's view, though expressed with understandable intemperance, is substantially correct. Sholto Douglas wrote to his boss Portal, the Chief of the Air Staff, on 1 October 1941 agreeing to send six squadrons of fighters to the Middle East as long as they were replaced by the spring. However, he added, he did 'feel very anxious about the rumour which reaches me that you are proposing to send Spitfires to the Middle East'. Spitfire production, Douglas wrote, was barely enough to keep up the flow of replacements needed by the 69 squadrons he would have left out of the current 75. (His protégé Leigh-Mallory was indeed losing large numbers of Spitfires – and their pilots – over France.) In any case, Spitfires might not be able to stand up to the rigours of the desert as well as Hurricanes. Above all,

Douglas feared that Portal would turn on a 'tap' which would put Fighter Command into 'a parlous condition'. If Russia, already in receipt of Hurricanes, and still reeling from the first blows of the German invasion, were to go under during the winter, Britain could be open to 'a mortal blow next spring'. Four days later, Portal sent Douglas a soothing reply, suggesting that he was being 'unduly pessimistic', that plenty of Spitfires were rolling off the production lines and that the Germans could not invade Britain against as few as sixty squadrons of them even if Russia did surrender. He added some diplomatic advice about reducing Spitfire wastage in France. There was a further exchange, but in the end, Douglas wrote to Tedder at the beginning of November, telling him that he was to get seven fighter squadrons – though he did not say what type of aircraft they would have. None arrived during the winter, but the cogs in the Air Ministry ground away to the extent that a worried Douglas was moved to write to Portal's deputy, Wilfred Freeman, on 7 February 1942 asking that the number of Spitfires sent to the Middle East be restricted to twenty a month.[20]

The first few Spitfires finally got to Malta in March 1942, but the Desert Air Force had to wait until May, when 145 Squadron got Spitfire Vs which became operational in June. Not only that – when war broke out in the Far East in December 1941, Tedder had to send out 450 aircraft from the Middle East. None were sent from England. Despite the misleading claims filed by Leigh-Mallory's pilots, the small Luftwaffe fighter force in France was shooting down far more RAF aircraft than it lost itself, and the losses were all for nothing.[21] The idea was to tie down the Luftwaffe and force it to withdraw fighters from Russia. The only Luftwaffe units ever actually withdrawn from Russia were sent to the Middle East because of the RAF's activities in Malta and the desert.

So when Rommel attacked the Gazala line in late May 1942, the Desert Air Force had about 300 serviceable aircraft, but none of them were Spitfires. They had to deal with 500 Axis ones, of which about 120 were Bf 109Fs. The Desert Air Force claimed to destroy 200 Axis vehicles, but paid a heavy price. The greatest RAF bombing effort was put in at Bir Hacheim and 'the Cauldron', the greatest Luftwaffe bombing effort over Tobruk. Both sides challenged each other in the air. Rommel challenged von Waldau on the ground, criticising the Luftwaffe's performance over Bir Hacheim. This provoked an irate response from the *Fliegerführer Afrika*, who threw figures about the number of Luftwaffe sorties and the resulting losses back in Rommel's face. The Luftwaffe, he claimed, was being asked to sacrifice itself in support of operations which could not lead to success. In high dudgeon, he claimed that he was being slurred, and demanded that his own conduct be examined by a court martial. An emollient Kesselring got everyone to calm down and forget about courts martial.[22] Announcing Kesselring's imminent arrival in a letter home, Rommel wrote to his wife: 'Kesselring is coming again this morning. Commander-in-Chief South! That just applies to the Luftwaffe, though. He would like to worm his way into the role of a Wehrmacht commander. Over my dead body!'[23] With that sort of attitude, the Axis air and ground forces were never going to work together effectively.

By June both air forces were worn out, the Luftwaffe more through lack of spare parts and petrol and the attention the Desert Air Force paid to their airfields than through losses in the air. Tedder pillaged the rest of the Middle East for aircraft and crews, and finally, two experienced Spitfire squadrons, 92 Squadron from England and 601 Squadron from Malta, arrived to join 145 Squadron.[24] Their impact on morale was as great as their impact on the fighting. Knowing that there were a few Spitfires around to keep the 109s off their backs made the Desert Air Force pilots more confident. Equally, the 109 pilots had to be careful to make sure there was nobody on their tail and that they were bouncing P-40s or Hurricanes rather than Spitfires, so they were more circumspect. It took a six-line memo from Churchill, who had had his ear bent by Tedder and Coningham, addressed to the Secretary of State for Air and the Chief of the Air Staff to get Spitfires over the desert in any numbers.[25] Unfortunately, the memo did not hit their desks until 9 August and the Spitfires did not get to the desert until November, when seven RAF squadrons and two US fighter groups flying Mark Vs arrived in Tunisia after the desert war in a strict sense was over.[26]

The result of all this was that the Desert Air Force kept going and the Luftwaffe faded away. During the Eighth Army's retreat from Mersa Matruh, when the narrow coastal road was crowded with trucks and the Messerschmitts were only 40 miles away, the number of casualties inflicted by the combined power of the Luftwaffe and the Italian Air Force was six unlucky men.[27]

The losses in the air during the battle were about the same: 173 British and 181 Axis. What mattered was that in the first week of July, the RAF flew 5,458 sorties, more than the Luftwaffe flew in the whole *month*. This meant that Auchinleck's men had air cover, and Rommel's were constantly bombed.[28] On 16 July Rommel found out for himself what this was like when the car he was sitting in was shot up seconds after he had made a timely exit from it when he heard aircraft approaching.[29] This experience did not put him in the best of moods for his meeting with Kesselring the next day. There was something of an omen about it. Two years and one day later in Normandy, he was not so lucky.

The Luftwaffe was also plagued by raiders on the ground. Inspired by the successes of the Long Range Desert Group, formed with Wavell's support to carry out long-range reconnaissance and raids, Lieutenant David Stirling got Auchinleck's approval in mid-1941 to set up a group of men to attack enemy airfields behind the lines. Originally conceived as paratroopers, the force was called the Special Air Service, or SAS. After a disastrous first operation from which only a third of their men returned, the SAS enjoyed a string of successes and by the end of 1942 was able to claim the destruction of some 250 Axis aircraft on the ground. It never lacked recruits. Its members ranged from the homicidal Ulsterman Paddy Mayne, who 'possessed a total disregard of danger and a genuine love of fighting for fighting's sake', to the artist John Verney, who saw in the SAS 'a pleasant, if hazardous, solution to the problem of being a soldier … the war without the army'.[30] By the time the desert war was over the original 66 officers and men had grown to some 700.[31]

For the Eighth Army, it was as well the RAF was there, for it had needed all the help it could get. Auchinleck had seen the weaknesses at first hand: the radio issue, the insularity of the different arms, the continued naivety of armoured tactics, the lack of initiative shown by middle ranking officers. Staff work, right down the line, was slow and attacks were planned according to the book. There was a lack of attention to detail, such as how wide a path to clear in a minefield to allow tanks through. He could also see that as a result of all the failures there was a lack of trust between senior officers, a tendency to look for scapegoats and pass the buck, a lack of energy and conviction. When things went wrong, officers stopped and had a row instead of sorting it out. There was a lot to put right, but the worst thing was lack of trust. Morshead's rebellion had showed how bad it was, and events had proved that Morshead had had a point. Kippenberger of the New Zealand Division has described the relationship between infantry and armour, not just in his division but throughout the Eighth Army, as 'a most intense distrust, almost hatred'. Infantry commanders assumed the armour would never show up when they said they would.[32] No army could work like that. Auchinleck had first to reinvent the Eighth Army and then finish Rommel.

To do that he needed some new people. He had removed Ritchie on 25 June. On 25 July, Auchinleck wrote to his direct superior, the Chief of the Imperial General Staff Sir Alan Brooke. He reported on the latest fighting, the Army's position and raised once more the need for a new commander for the Eighth Army. Auchinleck himself was still C-in-C Middle East. He had just been standing in and could not simultaneously run a crucial theatre of war and command in battle the only British army fighting the Germans. Perhaps Gott could do the job. Perhaps there was someone in the Far East or in England. What did Brookie think?

On the same 25 July, the Auk addressed a special Order of the Day to his men. He told them they had done well and stopped the enemy through sheer guts. The enemy was trying to get reinforcements, but the Navy and Air Force were after his ships and would stop him. Their own job was to finish him. 'We must not slacken,' Auchinleck wrote. 'If we can stick to it, we will break him. STICK TO IT.'[33]

On the afternoon of 27 July, just as the Battle of El Alamein, the beginning of which he had recorded in his diary, was ending, Major General Dorman-Smith handed his boss a report called 'Appreciation of the Situation in the Western Desert'. 'Chink' Dorman-Smith was a controversial figure. He was clearly brilliant, having enjoyed a meteoric rise, but was regarded by many as mad, bad and dangerous to know. He had worked with Wavell, and Auchinleck found him stimulating. Some of his ideas were crazy, Auchinleck thought, but he did have ideas, and once sorted out, some of them he thought very good. He read Dorman-Smith's report and agreed with it.

The 'Appreciation' considered that Panzerarmee Afrika was too weak to launch an offensive immediately, but would build up its strength and would be ready to attack by the end of August. Eighth Army's morale was high despite everything, but none of its

formations were 'now sufficiently well-trained for offensive operations'. The Army needed well-trained reinforcements and a period in
which to train. Dorman-Smith recommended strengthening the front
and preparing for an enemy attack in August, funnelling it through
the south and meeting it with strong armoured formations from El
Alamein. After holding the enemy and further weakening him in
August, Eighth Army would be strong enough to counter-attack in
mid-September.[34]

So there would be further battles at the Alamein position. This one
had only been the First Battle of El Alamein. How many more would
there be? Just two, if all went according to plan – one to hold
Rommel again, and then one more to finish him.

Dorman-Smith was not the only one to write an appreciation of
the situation. On the same 27 July, the British Ambassador in Cairo,
Sir Miles Lampson, sent a telegram to London saying that local
morale was very bad and that the pause in the fighting was causing
dismay amongst the Egyptians. Lampson had never got on very well
with Auchinleck, who was furious when he found out about the
telegram.[35] There was not much he could do about it, so he just got
on with planning the next battle.

Three days later, on 30 July, Auchinleck summoned his Corps
commanders and discussed the plan. He wanted to fight the next
engagement as a set-piece battle from a defensive position because
that played to the Eighth Army's strengths and annulled Rommel's.
He wanted the Army re-organized into fully mobile divisions, each
with varying proportions of infantry, armour and artillery. They left
the conference to start preparing for the battle. Auchinleck sent a
telegram to London explaining the plan in broad terms, and went to
Cairo for a day's leave.[36]

Early on the morning of 4 August, a Liberator bomber which had
flown from London via Gibraltar landed in Cairo. The large,
inelegant machine taxied in and stopped on the tarmac. The dust
settled. After a few minutes, some papers floated out of the craft's
whale-like belly and drifted down the runway. They were followed by
a pair of short legs clad in RAF blue, which waggled in search of the
ground. They belonged to the Prime Minister, Winston Churchill,
who presently revealed his full cherubic form resplendent in the
uniform of an air marshal, jaws clenching a cigar. He was
accompanied by Sir Alexander Cadogan of the Foreign Office. Sir

Alan Brooke had landed on a different aircraft a few hours earlier, having just visited Malta.[37] A visit from Churchill was always good for morale, but no one in Cairo was quite sure why he had decided to come along as well as Brooke. Perhaps something was up.

THE
POLITICAL
WAR

F OR BRITAIN, THE FIRST NINE months of 1942 were the worst of the whole war.

In 1940, catastrophe had been followed by defiance. After the disasters in Norway, the Low Countries and France, Wavell and O'Connor had delivered victories in the desert. The Battle of Britain had been won, there had been no invasion and London had taken the Blitz and endured. This meant Britain's survival.

In 1941, defeats had been followed by salvation. After British setbacks in the desert and the evacuations from the Balkans and Crete, the Soviet Union had siphoned the Wehrmacht away into its distant vastness. On 5 December, despite having lost some 3 million men, the Red Army launched a successful counter-attack which saved Moscow. On 7 December, Japan entered the war against Britain, simultaneously attacking the United States at Pearl Harbor. That evening on going to bed, Churchill wrote, 'I slept the sleep of the saved and the thankful.'[1] On 11 December, anxious to support his Japanese ally who had 'never been vanquished in 3,000 years', Hitler declared war on the United States.[2] This meant Britain's deliverance.

But 1941 ended with disasters which presaged the year to come. On 10 December, two British capital ships, the *Prince of Wales* and

Repulse, were sunk off the coast of Malaya by Japanese torpedo-bombers. On Christmas day, Hong Kong fell.

On 11 January 1942, the Japanese entered Kuala Lumpur, the capital of Malaya. By the end of the month, their outnumbered forces had occupied the whole of Malaya and invaded Burma. In the North Atlantic, there began a period Churchill called 'the U-boat paradise'.[3] On 21 January, after 'Crusader' had petered out, Rommel began his surprise offensive and the Eighth Army retreated.

On 12 February, the German battlecruisers *Scharnhorst* and *Gneisenau* slipped swiftly through the Channel from Brest to Wilhelmshaven. This 'Channel dash' was of no great military significance, but it was a humiliation for the Royal Navy and the RAF. The British public were outraged. There was an enquiry.

On 15 February, the garrison of Singapore surrendered, leaving 130,000 British, Indian and Australian prisoners in the hands of their 35,000 Japanese conquerors. Singapore was Britain's main naval base in the Far East, and the greatest symbol of European power in Asia. The British public had been told that it was impregnable. Its capitulation was the greatest disaster in the history of the British Army. Britain's loss of prestige was permanent. Most of the captured Indians joined the Indian National Army to fight on Japan's side in Burma. Churchill conducted a series of painful exchanges with the Australian Prime Minister, who questioned British military competence and insisted that Australian troops be sent to defend Australia itself rather than Burma.[4]

In the month of February, the U-boats set a new record of tonnage sunk. In March they surpassed it. Allied attempts to counter them seemed to be ineffective. On 7 March, Rangoon, the capital of Burma, fell to the Japanese.

In April came the blitz on Malta. In Burma, Mandalay fell on the last day of the month.

In May, shipping losses rose again. The Japanese were as unstoppable as the U-boats. By the end of the month they had occupied the whole of Burma and were on the border with India. The Germans defeated a Russian offensive at Kharkov, destroying three Soviet armies and inflicting 250,000 casualties. On 26 May, Rommel attacked the Gazala line.

In June, U-boat sinkings matched their March record. Total shipping losses in the Atlantic for the year to date exceeded those for the whole of 1941. On 21 June, Tobruk surrendered. Churchill was in America with President Roosevelt, discussing various plans for invading Europe and finalizing an agreement to pool research on the atomic bomb. In the evening Churchill was handed a telegram which had the effect of an atom bomb on him. He phoned London in disbelief. Roosevelt expressed sympathy and asked how he could help. 'Give us as many Sherman tanks as you can spare,' Churchill replied, which the Americans agreed to do. The following morning he was able to read the headlines in various New York newspapers: 'Anger in England'; 'Tobruk Fall May Bring Change of Government'.[5]

When Churchill landed back in England on 26 June, he learned that the one-time Communist Tom Driberg, standing as an independent candidate, had won the Essex seat of Maldon in a by-election, with a 22 per cent swing away from the Prime Minster's Conservative Party.[6] 'This seemed to me,' he observed in his memoirs, 'to be a bad time.'[7]

On 30 November 1941, this extraordinary man had turned 67. He had been Prime Minister and Minister of Defence for some eighteen months. On Boxing Day, while he was in Washington, he suffered a minor heart attack which his doctor, Lord Moran, kept quiet, even from his patient. The events of the next six months sapped Churchill's energy and morale like those of no other period. The fall of Singapore and then of Tobruk made him wonder whether the soldiers of 1942 could fight like those of World War I. He kept his fears and feelings largely to himself, but now and again his guard dropped. One of his doctors chanced across him in the map-room one day, staring at a chart of U-boat sinkings and overheard him muttering, 'Terrible'. On another occasion he confessed to a naval officer that he was tired of it all and was thinking of handing over to someone else. Roosevelt's special envoy Averell Harriman observed how Singapore had shaken him. His daughter Mary noted in her diary that her father was 'saddened – appalled by events' and that he was 'desperately taxed'. Despite everything, he applied the dictum he used to his staff: 'KBO'. It stood for 'keep buggering on'.[8]

On 25 June a motion was put before the House of Commons to the effect that the House 'had no confidence in the central direction of the war'.

On 28 June, Hitler launched operation 'Blue', sending 68 German and 50 Rumanian, Hungarian and Italian divisions surging into southern Russia and down towards the oilfields of the Caucasus. If 'Blue' achieved its goals and Rommel's dash for the Nile were successful, the two forces could eventually link up. On 30 June, the DAK reached El Alamein.

On 1 July, Churchill faced a Commons debate on the vote of censure. He had faced a vote of confidence at his own request at the end of January, and won by 464 votes to one. He felt very confident, for the all-party national government was very strong. Nevertheless, he has admitted that a party government could have been overturned at this point, 'if not by a vote, then by the kind of intensity of opinion which led Mr Chamberlain to relinquish power in May 1940'. Most of his critics were inept debaters, and Churchill swept them aside in a masterly speech. The motion was defeated by 475 votes to 25, but there were 40 abstentions. Many of those who did vote for the government were beset with reservations. As Aneurin Bevan remarked, how long could Churchill keep winning every debate and losing every battle?[9]

Nor did the debate put an end to the disquiet which had been growing throughout the Commonwealth. After the fall of Singapore, the Sydney *Bulletin* had described Churchill's government as 'the greatest calamity that Britain has had in the line of governments since the administration of Lord North', who had presided over the loss of the American colonies. It did not shrink from pointing the finger of blame. 'Mr Churchill may be the world's greatest spellbinder but he has proved himself the world's worst campaign planner. The direction of strategy and the disposition of forces, weapons and munitions must once and for all be taken from his guilty and incapable hands.' Britain had decided to keep him. Australia would look increasingly to America for help in defending itself against the Japanese.[10]

Churchill desperately needed someone to win a battle. He was already convinced that that person was not Auchinleck.

Churchill did not like generals. When Sir Alan Brooke became CIGS in December 1941, he found he had to devote a lot of his energies towards defending his subordinates from the Prime Minister. 'Have you got a single general in the army,' Churchill would ask him, 'who can win battles? Have none of them any ideas? Must we continually lose battles in this way?' He never let up on the size of the army's tail: 'Pray explain, CIGS, how it is that in the

Middle East 750,000 men always turn up for their pay and rations, but when it comes to fighting only 100,000 turn up.'[11] Generals hoarded resources, tried not to fight battles at all and lost them when they did.[12]

At every point in the desert war, Churchill goaded his commanders to attack, and when they did attack, berated them for not having done so sooner. Auchinleck was a prime target. It reached a peak in the spring of 1942 when Ritchie was encamped at Gazala. Churchill formulated abusive memos to Auchinleck, and Brooke tried to intercept them. He found protecting Auchinleck 'very exhausting'. In May, he only just succeeded in dissuading Churchill from replacing Auchinleck with Alexander. The fall of Tobruk finally blew away any credibility Auchinleck had left. The day after the Commons vote, Churchill wanted to fly out to the Middle East and find out for himself what the 750,000 men there were up to, apart from taking their rations. As news came through that Auchinleck had stopped Rommel, he relented, and contented himself with what Brooke called 'unpleasant wires'.[13]

Churchill did this in part because Enigma revealed Rommel's weaknesses to him, while those of his own forces were sometimes less apparent. In part, too, he was passing on some of the political pressure he was under, pressure clearly revealed by the vote of censure debate. In the main, though, it was his own impatient, aggressive nature. 'I am certainly not one of those who need to be prodded,' he explained to the House of Commons later in the year. 'In fact, if anything, I am a prod,' and he added 'My difficulties rather lie in finding the patience and self-restraint to wait through many anxious weeks for the results to be achieved.'[14] Many of those he prodded considered themselves to be prods as well, and found the efforts of the prodder-in-chief singularly unhelpful.

Brooke wanted to go out to Egypt himself – by himself – to find out what was wrong, for it was clear to him that something was. He had thought that Auchinleck's appointment of Ritchie had been an error, for though he liked and respected Ritchie, he had never held an operational command. He obtained Churchill's permission for the trip, but on 30 July he learned that Churchill had changed his mind and was going to come too, feeling that only his own presence could galvanize the 'inexplicable inertia of Middle East Command'. That idea had first been put in his head by a young officer called Julian

Amery, the son of the Secretary of State for India Leo Amery. He had recently returned from Cairo and saw Churchill on the afternoon of the censure debate. He spoke of low morale and loss of confidence in the command and suggested that only the presence of Churchill himself in the desert would give the men the boost they needed.[15] In addition, given the terrifying progress of the Wehrmacht's offensive in Russia, Churchill thought that he and Brooke should fly on from Egypt and drop in on Stalin as well.[16]

Auchinleck had not done himself any favours in handling the Prime Minister. Auchinleck was unfocused and unclear on paper and often verbally inarticulate as well. After the fall of Tobruk he had written to Brooke on 23 June, when Brooke was still in America, offering to resign. The offer was refused, and instead he took over the Eighth Army from Ritchie. The next day, Auchinleck wrote to Churchill, thanking him for his support but starting with a modest apology: 'I fear that the position is now much what it was a year ago when I took over command, except that the enemy now has Tobruk, which may be of considerable advantage to him.' In other words, he had failed. Churchill wrote back assuring him of his complete confidence, but in fact he agreed with him.[17]

The Tobruk débâcle had been the result of a messy confusion of desires and commands. Auchinleck had never intended to hold it at all if holding it meant another siege. He thought garrisoning and supplying it to be a waste of manpower, as did Admiral Cunningham and Air Marshal Tedder, and had written to London on 19 January to that effect.[18] Churchill disagreed. Apart from its importance as a port, the defence of Tobruk had been one of the heroic highlights of 1941. When it came to the crunch in June, it was up to Ritchie. As Ritchie was pulling back on 14 June, Auchinleck ordered him to form a line in front of Tobruk. On the same day, Auchinleck received a message from Churchill saying: 'Presume there is no question in any case of giving up Tobruk.' The next day, Ritchie announced that he could not hold the line west of Tobruk as Auchinleck had ordered. By leaving that line he would have to abandon Tobruk as well, as it was no longer the fortress it had once been. Its defences were in ruins, and the minefields had been cleared to aid British movement. Sitting in London, Churchill sent Auchinleck a telegram the same day saying: 'We are glad to have your assurance that you have no intention of giving up Tobruk. War Cabinet interpret your telegram to mean that, if the need arises, General Ritchie would leave as many troops in Tobruk as are necessary to hold the place for certain.' Auchinleck took this to be an order. Ritchie began organizing a striking force outside Tobruk to take Rommel in the rear if he tried to assault the town, but as usual Rommel was too quick for him. In the confusion, disaster was all but inevitable.[19] A court of enquiry concluded in August 1942 that Tobruk had fallen because of 'the eleventh hour reversal of policy'.[20] Churchill did not want to know *what* was to blame but *who* was to blame. It never occurred to him that he might be one of the guilty – after all, *he* had never changed his mind. The court's report covered the whole of the battle of Gazala as well as Tobruk, and specified thirteen lessons from the events which revealed embarrassing shortcomings in the Army's operating practices. They ranged from the reiteration of very basic military principles like the need to concentrate forces, through basic operating procedures such as the need to repeat back orders given by radio to check that they had been understood, to basic common sense, like marking minefields in rear areas.[21] As far as Churchill was concerned, it was clear who was to blame for all that.

He was not alone in his opinion. In order to prepare Churchill for the censure debate, the Leader of the House of Commons, Sir Stafford Cripps, had composed a report summarizing the charges Churchill could expect to meet. It must therefore have reflected the views of the general body of MPs. It was all about the desert. It attributed the loss of the Maldon by-election to 'results in Libya', raised serious issues about the quality of equipment, criticized the handling of the press in Cairo, and lambasted the generals for 'lack of leadership' and being 'out of date'. On one point it was quite specific: 'This line of criticism has led to doubts as to whether either the Commander-in-Chief or the Army Commander have a real appreciation of the tactics and strategy of modern mechanized warfare, and as to whether it is not necessary to have a complete change in command, putting in the place of those now there men more experienced in and with more aptitude for mechanized warfare.'[22]

There were in fact no such men in the higher echelons of the British Army. All the senior officers with actual experience of mechanized warfare were in the desert. The real issue was confidence. Churchill had none in Auchinleck, and as he and Brooke, aided by the South African Premier General Smuts, did their round of interviews in Egypt, they also took a dim view of many around him. They were not alone in regarding the Auk as a very poor judge of people. Both his army commanders had clearly been mistakes, and they found his staff a motley crew. His Chief-of-Staff, Corbett, was regarded by many to be utterly incapable in that role, yet Auchinleck had even raised his name as a candidate for the Eighth Army.[23] Then there was the strange 'Chink' Dorman-Smith, of whom Brooke was deeply suspicious. Beyond this, though, they believed those who blamed Auchinleck for their own problems. Another member of their party, Colonel Ian Jacob, conducted a series of discussions of his own, and concluded: 'There is universal respect for General Auchinleck as a big man, and a strong personality. No one openly criticizes him. Nevertheless, he has not created a coherent army.'[24] It had ultimately been his responsibility to do so, or to find a commander who would. Now, that incoherence, with its blame culture, became part of his undoing.

Clearly, the army needed fresh blood, but Churchill was also mindful of the need for experience. He first offered Brooke the job of C-in-C Middle East, but Brooke refused. He then suggested Alexander as C-in-C, and Gott to command Eighth Army. Brooke did not object to Alexander, but thought Gott was too tired. He thought the army needed above all else to be given self-confidence, and that required someone who brimmed with self-confidence himself. He knew just the fellow, the commander of South-Eastern Command in England, one Lieutenant-General Bernard Montgomery. Montgomery had commanded 3rd Division in Brooke's Corps in France in 1940 and not seen action since then, but he had proved to be a very good trainer of men. Brooke doubted that he could get along with Auchinleck, who was much too 'hands-on'. Indeed, as he well knew, they had clashed before when both served under him when he was C-in-C Home Forces in 1940.[25] However, he might work well with Alexander who had once been his pupil at staff college and would in any case leave him to get on with it.

Churchill did not know Montgomery well, but had enjoyed a day's outing at the Third Division near Brighton in June 1940, at the end of which they had 'very good talks' over dinner at the Royal Albion Hotel. When Churchill asked Montgomery what he would drink, he replied, 'Water', and added that he neither drank nor smoked and was 100 per cent fit. Churchill observed that he himself both drank and smoked and was 200 per cent fit. During dinner they agreed that however fit the troops may or may not have been they certainly needed more transport. Back in London, Churchill wrote a memo to the Secretary of State for War marked 'Action this Day', and Brighton's bus fleet was requisitioned for Montgomery.[26]

Churchill had never met Gott, but was impressed that many held him in high regard. Brooke and Churchill went out to see Auchinleck himself at his HQ, which Churchill described as 'a wire-netted cube, full of flies and important military personages'.[27] Pretending not to notice the piles of camel dung outside, Churchill interviewed Auchinleck alone in his caravan. According to some who overheard, 'the Auk wasn't very articulate then'.[28] For a man like Churchill, that probably sealed his fate. Brooke had also been talking to Auchinleck, and discovered, to his surprise and delight, that all in all the Auk also thought Montgomery the best man for the Eighth Army job.[29] Churchill asked Gott to drive him back to the airfield, and questioned him during the journey. He decided that Gott was fit enough, ignored Brooke's advice, and sent a telegram to the Cabinet the next day, outlining a reorganization of the whole theatre.

The existing Command was to be split in two with Alexander as C-in-C Near East, where the action was, Auchinleck C-in-C Middle East, (i.e. Iraq and Persia) where nothing was happening, and Gott as Eighth Army commander. Three of the men around Auchinleck, Corbett, Dorman-Smith, and Ramsden, were to be relieved of their commands. These measures, Churchill wrote, would 'restore confidence in the Command, which I regret does not exist at the present time'.[30]

But it was not to be. At 16:00 hours on 7 August, Gott boarded an old Bombay transport aircraft at Burg el Arab taking some wounded soldiers and a few passengers to Cairo, following the same route the Prime Minster's plane had flown. The area was considered to be so safe that no fighter escort was provided. The Bombay was intercepted by a pair of Bf 109s, which set two of its engines on fire. The pilot ordered the rear door to be removed and force-landed, ordering the passengers to get out through the opening before the plane had come to a stop. The crew exited through the cockpit escape hatch, and as they did so the Messerschmitts strafed the wreck, setting it on fire. To their horror, the airmen discovered that the rear door was still closed.

The fuselage was engulfed in flames and all inside were killed.[31]

The news of Gott's death reached Brooke in the evening. Coming on top of everything else, he felt it to be 'a very hard blow'. After dinner he conferred with Smuts and Churchill, pressing the case for Montgomery. 'Had some difficulty,' he wrote in his diary that night. 'PM rather in favour of Wilson. However, Smuts assisted me, and telegram has now been sent off to Cabinet ordering Montgomery out to take command of Eighth Army.' Reflecting on the episode after the war, Brooke felt that 'the whole course of the war might have been altered if Gott had been in command of the Eighth Army'. He held Gott in great esteem, but felt he was indeed too tired to have fought the coming battle to a decisive conclusion.[32] Churchill was prepared to give way on this occasion. In a long letter to his wife on 9 August he told her that Montgomery was 'competent, daring and energetic'. 'If he is disagreeable to those about him he is also disagreeable to the enemy', he added.[33]

On 8 August, Colonel Jacob took Auchinleck Churchill's letter offering him the new post. Auchinleck read it and turned the offer down. At the end of the month, he left the desert for India, and never returned.[34]

On 10 August, Churchill wrote a report for London, in which he recorded the instructions he had issued to the newly arrived General Alexander two days before: 'Your prime and main duty will be to take or destroy at the earliest opportunity the German–Italian army commanded by Field-Marshal Rommel, together with all its supplies and establishments in Egypt and Libya.' Nothing was to divert him from that 'paramount' task. That evening after a genial dinner at the embassy in Cairo, the party of distinguished visitors left for Moscow.

As they did so, back in England Lieutenant-General Bernard Law Montgomery boarded a plane at RAF Lyneham 'with a light heart and great confidence'.[35] It took him to Gibraltar and then on to Cairo.

The desert war was to take a new turn in more ways than one. A week before leaving for Cairo, Churchill and Brooke had entertained a senior American delegation to London to discuss the thorny problem of opening a 'Second Front', for which Stalin had long been pressing. They had persuaded the sceptical Americans that the Mediterranean, rather than France, was the place to open it. Given President Roosevelt's insistence that the Germans rather than the

Japanese were the primary enemy and that American troops should go into battle against them in 1942, the Americans had agreed that a landing in French North Africa should take place not later than 30 October. Churchill named the operation 'Torch'.

'Torch' would render Rommel's position untenable. He could be starved out, or forced to retire to protect his rear and destroyed in the open desert. There was a case for the Eighth Army remaining on the defensive and joining the new army from the west to round up the Panzerarmee Afrika by completely encircling it with massively superior forces. The case was never made.

The first reason for this was that once he was back in the desert nobody knew what Rommel might come up with. The Desert Fox had slipped away before, and might defy the odds again. He had to be pinned down and forced to fight a static battle. The second was that Churchill could not wait. He knew that Stalin would give him a hard time anyway, and unless he delivered a clear military victory somewhere soon, so would the House of Commons.

There was a third reason. It was the most fundamental, running deeper than either battlefield tactics or grand strategy. The events of the year, particularly Singapore and Tobruk, had shaken Churchill's faith in Britain's armed forces. He had begun to doubt the ability and even the willingness of the Army to fight. 'Defeat is one thing,' he wrote on the fall of Tobruk, 'disgrace is another'.[36] The governments of South Africa, New Zealand and in particular Australia had clearly begun to lose faith in Britain's prosecution of the war. The commanders of their troops in the field were increasingly referring back to their own governments and questioning orders. Brooke too, tireless defender of the Army that he was, had had his dark nights of the soul. On the last day of March before going to bed he had confided to his diary: ' ... Have already lost a large proportion of the British Empire and are on the high road to lose a great deal more of it. During the last fortnight I have had a growing conviction that we are going to lose this war unless we control it very differently and fight it with more determination.' He felt better when he woke up the next day.[37] The problem remained. The real issue was the ability of the British Army to defeat the German Army in battle. If it could not do so, it was difficult to see how the war could be won. For the sake of honour, of international prestige, of Britain's status among her allies, of the credibility of the government, of public opinion, and of the morale of her fighting men, a British army had to win a clear victory on the battlefield. The only place it could do that was at El Alamein.

Montgomery arrived in Cairo on 12 August and at 11:00 was driven to GHQ to see Auchinleck, who had decided not to hand over to Alexander until 15 August. It was not their first meeting. In England just after Dunkirk, Montgomery had taken over V Corps from Auchinleck, and proceeded to loudly criticize the state of the Corps and its defence plans. Auchinleck had been promoted to be his direct superior. The conversation between the pert, shrew-like newcomer and the gentle, towering Auk was brief. Auchinleck explained his dispositions and plans to the man London had provided in answer to his request for a new Eighth Army commander. He disliked but respected him. The dislike was mutual, but the respect was not. As the briefing ended, Auchinleck decided that perhaps after all it was just as well that he had been replaced by Alexander.[38]

Montgomery then visited the Deputy Chief-of-Staff, Major-General John Harding, who made a very different impression from his boss, Corbett. Montgomery tasked Harding with working out how to form what he called a *corps de chasse*, an armoured Corps like the Afrika Korps, a task Harding had completed by the evening. Montgomery spent the afternoon shopping. He needed some clothes for the desert.[39]

At 5:00 the following morning, the new broom set out by car for the Eighth Army's desert headquarters, accompanied by Brigadier Freddie de Guingand from the Eighth Army staff. De Guingand had written a short paper for Montgomery, whom he knew from before the war, giving his views on the situation in the desert. Montgomery did not want to read the paper, so they talked during the journey. De Guingand told him that the army's policy was defensive, that everyone was looking over his shoulder, that divisions were split up into 'Jock Columns' instead of fighting together and that the headquarters set-up was wrong and should be next to the RAF at Burg el Arab.[40] Montgomery clearly took all this on board. They arrived at about 11:00 and stepped round the camel dung to meet Ramsden. Ramsden was on Churchill's hit list but did not know it, as he had been reprieved on the news of Gott's death and placed in temporary command of Eighth Army. De Guingand had informed Montgomery during the journey that most of the

Eighth Army staff regarded Ramsden as 'bloody useless'.

Ramsden briefed Montgomery on the situation, after which Montgomery sent him back to XXX Corps, ordered the demolition of the headquarters, which he called a 'meat-safe', and had lunch. He decided to take de Guingand's advice and set up a new HQ at Burg el Arab on the coast road a few miles from Alexandria next to the Desert Air Force HQ. After lunch, he sent a signal cancelling all orders for a withdrawal and another informing Auchinleck that he had decided not to wait until the 15th, but had taken over right away. He then asked de Guingand to assemble the staff at the 'meat-safe' at 18:00, and then disappeared into the desert to visit XIII Corps, just in case Auchinleck were to receive the signal and decide to reply.[41]

Montgomery got back half an hour late at 18:30, and found 50 to 60 officers gathered together to listen to what he had to say. They stood to attention and saluted. Montgomery returned the salute and walked over to the steps of the caravan. He stood on the steps with his hands behind his back and asked his audience to sit down on the sand. Given his lack of stature, this was the only way he could be sure they could see him. He was thin as well as small, looked strikingly white compared with the sunburnt desert veterans, and incongruous in his new shirt and slacks. He had a pointed face with high cheek bones and a long sharp nose protruded from under his red-banded peaked cap, adding its shadow to the slight colour of a neatly trimmed moustache. The sharpness of his features was exaggerated by the harsh light and shade of the desert sun. Montgomery looked straight at them with his piercing blue-grey eyes and began to speak. His voice was high, clipped and unmelodious. Its modulations were emphatic and sounded strangely unnatural. He talked without notes. However, someone took down what he said in shorthand.[42]

Montgomery introduced himself, said that in order to work together they must have confidence in each other, and expressed his confidence in them. They would work together as a team. They would then 'gain the confidence of this great army and go forward to final victory in Africa'.

He then said that one of the first duties of a commander is to create the 'atmosphere' in which everyone would live, work and fight. He did not like the general atmosphere he found there:

'It is an atmosphere of doubt, of looking back to select the next place to which to withdraw, of loss of confidence in our ability to defeat Rommel, of desperate defence measures by reserves in preparing positions in Cairo and the Delta. All that must cease. Let us have a new atmosphere.'

Egypt had to be defended at Alamein, he continued. There was no point in digging trenches in the Delta.

'I have ordered that all plans and instructions dealing with further withdrawal are to be burnt, and at once. We will stand and fight *here*. If we can't stay here alive, then let us stay here dead.'

Then he delivered the good news. 'I want to impress upon everyone', he said, 'that the bad times are over.' Reinforcements were arriving from the UK and at that very moment, three to four hundred Sherman tanks were coming over 'and these are being unloaded at Suez <u>now</u>'. He then told them about the order Churchill had sent to Alexander. It was their mission statement:

'Our mandate from the Prime Minister is to destroy the Axis forces in North Africa; I have seen it written on half-a-sheet of notepaper. And it will be done. If anyone here thinks it can't be done, let him go at once; I don't want any doubters in this party. It can be done, and it will be done: beyond any possibility of doubt.'

He understood that Rommel was expected to attack. Let him do so. After that, they would knock him for six, right out of Africa. But not at once. First he would create a British Panzer Corps like the Afrika Korps and train it out of the line. He had already given orders to form it.

'I have no intention of launching our attack until we are completely ready; there will be pressure from many quarters to attack soon; <u>I will not attack until we are ready</u>, and you can rest assured on that point.'

He introduced de Guingand who was to be his Chief-of-Staff. Orders from de Guingand were to be treated as orders from him, and would be acted on *at once*.

'I understand there has been a great deal of 'bellyaching' out here. By bellyaching I mean inventing poor reasons for not doing what one has been told to do. All this is to stop at once. I will tolerate no bellyaching. If anyone objects to doing what he is told, then he can get out of it; and at once. I want that made very clear right down through the Eighth Army.'

Some of them, he added, might think that he was slightly mad. He assured them he was quite sane. Having thus described the new atmosphere, he told them to see that it permeated right down through the Eighth Army. Every private must know what was wanted.

'When they see it coming to pass, there will be a surge of confidence throughout the Army. I ask you to give me your confidence and to have faith that what I have said will come to pass.'

Montgomery was the son of a bishop. He went on:

'There is much work to be done. The orders I have given about no further withdrawal will mean a complete change in the layout of our dispositions; also that we must begin to prepare for our own offensive.'

'The great point to remember,' he concluded,

'is that we are going to finish with this chap Rommel once and for all. It will be quite easy. There is no doubt about it. He is definitely a nuisance. Therefore we will hit him a crack and finish with him.'

It was pure theatre, and as at the end of many great shows, the audience sat in silence. Montgomery had taught himself to address audiences effectively. Memories of his first attempt at public speaking in 1940 when he addressed all the officers of his division after Dunkirk were that it was unimpressive. His voice was high pitched and he was verbose. A year later he seemed to have become far better. Now, a year after that, he matched content and delivery in a uniquely powerful way.[43]

The content contained some poetic licence – the Shermans were not unloading at Suez, but they were due in September, which was good enough. The cancellation of all plans for withdrawal was pure theatre too, for there were none to be cancelled. GHQ had contingency plans for the defence of the Delta – it would have been irresponsible not to have made them.[44] But nobody had ever had any intention of fighting anywhere other than at Alamein, and the plans Dorman-Smith and Auchinleck had conceived for a further offensive were already being worked on. Senior officers who later heard about Montgomery's claims were mystified.[45] But it was the spirit of the order, the gesture, that counted at the time. De Guingand described the impact of the speech as 'electric'.[46] His audience did not yet know whether Montgomery was any good or not, but he certainly was different. He told them what they needed to hear. He was the man for the hour.

It was a masterly performance. The language is very simple, sometimes Biblical, and very clear. There is nothing literary or rhetorical about it.[47] The most telling words are monosyllables, like: 'It can be done, and it will be done.' The sentences are short, and most of them are assertions. The army was baffled, but to the new commander, all was absolutely clear, in black and white. Everything to him was fact, and he delivered his speech in clipped, unemotional terms. Montgomery also put his finger on the core issue: the breakdown of trust between units and individuals, the issue he called 'confidence'. To have done this after seven hours in the desert shows remarkable acuity. He had started to do what all effective leaders do: to define and focus on the task – finishing Rommel – and to build a team – by creating mutual confidence.

On the morning of 14 August, Montgomery toured the northern sector held by XXX Corps. On arriving at 9th Australian Division, Montgomery took up the suggestion of a tanned liaison officer and swapped his peaked cap for an Australian slouch hat, which afforded better protection from the sun. He then stuck an Australian badge on it. At 14:00 he reached 5th Indian Division and, in the late afternoon, 2nd New Zealand Division, collecting unit badges as he went.[48] He knew all about the Rommel factor. If he was to defeat his army, he had also to defeat him, and this was a piece of psychological warfare. Auchinleck had written a memo about the hold Rommel had on the minds of his men. Montgomery was now taking action to loosen that hold and replace it with a hold of his own. It had aspects of a duel. A few days later, he had a portrait of Rommel by the German artist Willrich hung in his caravan.[49]

The team got more fresh blood. Ramsden stayed at XXX Corps,

but now that Gott was dead someone had to take over XIII Corps. Montgomery regarded people selection as critical and as his predecessor's greatest weakness. He later wrote that he devoted a third of his working hours to 'the consideration of personalities'.[50] He wanted people he knew – people in whom he 'had confidence'. He sent for the bright and enthusiastic Brian Horrocks, who had served under him in France and England. Horrocks arrived on 15 August. In briefing him, Montgomery told Horrocks – whom, probably in allusion to the protagonist of R.S. Surtees' nineteenth-century fox-hunting novels, he always called 'Jorrocks' – that he expected Rommel to attack soon and come round from the south. XIII Corps was to repel the attack without getting unduly mauled in the process. Montgomery had been told about the fate of 23rd Armoured Brigade, and he did not want another new boy from England doing the same thing again. It was especially important to preserve the armour, as Montgomery would be wanting it for his *corps de chasse*.

Horrocks had taken over 9th Armoured Division in England that March, so he had learned the basics about handling tanks, but he came from the infantry. Having last seen action as the commander of an infantry battalion in 1940, Horrocks now had to command an armoured Corps facing an attack led by the most celebrated Field Marshal in the German Army. He left the interview with a sinking feeling in his stomach. As Horrocks left the caravan, Montgomery stood at the door and wagged his finger at him, saying, 'Remember, Jorrocks, *you are not to get mauled*.'[51]

Having sent his pupil on his way, the schoolmaster returned to consider his plans. His own experience of active command was not in fact very great. He had seen action as a junior officer in 1914 and been badly wounded after less than two months. On recovering he became a staff officer and ended the war as Chief-of-Staff in an infantry division. In 1940 when Horrocks had commanded a battalion, he had commanded 3rd Division, and brought it back from Dunkirk more or less intact, a considerable feat. But that had been two and a half years ago. He had had no battlefield experience since then and no experience of armour beyond exercises. The trainer of 7th Armoured Division, Percy Hobart, was his brother-in-law, but had little influence on him. Hobart was one of the many with whom Montgomery did not get on.[52]

Alexander had held no active command since 1940 either. He had commanded an infantry Corps at Dunkirk, and his only experience of armour had been in an exercise run by Brooke and Montgomery in the Autumn of 1941, in which both his umpires agreed that he totally mishandled it. He had just returned from Burma, where he had managed the retreat. This consisted mainly in the considerable administrative feat of evacuating thousands of refugees. He was considered to be a man of very little brain, but Churchill admired his physical courage and liked his style. He had been Montgomery's pupil and despite the fact that he was now his former instructor's superior, the relationship did not change.[53]

Alexander was cool, brave and the son of an Earl. Montgomery was clear, confident and professional. But whatever their qualities, their combined experience did not make it look as if they would weigh very heavily in the balance against the Desert Fox and his sharp-toothed cubs. Many desert veterans remained sceptical and withheld their judgement.

Whilst thinking about his future offensive, Montgomery's immediate priority was repelling Rommel's next attack whilst keeping his own forces intact. The ground he was on offered Montgomery the opportunity, and he was getting the resources to make the opportunity real. The 44th Division, consisting of 131, 132 and 133 Brigades, was acclimatizing in the Delta and Montgomery moved it up to the Alam el Halfa Ridge, which he recognized, as Auchinleck had, to be a key position. Horrocks got 10th Armoured Division, with 66 Grants, as reinforcements, and had them join the 60 Grants of 22nd Armoured Brigade already at Alam el Halfa and dig in. People were aware that only Grants could take on Panzer IIIs and IVs. The 22nd Armoured Brigade were accordingly known as ELH – 'Egypt's last hope'. Horrocks hoped he would not lose it.

Seventh Armoured Division, now reduced to light tanks and a few cruisers, stayed out in the desert to the south, ready to harass Rommel and take him in the flank if he chose the expected route. To encourage him to do so, de Guingand arranged a deception. A map showing an area of soft going in the Ragil Depression to be hard, was carefully stained with NAAFI tea and put in a scout car which was then blown up in a minefield. The next morning the map had disappeared. In the event it had little effect on the outcome, but 'Jorrocks' enjoyed japes with the Jerries, and it was all good clean fun.[54]

On the evening of 17 August, Brooke and Churchill arrived back in Cairo after their week in Moscow. The following morning, Churchill bounded into Brooke's room in his dressing-gown while Brooke was still getting dressed and bent his ear about the need to attack Rommel immediately. Brooke pointed out that Monty had only been in command for two days, that there was a lot to sort out and that they might first listen to what he had to say before jumping on him.[55] On 19 August, they decamped to the desert. That evening, at the new HQ at Burg el Arab, Montgomery took them to his caravan and expounded his plan for meeting Rommel, who was expected to attack on or around 26 August, and then for his own offensive, which would take seven days of hard fighting. However, he would need six weeks to get ready – the end of September.

Both Brooke and Churchill found Montgomery's exposition masterly. He had 'gripped' the situation in just a few days, was clear, incisive and completely confident. Brooke went to bed pleased that Churchill had accepted the man he had recommended to him. He felt for the first time that year 'that at last we might begin to meet with some success'.[56] Churchill's reaction suggests that Montgomery must have been an extraordinarily good presenter, for though he was 'disappointed' at the timing of the offensive – the same timing suggested by Dorman-Smith – he accepted it. He even began to relish the prospect of Rommel 'breaking his teeth on us' before the main attack. But he was concerned about Cairo. He worried about whether there was time to organize its defences, and wanted 'every able-bodied man in uniform not required for Eighth Army' to defend it. Apparently, everyone agreed.[57]

At just about the time that they were all sitting down to listen to Montgomery, a convoy of ships was streaming across the Channel towards England. It was ferrying back the last survivors of a force of 4,963 men of the 2nd Canadian Division which had raided Dieppe in Operation 'Jubilee'. Of those men, over two thirds of them – 3,369 – stayed in Dieppe, dead, wounded or as prisoners. Casualties were higher than those to be suffered by either of the American divisions landing at 'bloody' Omaha beach on D-Day in 1944. At the time, and since, the raid was justified because of the lessons allegedly learned from it, such as the inadvisability of launching frontal attacks on strong coastal defences particularly if they had not been bombed and shelled beforehand. It was a high price to pay for wisdom of this quality. The original plans, conceived by Lord Mountbatten and his staff, had at some point in the murky planning process been approved by Lieutenant-General Montgomery as GOC South-Eastern Command. After the raid had had to be postponed in July, security was compromised and Montgomery had recommended its complete cancellation 'for all time'. Mountbatten got a new plan approved despite him, exchanging the original paratroopers with commandos and cancelling the preliminary bombing. Even the plan Montgomery had approved had been very risky. Was there a reckless gambler inside the meticulous planner? In the desert, nobody knew about it.[58]

The next day, the visitors inspected the troops in the field. Churchill felt the army's 'reviving ardour'. Everybody said there had been a tremendous change already. He did not like all he saw, however. Horrocks explained his plan of digging in his tanks defensively to meet the German armour and then attacking their soft-skinned trucks from the rear. 'Dog eat rabbit', 'Jorrocks' explained, helpfully. 'That's no good,' Churchill replied, 'Why don't you attack?' Churchill kept repeating 'dog eat rabbit' to himself, and as he drove off with Montgomery he leaned over and muttered 'He's no good, get rid of him.' Montgomery told him to mind his own business.[59] It was just as well he had picked up so many brownie points the previous evening.

At the end of the day, ignoring doctor's orders, Churchill bathed in the blue-green waters of the Mediterranean. He had no bathing costume, so he took his dip wearing a shirt. Looking like a pink pygmy hippopotamus, he was rolled over by the waves, and as his legs came up out of the water, he made them into a 'V' sign.[60] Now everything would be all right.

He was still worried about Cairo, though, and in the last days of his visit, Churchill busied himself with its defences. The 51st Highland Division, now re-formed after its destruction in France in 1940, had just arrived. As it was not 'desert-worthy', Churchill had it posted to man the new Nile front – a novelty indeed.[61]

Having got wind of an impending battle, Churchill wanted to stay for Rommel's attack. But Brooke prevailed, and got him on to a plane on the evening of 23 August. 'I heaved a sigh of relief as I saw his plane take to the air,' he wrote. Now it was all up to Monty. Brooke penned him a letter saying he had 'wonderful prospects' out there, and wished him the best of luck, before he boarded his own flight for Gibraltar, and England.[62]

EL ALAMEIN –
ROUND TWO

ERWIN ROMMEL WAS NOT A happy man. Supplies were becoming critical again. The Tobruk booty was long gone. The ammunition there had been useless anyway. In July, the DAK had actually received only 6,000 tons of supplies at the front, one fifth of its quota. The rest were on the road or stuck at Tripoli. In August it got 8,200 tons, still only a third of what was needed. In addition to 164th Light Division which had arrived in the nick of time in July, Rommel had now got the Italian Folgore Parachute Division and Ramcke's Parachute Brigade. The Folgore had been training for the assault on Malta. They were well-equipped, well-led and highly motivated, as were Ramcke's men, though apart from a few veterans of Crete they were raw. However, neither of them had any trucks. Adding them to Rommel's ration strength was a mixed blessing if he could not feed them. He had received 39 tanks. He was not getting any stronger. His enemies were. They were building defences. Intelligence reported that a large British convoy would reach Suez by early September. The clock was ticking.

Rommel was dispirited and he was also sick. He had a nasty sore on his lip and suffered from fainting attacks. His doctor diagnosed a combination of common desert ailments: chronic stomach and intestinal catarrh, nasal diphtheria and circulation problems.[1] On 22 August, Rommel told OKW that he was ill and suggested that Guderian take over the Panzerarmee Afrika. However, Hitler had sacked Guderian the previous year, and so suggested instead that Rommel hand over to the commander of the Afrika Korps, General Walter Nehring. Rommel changed his mind. He asked for a long stretch of leave, but not until September. He still wanted to take Alexandria and become the conqueror of Egypt. He would have one more go first.[2]

His attack would start at night, but he needed a full moon. The next one started on 26 August. Rommel also needed at least four days supply of petrol, which was more of a problem. The 26th passed. On 27 August, Kesselring flew in to see him, and promised that *in extremis*, 400 tons a day of aviation fuel would be flown in from Luftwaffe stocks. For once, Rommel expressed some sympathy for Kesselring in a letter home. 'He is in a tough position in Rome,' he wrote. 'They promise him the earth and deliver very little. His over-optimism as far as this crowd are concerned has earned him bitter disappointments.'[3] On 29 August, Rommel decided to attack the following night. Cavallero told him that tankers would arrive at Benghazi that day. The decryptors at Bletchley Park told Montgomery a few hours later.

The plan was to try another drive round the southern flank. The 15th and 21st Panzer Divisions would push out south of the Ragil Depression and then head north in an arc towards the back of Alam el Halfa, with the Ariete and Littorio Divisions on their left and 90th Light to the left of them. The threat to the British lines of communication would tempt them to counter-attack in the same old way and the DAK would then throw them back in the same old way. After they had won the ensuing tank battle, 21st Panzer would move east and cut off Alexandria from the south and 15th Panzer and 90th Light would head for Cairo, where the Ariete and Littorio would relieve them. That would make Mussolini happy.

The line of attack was obvious. There could be no surprise about that. Its success depended on surprise in the attack's timing, and its speed. Supplies also depended on speed. If the Axis forces got bogged down in a long battle, they would run out of petrol. It was a considerable risk, but Rommel was used to taking risks. It was worth it. 'There is still a lot left to be desired,' he wrote to Lucie on the morning of 30 August, 'and there are all sorts of shortcomings. Despite all of that I've decided to go for it ... The stakes are so high. If this blow succeeds, it could decide the war. If it doesn't, then at least we'll ruffle their feathers.'[4] He now had 200 German tanks, including a number with the new high-velocity guns, and 240 Italian ones, giving him 440 in all, plus a few light tanks. The British had no doubt guessed where he would come and could also work out for themselves that it would be any time during the full moon. They had 700 tanks, though only 160 of them were Grants. Would they come on in the same old way?

At about 22:00 hours on the night of 30 August, Nehring's Afrika Korps, with 15th Panzer under von Vaerst and 21st Panzer under von Bismarck, and de Stefanis' XX Italian Corps with 90th Light under Kleeman, began moving through their lines, with their artillery shelling gaps in the British minefields ahead. By some quirk of chance, the minefields were shaped like the foot of Italy. As the men of the Panzerarmee probed forwards in the darkness, they heard a rumbling from above and saw great flashes of light from behind them. The RAF were bombing their transport north west of Kalakh. They did not know it, but in an ominous reversal of past experience, the British radio interception service had been listening to their traffic as they assembled for the attack.[5] If the British had in fact got wise to their timing, the only card they had left to play was speed.

That evening, Brian Horrocks had dined on tinned oysters with General Freyberg at the HQ of 2nd New Zealand Division, and then gone out to visit a Maori battalion which was due to carry out a raid on the Italians opposite them. He was driving back to his Corps HQ in his jeep when the sky to the south lit up, and the boom of gunfire rolled across the desert. This was obviously it.

XIII Corps HQ was a hive of activity. Horrocks felt very excited, so he decided to adopt a nonchalant air and go to bed, for there was nothing he could do then and he needed to be fresh the next day. That would be his great test. He did not sleep much, but he did get some rest.

Whilst Horrocks was curled up in a hole in the sand for the night, far away in the north, Ramcke's parachutists attacked part of 5th Indian Division, and 164th Division raided the Australians. The Trento Division raided the South Africans just as the South Africans were setting out to raid them. This activity was supposed to pin down

XXX Corps, but it did not fool anybody.

When the sun rose the next morning, it turned the sky blood-red. Horrocks shaved, dressed and, summoning up all the *sang froid* which went with the red cap-band of a lieutenant-general of the British Army, walked at a carefully measured pace to his operations room. From there, on top of the Alam el Halfa Ridge, he peered through his binoculars. There was a haze in the sky above him, but between it and the ground the air was very clear. He could see a mass of German tanks and vehicles moving steadily eastwards. By 11:00, he had identified the whole of the DAK. They were doing what everyone had expected. He called Montgomery and asked for 23rd Armoured Brigade, which was in reserve under XXX Corps, to be transferred to his command. By 14:00, it was in position, blocking the gap between Alam el Halfa and the New Zealanders.

For Rommel, the light of the desert morning had brought hard and heavy tidings. He had received the first report at 8:00. His troops were under constant air attack, and there had been heavy casualties. General von Bismarck had been killed by a mortar. Nehring himself was wounded, hit by a bomb splinter, so Rommel ordered his own Chief-of-Staff, Fritz Bayerlein, to take over the Afrika Korps. Above all, progress had been very slow. The minefields had been thicker than expected, and they, the air attacks, and the harassing defensive fire from the forward units of 7th Armoured Division pulling back in front of them, had all slowed down the attack. It took until 10:00 to get the bulk of the DAK moving. When Horrocks first saw them, they were already way behind schedule. Rommel had lost his last card, speed.

Rommel may have been a risk-taker, but he wanted to call off the attack. Bayerlein persuaded him to go on, but, in view of the alerted state of the defences, and the bombing of the petrol supplies, to turn north earlier than planned. The drive would be a lot shorter than the planned long hook carrying beyond the Alam el Halfa Ridge, and so save petrol. As it was, they needed to stop soon to refuel.

As Horrocks and his staff watched the German columns from their vantage point on Alam el Halfa, their view became gradually obscured. A dust-storm was blowing up from the south. By midday, they could see nothing, and the Desert Air Force was grounded. For the Germans and Italians refuelling under such conditions was a trying experience, but it was better than getting bombed. By 13:00,

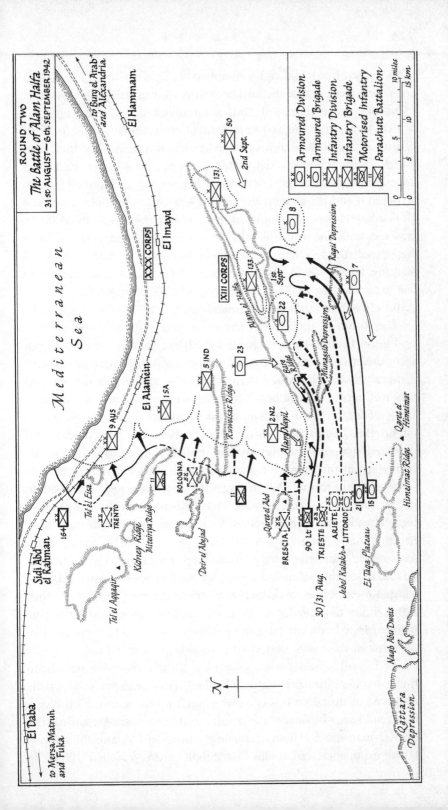

with the storm at its height, they had done it and the tanks began squeaking their way northwards, towards the western edge of Alam el Halfa, where the Grants of 22nd Armoured Brigade were dug in.

As the German tanks ground their way towards him, Horrocks was visited by Montgomery. The only real uncertainty had been whether Rommel would deliver a long hook past Alam el Halfa, or a short hook in front of it. A long hook would be stopped by 8th Armoured Brigade and Horrock's old command, 44th Infantry Division, but they were both untried units. It was clear now that it was a short hook, which would be stopped by the veterans of 22nd Armoured Brigade, under their bright young commander 'Pip' Roberts, backed up by 23rd Armoured Brigade, who had hopefully learned some lessons. That was better. Montgomery gave his new boy some advice and then, as he seemed to be getting on quite well, left to see Ramsden.

Rommel's battle plan was his old classic, a flanking attack from the south. But the grinding pace, in full view of his enemies, was very different from his earlier surprise dashes across the desert. The position and the defences did not allow that any more. The engagement about to be fought out was more characteristic of the Grand Old Duke of York than of the Desert Fox. He marched his tanks right up to the hill he had hoped to pass round; had an ineffectual fire-fight; and then marched them back again.

The Axis columns were making painful progress. They could hardly see. They hit soft ground, which slowed them down and made them burn up more fuel. On the left, the Italians were still caught up in the edges of the minefields. They were all still harried by 7th Armoured. Roberts and his men had been ready since dawn. No one was quite sure what was going on, but they all knew something was. At about 17:30, the storm began to abate. As the air cleared, about 120 German tanks emerged from the subsiding clouds of dust some 1,000 yards in front of Roberts' position.

Some of the tanks moved east, across the British position, while others moved towards them, paused and then also wheeled round. Roberts ordered a flank attack. The Germans saw them, lined up for action and a gun fight began. Most of the leading German tanks were new ones with the longer-range guns and they opened up while the British were still out of range, causing casualties among the Grants. However, they closed in, allowing Roberts' men to hit back. Probing for a way through, the attackers edged west, towards pre-sited anti-tank guns, which they could not see. The British gunners now had 6-pounders, not 2-pounders, and they held their fire until the range had closed to as little as 300 yards. Now it was German tanks which had to charge. They overran a few of the guns, but took heavy losses and could not break through. Roberts called down artillery fire on them. Dusk fell within an hour, and the DAK withdrew a few miles south towards Ragil. Both sides had lost something in excess of 20 tanks in the action.

That night, Montgomery issued orders to shell soft-skinned transport vehicles and asked the Air Force to bomb them as well. It was a night of rabbit hunting, but the dogs stayed in their kennels. Montgomery was hitting his enemy at his weakest point, as well he knew. The Fox could not live in the desert without his rabbits to feed him. Now it was clear what Rommel was up to, 8th Armoured Brigade was moved round to the west of Alam el Halfa.

The next morning, 1 September, Rommel was further frustrated. The British tanks were not trying to attack him. Much as Churchill might have been stirred by the thought of Horrocks emulating his own participation in the last British cavalry charge at Omdurman, 'Jorrocks' stayed where he was, as he had been told to, though his commanders were difficult to restrain.[6] So Rommel tried a second push on the ridge, perhaps still in the hope of luring his opponents into the open. Because of a lack of petrol he had to restrict the attack to 15th Panzer Division. It achieved nothing, and von Vaerst withdrew to sit in the desert, where he was shelled and bombed all day. Seven of his headquarters staff were killed and Rommel had a narrow shave when he came up to see him. The Desert Air Force flew 122 bomber sorties, mostly in the Ragil area. Rommel's position was hopeless, and he decided the next morning to retreat. However, he had to wait until nightfall to do so, so his men had to sit out yet another day under a rain of shells and bombs. The British seemed to have plenty of both. Coningham's crews flew another 167 bomber sorties which were hardly disturbed. Where was his petrol? Where was the Luftwaffe? Bloody Kesselring!

The Luftwaffe was there all right, but it was pursuing an agenda of its own. Since the first wing of JG27 had arrived in North Africa in April 1941, it had become apparent that they had in their ranks a real superstar, the twenty-one year old Hans-Joachim Marseille, who was indeed to become known as 'the Star of Africa'. He had first flown in action in the Battle of Britain in mid-August 1940. He was shot up several times, making a forced-landing after two weeks, and baling out into the Channel two weeks after that. He was posted to another unit, JG52, but his commander, the future head of the post-war Luftwaffe, Johannes Steinhoff, found him to be unmanageable and transferred him to I./JG27 to get rid of him. He arrived in the desert having filed seven claims. Marseille spent hours alone practising. He had a wonderful feel for an aircraft and an amazing eye for judging speed and distance, the rarest of all gifts. He honed those skills until he was the best shot in the Luftwaffe. He perfected the technique of diving on a circle of P-40s or Hurricanes, knocking one down with a few shells, zooming up and then doing it again. On 6 June 1942, he shot down six P-40s of 5 Squadron SAAF in twelve minutes in this way, taking his score to 81. On 18 June, he passed 100 and was whisked off to Berlin to pick up a Knight's Cross with Swords and Oak Leaves and do some photo-shoots. However, his greatest day was 1 September. Flying three bomber escort missions, he claimed 17 British fighters. Fifteen of them correspond to actual British losses. No other pilot had ever shot down so many of the enemy on a single day. His armourer calculated that he had expended the astonishingly low average of 15 shells on each victim.[7]

Marseille made a wonderful warrior-hero, and was the most famous German serviceman in Africa after Rommel, a real Aryan superman. However, warrior-heroes do not win modern wars. Shooting down British fighters did not stop the bombers. Instead of attacking them, which would in any case have been rather a dangerous thing to do, most of the pilots of JG27 milled about watching in awe as Marseille exhibited his graceful if gory skills, and making sure that nobody interfered. Protecting their superstars was a full-time job. Marseille's own wingman flew 100 sorties before making his first claim. On 1 September, German pilots only made 26 claims in all. The British actually lost 20 fighters. Therefore, assuming, as seems most likely, that Marseille got 15 of the 17 he claimed, all the rest of the 100 or so German fighter pilots between them only got five. The British lost no bombers at all.[8]

The Luftwaffe's emphasis on creating superstars had created a very strange culture in the fighter units. The commander of JG27, Eduard Neumann, commented after the war that 'most of the pilots in

Marseille's Staffel acted in a secondary role as escort to the "master"'. It was hard, he added, for newcomers to gain successes. Given the nature of air fighting, it was difficult for any new pilot in any air force, but some of the old hands in JG27 appear to have actively discouraged them from doing so. Another pilot of I./JG27 has observed that some squadron leaders had the attitude, 'There is only one man who has the right to shoot down enemy aircraft – me!' Internal rivalry over star status took precedence over military effectiveness. The events in the air on 1 September are an extreme illustration of the impact these prima donnas had on the furtherance of the Axis cause.[9]

Realising that Rommel's attack had been stopped, Montgomery prepared to push south across his line of retreat with the New Zealand Division, but he told Horrocks to close the gap 'gradually and methodically'. He did not want any cavalry charges. Rommel was dangerous in the open. Nevertheless, when Horrocks asked Freyberg to prepare an attack, a 'bellyaching' session began. Freyberg first asked for the 5th Indian Division to carry out the attack, and when this was refused, the new 44th Division.[10]

On the evening of 2 September, Rommel had a discussion with Kesselring. Rommel accused him of having led him up the garden path over the 400 tons a day of aviation fuel. It seems that although he did indeed order the fuel to be sent by air, the transport aircraft themselves used up 280 tons a day in moving it, with the result that only about 100 tons arrived at the most forward airfield at El Daba. It then had to be taken to the troops in trucks, which was the old problem, so hardly any arrived. All Rommel cared about was how much went into the petrol tanks of his vehicles. Kesselring had set himself up as a useful scapegoat.[11]

Rommel sent a signal to OKW, explaining that he had to break off the attack because of lack of surprise, heavy air attacks and above all lack of petrol, which is what he told his wife in a letter two days later. The cryptographers at Bletchley Park received the news gratefully. The withdrawal began on the morning of 3 September. Montgomery ordered that there was to be no forward movement except by patrols. Rommel's men were left to the mercies of the RAF and when reports from the air about the withdrawal came through, 7th Armoured Division staged local attacks in the south as well.

Horrocks finally struck a deal with Freyberg. That night, 3

September, the New Zealanders and a fresh brigade from 44th Division staged their attack on the Italian Folgore Parachute Division and Ramcke's brigade, who were expecting them. Communications broke down and there was chaos in the assembly area before the attack even started. Some units got lost, others veered off their planned route and the supporting tanks mistook some German lights for lamps marking their lanes through a minefield. The veteran New Zealand division had 300 casualties, but the single brigade of newcomers from the English home counties suffered over 700. Some ground was gained, but the following evening, Montgomery ordered Freyberg to withdraw.

Far from being dismayed at this set-back, Montgomery spent the rest of the evening explaining to a dinner guest how Egypt had been saved. President Roosevelt's personal emissary, Mr Wendell Willkie, had arrived in Cairo, having been warned by the President before he left Washington that it might be in German hands before he got there. Showing a political awareness unusual in soldiers of the time, Montgomery invited Willkie without prompting to Burg el Arab. Willkie found his host to be 'wiry, scholarly, intense, almost fanatical', and Montgomery made a deep impression on him. In the morning, Montgomery took him to see the wrecked tanks the Germans had left behind in the desert, explaining everything in great detail to the impressionable layman. He told Willkie he did not want to trumpet Alam Halfa as a great victory, for fear that it would frighten Rommel into leaving the Alamein line. He wanted Rommel to stay put. He therefore asked Willkie if he would talk to the press unofficially in a way that would restore morale in Egypt without sounding too threatening to Rommel. So, on 9 September, in what was probably the first stage-managed press conference in the history of the British army, Willkie gave the press an informal, low-key briefing. Most of them remained sceptical. But when Willkie returned to Washington, Montgomery could not have had a better ambassador.[12]

Rommel fell back slowly, but in good order. By the evening of 6 September, he had got all his forces out. His only net gain in territory was the Himeimat Ridge in the far south. Horrocks suggesting evicting him, but Montgomery said 'no' because he wanted Rommel to see the dummy installations he was preparing to put in front of it. The Second Battle of El Alamein was over. In the Italian Army, it was officially known as Operation 'Caballo', and unofficially as 'Santa Rosa', whose day was 30 August, when the operation was launched. Because of the feature which dominated it, it became known in the Eighth Army as the Battle of Alam Halfa, the name chosen by Montgomery and most British historians. The name most popular in the Panzerarmee Afrika was 'The Six-Day Race'.[13]

It had not been a big battle. Nor, in comparison with the month-long slog of First Alamein, had it been a long one. Casualties of all kinds amounted to about 1,750 for Eighth Army – two thirds of them in Freyberg's abortive counter-attack – and 2,800 in the Panzerarmee Afrika. The Panzerarmee had lost 47 tanks, having recovered 76 which had been damaged. But it had also lost almost 400 other vehicles, which was in many ways more serious. The rabbits had been gobbled up at a frightening rate. Some had been smashed by artillery fire, but worst of all was the bombing. Most of the rabbits had been snapped up by eagles.

The RAF had made its presence felt on the first night. Having flown 482 sorties on 31 August, they raised the level of effort on every day of the battle, culminating in 902 sorties flown on 3 September. The Luftwaffe had moved forward and reorganized itself since July, albeit with never more than 300 aircraft on strength. However, they were hampered by lack of spares to keep aircraft in flying condition and lack of aviation fuel to get them into the air, for Kesselring was now sharing it with the DAK. As a result, the Luftwaffe averaged only about 300 sorties a day, and just a third of those were bomber sorties. As Marseille and his pals had discovered more lucrative ways of advancing their scores than by attacking the bombers destroying the Afrika Korps, the British bombers had been left in peace. 'We were very heavily attacked every hour of the day and night,' commented Bayerlein, 'and had very heavy losses, more than from any other cause. Your air superiority was most important, perhaps decisive.' Even if Coningham had sent up his P-40s and Hurricanes as deliberate decoys, their losses would have been worth it to keep the 109s away from his bombers.[14]

Alam el Halfa was the beginning of something new. On the British side, air–ground co-operation had always been good, but now it went up a gear. In the desert, air superiority paid extra dividends. The land was flat and there no woods in which to hide. Every moving vehicle left tracks and raised a cloud of dust. Every extra mile a supply column had to travel from its base to the front was an extra mile of opportunity for a fighter-bomber. Every new supply dump was a new target for formations of medium bombers. Tedder and Coningham had grasped this from the first and so did Montgomery. It was one reason why he wanted to be at Burg el Arab next to Coningham. He told Horrocks and kept on telling everyone else that the air and the ground were one : 'It is one battle, not two'. Despite agreements in principle, personalities interfered, for Montgomery and Coningham, whom one of Montgomery's staff has described as 'bloody-minded' and 'prima donna-ish', did not get on.[15] This merely mirrored the established state of affairs on the other side, where the conflicts were not just between personalities, but had some substance.

However, despite being pounded from the air, the Fox had got away. Stranded in front of the Alam el Halfa Ridge, he had been at Montgomery's mercy. Montgomery knew exactly what the condition of his forces was. Why did he not let loose his dogs and 'finish' him?

This was no oversight. Montgomery's decision not to advance was quite deliberate. 'I issued very precise instructions at this stage,' he has recorded, 'since it was important to resist any temptation to rush into the attack.' Such temptations were widely felt amongst subordinate commanders at the time.[16] Montgomery's reason for resistance is very clear: 'The standard of training of the Eighth Army formations was such that I was not prepared to loose them headlong into the enemy; moreover, my purpose was to restore the line, and to proceed methodically with my own preparations for the big offensive later on.'[17] Montgomery did not believe that the weapon he had was capable of defeating Rommel in the open field. Most past experience and the execution of the one counter-attack which was launched on 3 September suggested he was right. Auchinleck would have been unlikely to demur. The skills were not there.

Montgomery had secured his reputation with Brooke on his ability to train. He had a good eye for what was needed, and knew how to develop it. He wanted to put the skills in place first and then fight a battle which played to *those*, not the ones which the DAK clearly had in abundance. Nobody will ever know whether or not, if he had decided differently, the Panzerarmee Afrika could have been annihilated in the desert south of Alam el Halfa in September. But the attempt would certainly have involved considerable risk. He had to fight a decisive battle – but first he had to forge the weapon to win it.

Montgomery started at the top. The day after the battle ended, he wrote a letter to Horrocks, saying: 'Dear Jorrocks, Well done – but you must remember that you are now a corps commander and not a divisional commander', and went on to list Horrocks' mistakes, mainly interfering too much in the affairs of his subordinates. Horrocks had been feeling quite pleased with himself for not getting mauled and eating lots of rabbits as well, and this brought him up short. Then he thought about it and rang up Montgomery to say 'thank you'.[18] Montgomery included himself amongst his own pupils. After Alam el Halfa, as after every exercise he conducted, he wrote down the lessons for himself, ten of them, in numbered paragraphs.[19]

Ramsden was a different case. A week after the battle, Montgomery sacked him and on 15 September, Oliver Leese arrived from England to take over XXX Corps. Leese had never had a major field command, having been Deputy Chief-of-Staff with the BEF at Dunkirk. Like almost all senior British officers, he had been trained in the infantry. But in 1941 he had been tasked with forming and training the Guards Armoured Division, and had thus spent over a year studying, if not practising, armoured warfare. He had also been one of Montgomery's students at Camberley Staff College. Montgomery was out to change the culture of the Eighth Army and he wanted to do it with people in whom he had confidence.

He had a third corps commander to appoint. He had decided that his armoured *corps de chasse* would be X Corps, and offered the job to Horrocks. Horrocks demurred. He came from a very humble regiment, he said, the Middlesex. The cavalry would resent him. Montgomery should put in Lumsden, who had won the Grand National. Alexander also took the view that champion jockeys were the best men to lead tanks – and after all, Lumsden was an old desert hand. Montgomery gave in, only to discover that this was the tip of the iceberg. One of his staff officers has explained that there was in the desert an informal, but very tight 'trades union operation, which was governed by the "cavalry", the Guards and the Greenjackets, and all the old sweats'.[20] Keith Douglas recognized that there was an 'unbridgeable gap' between 'the original horsed officers' of his regiment who spent their time in this social network and the newer officers who 'had mostly completed a mechanized training and knew their work reasonably well'.[21] With Thatcherite zeal, Montgomery introduced a meritocracy based on professionalism. The three corps and many of the divisions and brigades were reorganized, and at 7th Armoured Division John Harding replaced Renton, who had bellyached a lot with Horrocks. There was no Arthur Scargill in the Eighth Army and there was a war on, so instead of going on strike, the middle-class brothers of the desert trades union just bellyached quietly and illicitly to each other.

There was another less public but no less important appointment to make – that of chief gunner. Montgomery sent for Brigadier Sidney Kirkman who had worked for him in that role at South-Eastern Command. The artillery would be critical in what was to come. Montgomery knew that in modern warfare, most casualties are inflicted by shelling. He also knew that an attacker needs skilfully handled artillery to have any chance of success, and that artillery played a crucial role in the British Army's great run of victories in 1918. He had also realized, as Auchinleck had, that part of the Eighth Army's problem was that firepower was not concentrated, so he needed a good man at the centre to handle it. He was also aware that if the British Army was going to continue to fight the war at all, it had to substitute materiel for manpower. By mid-1942, the British war economy was producing plenty of armaments, but the expansion of the Army was slowing down because of a lack of men. Britain's demographics meant that the situation would get worse through the mid-1940s. For that reason alone, the Army could not face another Somme. Casualties had to be kept down, for they could not be replaced. Shells could. There were tactical, strategic and political reasons why Kirkman's guns had to do their job well.

Alexander did not like paperwork, so he used to come and visit Montgomery at Burg el Arab, and stayed there throughout the Six Day Race. This enabled Montgomery to keep an eye on him, and he was only rude to his chief on those rare occasions on which Alexander had the temerity to make suggestions about military matters. Otherwise, Alexander made notes of Montgomery's requests.[22] His main tasks were keeping London happy and getting equipment, and he was very good at both. The 300 Shermans arrived on 3 September. They carried the same dual-purpose 75-mm gun first used in the Grant, but instead of poking out of the tall, vulnerable hull, it was mounted in the turret, allowing the Sherman to fire 'hull-down' and engage anti-tank guns as well as tanks. By 1942 standards the machine was well armoured, and, a novelty for many British crews, mechanically reliable. The only thing which had not changed was the tendency it shared with all other British and American tanks to catch fire and 'brew-up' when hit. In Normandy, the Germans were to christen them 'Tommy-cookers' and their crews called them 'Ronsons' after the cigarette lighter. A report from 1941 concluded that the main cause with British tanks of the period was that red hot splinters from a penetrating shell set fire to the ammunition stowed in the turret. German tanks carried their ammunition in armoured bins. The British reduced the incidence of fires by adopting the same practice, and even filling the bins with water, but the Americans did not. Although British experts criticized the stowage provisions of the Grant, the problem remained with the Sherman.[23] Apart from that, it was a good match for the Panzer IV.

The number of 6-pounder anti-tank guns doubled, allowing the specialist anti-tank units to hand over many of their old 2-pounders to infantry battalions. For the first time the infantry acquired some anti-tank capability of their own. The 2-pounders were not great, but they were better than nothing and nobody was complaining. The medium and field artillery establishments of brigades and divisions were both substantially increased.

There was also plenty of radio equipment. When Seebohm's unit had been over-run in July, a lot of its equipment had been captured and its methods revealed. The British tightened up their own system accordingly and, by September, were well on the way to creating what was to become the most effective and secure communications system amongst all of the German Army's opponents.[24] Having started way behind, failure stimulated the Eighth Army to move steadily ahead.

In logistics it had always been ahead, and it lengthened its lead. Supply dumps were constructed, ammunition was stockpiled and transport depots were built up. Between 1 August and 23 October alone, Eighth Army had an intake of 10,300 vehicles, more than twice as many as the DAK possessed in total. Only 8,700 were issued, with the remainder forming a reserve.[25]

As the equipment flowed in, Montgomery devoted most of his energies to two things in which he had enormous experience and an outstanding track record: planning and training. They went hand in hand, for as he planned he considered what he thought the army could do, and as he trained, he focused on building up the skills his plan would require. Training was focused exclusively on those –

everything else was ignored. The whole process would at the same time create the 'atmosphere' he wanted and change the culture of the organization. The process was intricate, detailed and complex. His gift – an extraordinary gift, commented upon by every senior officer who worked with him – was to be able to make it sound straightforward, clear and simple. On 10 September, Montgomery issued 'Eighth Army Training Memorandum No.1', which he wrote himself, spelling out every requirement in detail.[26]

Physical fitness was first. Soldiers need to be fit, and most of the infantry spent much of their time sitting in trenches and moving in lorries. They would probably not be doing much fighting for several weeks, so they had to have something to do. The coming battle would require physical and mental hardness, and doing physical exercises together also improved units' morale. With Montgomery, it went deeper. He was a fitness fanatic, and was wont to quote some lines of Kipling which explained that nations 'fell because their peoples were not fit'.[27] He had introduced physical training for the first time in his commands in England and encountered considerable opposition. Montgomery's senior medical officer had protested that one colonel in particular must not run, or he would probably die. 'Let him die,' Montgomery replied. 'Much better to die now rather than in the midst of battle when it might be awkward to find a replacement.'[28] Some of the men, like Gunner Terence Milligan, still associate Montgomery's arrival on the scene with the 'chill of horror' they felt on being told to assemble at 6:00 am for a five mile run. Milligan planned to hide in a haystack and rejoin the group on the way back. Montgomery had thought of that. They were all put into trucks, driven five miles out and dropped. Some, he reports, were exhausted by having to climb off the lorry. Others 'tried to husband their energy by running on one leg'. But it was too cold to walk. They left their C/O by the roadside and never saw him again. His replacement was a keen runner.[29] In the desert most of the opposition came from 'old sweats' who had done plenty of fighting and thought that that was the best training. [30] Young or old, the sweats sweated at PT when the schoolmaster turned up to inspect them.

Skills were second. Some were specialized. A mine-clearance school was set up. XIII Corps developed some flail tanks called 'Scorpions', which beat the ground in front of them with a rotating drum fitted with chains to set off the mines. The resulting dust often caused the tanks' engines to overheat and stop, so XXX and X Corps steered clear of them, fearing that broken down flail tanks would block the very paths they were clearing. The other methods were the mine-detector, and, most reliable but also slowest of all, prodding with a bayonet. Everybody practised that.

Other skills were basic. Crews had to become familiar with their new tanks, and the infantry practised rifle and mortar firing. In order to learn how to use tanks and infantry together, clear minefields at night, use creeping barrages, master wireless security and so on, units held exercises based on the emerging plan. Rommel was particularly impressed by the Eighth Army's night attacks. They were something the Panzerarmee did not practice. The training took considerable effort. The line still had to be held, and a few units had to stay there come what may, but most divisions managed to rotate their brigades so that everyone could go through the 'Monty' mill. He had pioneered the use of realistic battle exercises when in command of 3rd Division in France, when he based them on what he thought was likely to happen for real. No other Division 'practised' in this way, which is one of the reasons 3rd Division was the only one to emerge from Dunkirk in good shape. By 1941, Montgomery was generally acknowledged to be the most professional trainer anyone could remember. His exercises had become the standard for the British Army as a whole.[31] The desert exercises were also based on what was expected to happen for real, and as the plan solidified, so they turned into rehearsals. The Highland Division held four in September and October. Divisions were to fight together, so as far as possible they trained together. Auchinleck's mixed 'brigade groups' combining all arms were abandoned, a move welcomed in particular by the Commonwealth commanders who wanted control over their own men, but which did not in itself further inter-arm co-operation.

The plan itself developed in two major phases, the first marked by one of Montgomery's crisp conferences, held on 16 September. He gathered together all thirteen corps and divisional commanders and their senior staff officers at Burg el Arab, and gave his first exposition of Operation 'Lightfoot', which he had written down on fourteen sheets of paper two days before. Given the number of mines the enemy were laying, light feet would be needed.

In essence, the plan was to attack simultaneously in the north and the south, making it hard for Rommel to ascertain the direction of the main effort. The main effort would in fact be in the north, where XXX Corps would break in between the Miteiriya Ridge and the sea and clear a bridgehead. X Corps would then pass through them, and engage the Afrika Korps in the sandy plains beyond. In the south, XIII Corps would capture Himeimat and by thus threatening Rommel's flank, force him to send his armoured reserves down to plug the gap, as he had done in his attempts to thwart Auchinleck in July. At the same time, part of 7th Armoured Division would turn Rommel's southern flank and go rabbit-shooting among his supply dumps.

The attack would be launched at night after a massive artillery barrage. XXX Corps was to clear a path through the minefields during the first night and also clear the area of enemy troops. In order to do so, it would deploy the concentrated firepower of about 450 guns. X Corps would move through them the following morning, and straddle Rommel's supply routes west of the Miteiriya Ridge. There would also be a small sea landing behind the lines to assist the northern thrust.

Montgomery's exposition ended by stressing the importance of morale. The battle, he said, 'would be a real rough-house'. It would also be 'the turning point of the whole war'. The result would largely depend on which side could stand up to the 'buffeting' longest. That was why the soldiers needed to be physically hardened up. 'There will be no tip and run tactics in this battle,' he concluded. 'It will be a killing match. The German soldier is a good soldier and the only way to beat him is to kill him in battle.'[32]

So there it was. It was to be a battle of attrition, a World War I killing match. The skills of the Afrika Korps would be nullified and Rommel's cunning would count for nothing. The Fox would not be chased across open fields and killed in the open, but cornered in his den and pinned down. Then the dogs would tear him to pieces.

Yet he was still a wily animal, so he had to be tricked. The plan included a series of elaborate deception measures. They were put under the control of one man, Lieutenant-Colonel Richardson. The first aim was to make Rommel think the main thrust would come in the south. In the north, therefore, tracks for vehicles were not laid until the last moment, but jump-off positions were started early and then camouflaged. Stores were stacked to look like trucks or tents from the air, and vehicle movements were discouraged. In the south, new tracks were laid, dummy dumps and a dummy pipeline built, vehicles were driven around as much as possible, and wireless traffic was simulated. The second aim was to disguise the attack's timing. The clearest indication of an imminent attack would be the concentration of forces near the front. So when X Corps went to the rear to train, dummy stores were erected to make it look as if they had not moved. When they did move, they took their real stores with them and replaced them with the dummies so it looked as if nothing had changed. A signals unit was left behind to keep the airwaves busy.[33]

Not all the unit commanders were happy with the plan, however. Experience dies hard. The infantry were worried about being left deep in enemy lines with no armoured support. The armour were worried about being trapped in narrow lanes which the 88s could turn into killing fields. There was bellyaching and the desert trades union reps raised points of order. On taking over XXX Corps, Leese had been horrified by the state of relations between infantry and armour. When he explained to the commanders of his infantry divisions that the armour would pass through the gaps in the minefields, they quietly opined that they would not. He was shocked and said that of course they would because it was an order from the army commander. His officers simply told him once again that in their opinion the armour would not do so. All became clear when at a conference at X Corps Lumsden told his commanders that there was one point in the plan with which he did not agree. 'Tanks,' he stated, 'must be used as cavalry ... and not kept as supporters of infantry. So I don't propose to do that.'[34] Monty had a word with Lumsden, and he backed down. However, the issue was not going to go away. Perhaps the *corps de chasse* had not been such a good idea after all.

As he took on board the views of his most senior generals and observed the preparations with his own critical eye, Montgomery decided that the army was not up to it. 'The training was not good,' he wrote in his diary. He felt he had to be very careful and ensure that 'units were not given tasks which were likely to end in failure because of their low standard of training'. Accordingly, on 6 October he issued a five-page memo. The sea-landing was dropped. There was not enough time to reorganize and integrate the armour and infantry under a single command structure. So the two corps in the north would fight together. XXX Corps would create a path, but not clear it of enemy troops on the first night. X Corps was to move through and then, instead of breaking into the open, shield the infantry of XXX Corps from the Axis armour by taking up defensive positions, as at Alam el Halfa, on ground of its own choosing. Thus protected, XXX Corps would engage in a drawn-out 'dog-fight' designed to 'crumble' away the holding infantry. Montgomery allowed ten days for this. There would be three phases: the 'break-in'; the 'dog-fight'; and the 'break-out'. He would win. It was just a question of time.[35]

Whilst the two armies were preparing for the showdown, the front was fairly quiet. Middle East Headquarters decided that the Axis should be distracted by some activity aimed at further disrupting their supplies lines, so they dusted off a plan originally suggested by the Navy for a raid on Tobruk. The Navy staff were no longer very keen, but were overruled by Admiral Harwood. The Long Range Desert Group and the SAS had been hatching plans of their own for land-based raids on the petrol dumps at Tobruk and some neighbouring airfields, so all these initiatives were drawn together into a complex series of co-ordinated raids on Tobruk, Barce and Benghazi involving several hundred commandos landed from two destroyers and various groups of special forces. The combined plan soon became the number one item of gossip in the bars of Cairo. Montgomery did not like special forces and was deeply sceptical about the whole thing, but it was launched on the night of 13 September. It was a disaster. It ended with the loss of the two destroyers and a cruiser, and some 700 sailors and soldiers, of whom about 100 were killed. Little damage was done. Montgomery was not surprised. He had not been involved in any of it and did not allow the outcome to distract him from the main business in hand.[36]

While all this was happening on the ground, the war in the air continued. The Desert Air Force had dominated the air at Alam el Halfa, but events in September served to render its superiority unchallenged for the rest of the desert war. After Marseille's record-breaking start, it was a disastrous month for the Luftwaffe, and for JG27 in particular.

In the first five days, the Geschwader lost six young pilots, five of them to Spitfires and one in an accident. On 6 September, one star ace with 40 claims, Gunther Steinhausen, and another pilot were shot down by Hurricanes. The next day, a second top-scorer, Hans-Arnold Stahlschmidt with 59 claims, was killed by a Spitfire of 601 Squadron.

In the next fortnight, JG27 lost six more pilots, two of them in a mid-air collision. This was despite deliveries of the latest version of the Messerschmitt 109, the 109G, with a powerful new Daimler-Benz engine. On the last day of the month, Marseille himself joined his Staffel on a patrol in a brand new Bf 109G. The patrol was uneventful. On the way home to base, Marseille reported smoke in the cockpit. He kept flying, but the smoke was making vision difficult. Finally he decided to bale out. Marseille turned the machine on its back, but he could not see and did not realize that the Messerschmitt was in an inverted dive. He fell to earth with his parachute unopened. It is thought that the tailplane hit his chest as he left the aircraft and knocked him unconscious. Unable to pull the rip-cord, he was killed when he hit the ground.[37] Having already lost 15 pilots, the heaviest losses of any month so far, the death of their top-scorer was the last straw for JG27. Marseille's I. Gruppe was withdrawn from operations for a month – one which was to prove critical. Marseille's total claims of 158 were exceeded by 29 other German fighter pilots, but all of those got most of their total in Russia. He remained the top-scorer against the Western Allies, and made 151 of his claims in Africa. Just four of them were for bombers.

Marseille may have died unconquered, but the cult built around him now came back to haunt its creators. The loss of their heroes was a terrible blow to morale, and to efficiency. Marseille, Stahlschmidt and Steinhausen between them accounted for almost 20 per cent of all the British aircraft claimed by the Luftwaffe in Africa. A lot of the boys they left behind claimed none at all. In any case, the easy days of picking off obsolete P-40s and Hurricanes were numbered. The Desert Air Force still only had three squadrons of Spitfires, but between them they certainly accounted for a third, and maybe as many as half of JG27's losses in September.[38]

The RAF was now steadily building up its forces. By mid-October, Tedder had a total of about 1,500 aircraft, 1,200 of them in Egypt and Palestine. Whilst the two Axis air forces between them had 3,000 aircraft in the Mediterranean, just 575 of these were in Africa, and their serviceability rate was only about 50 per cent. The Luftwaffe fielded about 325 of the total, but their offensive strength was largely limited to Ju 87 Stuka dive-bombers, which were extremely vulnerable. They had no medium bombers to speak of. Apart from some ineffective twin-engined Messerschmitt 110s, their fighters consisted of just over 100 Bf 109s, only 65 of which were serviceable. After I./JG27 were withdrawn, the remaining force could not possibly both protect the Stukas and disrupt the RAF's bombers, even if it had changed its ways and made determined attempts to do so. Tedder on the other hand had a new source of strength. The Yanks were coming. As early as 25 June the American Major-General Brereton had been tasked with creating an air force in the Middle East, and by October, both bomber and fighter units were operating with the RAF, with all but the heavy bombers directly under Coningham. Thirteen of Tedder's 96 squadrons were American. On 12 November these were to become the US Ninth Air Force.

These forces were aggressively handled. In the second week of October, heavy rain in the west trapped the Axis aircraft on water-logged airstrips and Coningham seized the opportunity to attack them on the ground, damaging their infrastructure and destroying about 30 aircraft. Tedder wanted to extend the attacks to Rommel's ground forces, urging Montgomery to make a threatening move so that Rommel would concentrate them together. He then wanted to attack them round the clock for three to four days so that they were seriously weakened, and the survivors demoralized and physically exhausted before the Eighth Army attacked. It was too late to put this idea into action.[39]

So it was all coming together. Montgomery had said he would attack when he was ready. The question was when that would be. This was a matter of some interest in London.

After their return to London, Churchill and Brooke had been preoccupied with the planning of 'Torch'. It had been agreed that the operation would be commanded by a quiet American staff officer called Eisenhower. Eisenhower had set up a headquarters in London and dined with Churchill the day after his arrival from the desert. In the days that followed there were some vigorous discussions between the British and US staffs about the scope of the operations 'Torch' was to lead to. There was then some shilly-shallying about dates, which drove the Prime Minister frantic – there were problems finding enough ships, then with equipment for the American infantry, and so on. The original date had been 30 October at the latest. That had been quite late enough for him.

In the middle of all this, Churchill had been gently prodding Alexander about when he was going to hit Rommel a crack. Having got used to nasty surprises he had been nervous about Rommel's expected attack. News of his repulse relieved him, but did no more than that. Alexander suggested that the disorganization caused by Alam el Halfa would delay the Eighth Army's offensive. Churchill wrote to Alexander on 17 September, saying that he understood the date to be the fourth week of September. When the message arrived, Alexander showed it to Montgomery. Montgomery told him that he would not do it in September. Alexander then asked him what he should tell the Prime Minister. So Montgomery took a pad and wrote down a reply. He stated that firstly Rommel's attack had caused some delay to preparations, that secondly the attack needed the right moon conditions, that thirdly the troops would be insufficiently equipped and trained in September and that therefore, fourthly, an attack in September would result in failure but an attack in October would result in victory. Alexander sent it unaltered on 19 September.[40]

Sir Alan Brooke had had no leave all year, so he asked Churchill if he might combine a visit to the Infantry School at Barnard Castle with three days' grouse shooting on the Durham moors. Churchill thought this was an excellent idea, so Brooke conducted his visit and took off to the moors. On the evening of 19 September, Brooke had come in from his first day on the butts to be told to go at once to the nearest scrambler telephone. The nearest such device was at Catterick aerodrome, 15 miles away. When Brooke got to the phone, he found it was Churchill, who wanted to know what he thought about Alexander's telegram. Brooke informed him that he had not seen it. Churchill accused him of being out of touch with the strategic situation. Brooke reminded him that he had been on the grouse moors all day, with his approval. 'Well, what are you going to do about it now?', Churchill asked him. Brooke asked him to send the telegram up for him to look at, and he would reply the next day. Churchill asked him how he would reply, and whether he had a cipher office with him. Brooke replied that he did not usually pack cipher offices when he went shooting, and would come back to the phone and speak to Churchill directly. A motorcyclist delivered Alexander's telegram from London that night. There was nothing the least bit urgent about it. Perhaps that was the problem.

Brooke returned in the rain to the telephone in Catterick the following day. He told Churchill that he thought the reasons given for attacking in October rather than September were excellent. The conversation got a bit vague after that, but Brooke thought he heard Churchill agree with him. When Brooke got back to London, Churchill had written a message to Alexander explaining that unless he attacked immediately Rommel would have built a Maginot line in the desert and the attack would fail. Brooke managed to tone it down.[41]

The pressure on Churchill had not waned. The Leader of the House, Sir Stafford Cripps, had been restless ever since the censure debate, and on 21 September was only just dissuaded from resigning in protest at the misconduct of the war. Had he done so, it would have dealt Churchill a very severe political blow.

Finally, on 22 September, the date of 'Torch' was fixed for 8 November. Montgomery (in the form of Alexander) had told Churchill he wanted to launch the attack 13 days prior to the landings, which would be 26 October. The other criterion was a full moon, as was usual in the desert, to help the troops clearing minefields. The next full moon was on 23 October.

On 11 October, the final 'Malta blitz' began, causing a further bout of anxiety in London. The airfields in Cyrenaica had to be captured soon so that aircraft could operate from them to protect the Malta convoys.

On 14 October, Brooke received a telegram announcing the date of operation 'Lightfoot'. It was so secret that he was asked to tell no one, not even Churchill. Brooke worried that if he did not, Churchill would keep on sending wires to Cairo and upset things. Lunching with Churchill on 16 October, he found he was on good form, so he gave him the news. It was 23 October.[42]

Rommel knew what was coming, or he thought he did. He had noted the change of command in the Eighth Army, but he had never heard of Montgomery, so it meant nothing to him, and he had no portrait to hang up in his headquarters. In Montgomery's position, he would launch attacks in a number of places, probe for weaknesses and then exploit the most promising. He therefore made his defences strong enough everywhere to give him time, and held back the DAK so that it could then counter-attack wherever a breakthrough seemed to threaten. He kept the armour out of the line, and sandwiched battalions of Ramcke's paratroopers between the Italian infantry so that they could stiffen them up and 'make suggestions' to their neighbours. The defences themselves looked rather like those used in

World War I, with rows of barbed wire. However, the basis of them was not wire and trenches, but minefields. Rommel had his engineers prepare particularly elaborate ones which he called 'Devil's gardens'. Anti-tank and anti-personnel mines of different designs and origins were placed in layers, and mixed with wired-up bombs and shells, many of those from captured stock. The first minefields were held by section posts. There was a second line of minefields a mile behind those, followed by the main defensive line with anti-tank guns. That way, the initial British artillery barrage would fall on almost empty forward positions, and the infantry assault would get held up on the second line, giving the defenders in the main line plenty of warning. The whole position contained an estimated 445,000 mines, most of them anti-tank devices, and was five miles deep.[43]

Rommel needed to restore his health, and on 19 September, General Stumme arrived from Russia to take over while he was away. Rommel announced that he would return as soon as the attack came. With Nehring in hospital, the Afrika Korps was taken over by General von Thoma, and both 21st Panzer and 90th Light got new commanders. The biggest worry, as usual, was supplies. Rations were being cut. Issues of butter and margarine were stopped, bread was reduced to 375 grams a day and the third water ration of the day was cancelled. The only potatoes left were canned ones captured at Tobruk.[44] There were 10,000 tons of supplies still at Tobruk, which was bombed almost every night. Someone had to sort it out. That was out of his hands.

On 24 September, Rommel left the desert. He called in on Mussolini in Rome. Mussolini told Rommel that in his view they had for the time being lost the battle in the Mediterranean because Italy did not have enough shipping capacity left. In any case he expected the Americans to invade North Africa the following year. Asked about his intentions, Rommel disingenuously replied that he thought it might be feasible to launch a feint attack in October, and a decisive offensive in the winter if supplies were forthcoming. Mussolini was happy with that timing, as it would thwart American intentions. It was important, he said, to capture the Nile Delta before they arrived. Rommel then asked Mussolini what he could do to get some proper anti-tank weapons and artillery for the Italian Army. Nothing, Mussolini told him. So they went off for lunch.[45]

After that, Rommel flew on to Germany. He spent a few days with

Goebbels and his family, who were his closest friends among the Party hierarchy, and had served him well. On 30 September, Hitler received him at the Chancellery to present his Field Marshal's baton, and he was a star guest at the Winter Relief Rally held in the Sportpalast that evening. There, Hitler announced that having reached the Volga at Stalingrad, he would never be shifted from the spot. On 1 October, Rommel had a private audience with Hitler at the Chancellery, and was promised new weapons. Being a celebrity, he had further duties to perform. On 3 October he held a press conference with newsreel cameras at the Propaganda Ministry, where he made some optimistic prognoses about the prospects of the defences at El Alamein. As he left, he stood briefly at the door and told his audience that they had the door to Egypt in their hands. That was a nice touch, though the cameras did not catch it. Goebbels and his paparazzi welcomed the chance to have a front page about the desert, as readers of the *Völkischer Beobachter* had been getting a bit bored with all the triumphs in Russia. After that, Rommel retired to the Austrian resort of Semmering to try to recover his health.[46]

He had left behind about 50,000 German and 54,000 Italian troops, 104,000 in all, with just under 500 battle tanks (206 German and 279 Italian) and about 1,200 guns. The Eighth Army had about 195,000 men with just over 900 battle tanks and 2,300 guns.[47] The headcount is misleading, however, for a lot of the men on both sides were engaged with some aspect of the tortuous logistics rather than manning the tanks and guns. At the sharpest end of the front line, the 86 infantry battalions of the Eighth Army, about 60,000 men, were confronting 70 Axis infantry battalions, 42 Italian and 28 German, with some 45,000 men. The 2:1 discrepancy in equipment was worrying for the Germans and Italians, but at 4:3 the discrepancy in actual fighting infantrymen was not that great. There was no opportunity for manoeuvre, but they were in strong prepared defences. The men of the Panzerarmee had faced comparable odds before even without the advantages which always accrue to the defenders. They should be able to hold. Both sides could do their own sums to estimate the numbers, but no one could assess the balance of quality. Equipment had changed, new troops had arrived, and there were many new commanders on both sides. As always, the goddess of fortune would reserve her favours until battle was met.

On the morning of Friday, 23 October 1942, Bernard Montgomery held a press conference. Things had changed since his arrival. Journalists and cameramen were encouraged to write not only about the Eighth Army but about its commander as well.

General Stumme spent the morning presenting German decorations to some Italians of the Bologna infantry division and an engineering battalion. As Stumme eyed them through his tightly clenched monocle, they noted that he was red-faced and seemed to be bursting out of a uniform at least one size too small. Clearly a man with high blood pressure. Two of the engineers were reluctant to accept the Iron Cross, as the father of one and the brother of the other had been killed fighting the Germans in World War I. In the end they saluted and kept quiet. Captain Giacomo Guiglia of the Italian radio interception unit did not keep quiet. He had been listening to British radio traffic, and spent the morning driving up and down the whole front visiting unit commanders to tell them that the British attack was only hours away. Nobody took any notice. The Germans thought it was just another jumpy Italian waving his arms in the air making a fuss about nothing.[48]

After the press briefing, Montgomery went forward to his tactical HQ near XXX Corps. Over the previous few days, some seasonal showers had brought the temperature down to a mild 15–20ºC. In the evening, a light north-westerly breeze added to the chill which always came to the desert after sunset. Montgomery went to bed at 9 o'clock, as was his habit, and read a book for half an hour before turning his light off, as was also his habit. As he lay down to sleep, his men received a 'Personal Message from the Army Commander', which proclaimed the imminent commencement of what he called 'one of the decisive battles of history'.

'When I assumed command of the Eighth Army,' he announced, 'I said that the mandate was to destroy ROMMEL and his Army, and that it would be done as soon as we were ready. We are ready NOW.'

VIII

EL ALAMEIN – ROUND THREE

B Y THE EVENING OF 23 October 1942, the pieces were lying out on the chess board for all to see.

Churchill and his chiefs-of-staff had won the strategic war. Rommel's army was at the end of its tenuous lines of communication in a hostile environment and was about to be cut off by an Allied army landing far in its rear.

Cunningham, Somerville and Park had won the supply war. If serious fighting started, no one in the Panzerarmee Afrika knew how long their stocks of fuel or ammunition would last. They were already on short rations. They were outnumbered two to one in tanks and guns.

Tedder and Coningham had won the air war over the desert. They had air superiority over the battle front and the RAF dominated the air on both sides of it.

The British had won the information war. The Axis dispositions were known. The deception in the south had worked. Battlefield communications were now secure, and people knew how to use them. Since the Germans had lost their ears on the battlefield in July, so the Eighth Army had sharpened their own, and radio interception units listened in to enemy conversations.

In an earlier age, perhaps, Montgomery would have sent Rommel a note and they would have met in the desert. Montgomery would have offered Rommel an honourable surrender. Rommel would have proffered his sword, which Montgomery would, of course, have returned. The Afrika Korps would have kept its arms, and marched home. But in the twentieth century, only killing would do.

For if the odds were clear, the outcome of the battle was not. The Eighth Army had not yet won the tactical war. It had practised how to use tanks, guns and infantry together, but nobody knew if it could do it for real. It had attacked before with more guns and more tanks than its enemy, and failed. Perhaps it would fail again. Perhaps the belts of mines would prove to be impenetrable. Perhaps the British would get stuck in them, and anti-tank guns and machine guns would turn them into a killing ground. Perhaps Montgomery would make a crucial mistake. Perhaps the fighting prowess and self-sacrificial heroism of the German soldier would see him through again.

The political war had not been won. If Hitler could not conquer, he wanted death. For Churchill, saving Egypt was not enough. He needed a victory in the field. So the armies had to fight a battle.

However, this battle would be one in which the strengths of the Eighth Army would count for most and the strengths of the Afrika Korps would count for least. They were going to play a different game, and Montgomery had set the rules. There would be no manoeuvring. Montgomery was going to use the Eighth Army like a steel-tipped drill to bore holes in the dam Rommel had created with his defensive positions. The defences, strong as they were, would be assaulted head-on in the 'break-in'. The artillery would be used to give the infantry some purchase on the sheer, unbroken wall they faced. The defending troops would then be pinned down and 'crumbled' away in a battle of attrition which would last over a week. The Eighth Army would win this phase because it could afford to take losses and the Panzerarmee could not. It would push the holes deeper and widen them as it went. Montgomery would bore and grind away at several points forcing Rommel to move his mobile armoured reserve to and fro to fill in one crack after another. Then, when he was off-balance, and aware that the drill could finally get through in any one of a number of places, the 'break-out' would be made by infantry and tanks at a point where he could not counter it. Like the water in the dam, armour would then pour in a torrent through the gap, burst it wide open and then inundate and wash away an already stricken enemy. Rommel's chance of victory was that the material of his dam would prove to be too hard, its width too great, and that the drill would break. Either way, unlike all previous encounters in the desert, this battle could only end with one side or the other meeting catastrophe.

The evening of Friday, 23 October 1942 was quiet in the desert. Far to the north-west, bombs from RAF Lancasters were falling on Genoa. Much further away to the north-east, shells howled and tommy-guns barked as the German Sixth Army squeezed the desperate Soviet defenders of Stalingrad into a few blasted pockets of land on the west bank of the Volga. Further away still, Army Group North was launching another attack on Leningrad. On the other side of the world, Japanese troops were launching another attack on the US Marines defending Henderson airfield on Guadalcanal in the Solomon Islands. During the day, the last two American fleet-carriers in the Pacific, which had been trying to reinforce the Marines, had been damaged and put out of action. The world was at war, and people were dying everywhere.

Behind the Eighth Army's forward lines, Keith Douglas had spent the October days working at the headquarters of 10th Armoured Division. He spent the evenings writing letters and working on some poems. He called one of them 'Moonlight, Wadi Natrun', changed the title later to 'Lines written before the Alamein offensive', and then to 'The Offensive 1':

'Tonight's a moonlit cup
and holds the liquid time
that will run out in flame,
in poison we shall sup.

The moon's at home in a passion
of foreboding. Her lord
the martial sun, abroad
this month will see Time fashion

the design we begin:
and Time will cage again
the devils we let run
whether we lose or win.'

The fox was still running. It had got inside him.

> 'So in conjecture stands
> my starlit body. The mind
> mobile as a fox goes round
> the sleepers waiting for their wounds.'

He posted three of the poems to his friend and fellow writer John Hall, adding: 'If you don't want any of these, please send them on to my mother, c/o National Provincial Bank Ltd., Staines, Middx., or any better address you know.'[1]

In London that Friday evening, Sir Alan Brooke got a call from the War Office after dinner to say that the attack was starting. Before going to bed in his flat in Westminster Gardens, he opened his diary. 'We are bound to have some desperately anxious moments,' he wrote. 'There are great possibilities and great dangers. It may mean the turning point of the war leading to further success combined with the North African attacks, or it may mean nothing. If it fails I don't quite know how I shall bear it. I have pinned such hopes on these two offensives.' After writing those lines, he sat at his desk staring into space.[2]

At twenty five minutes past nine Egyptian Summer Time, liquid time ran out and the killing began in the desert.

It began as the first shells landed in the southern sector, hurled from the mouths of the 288 guns of XIII Corps. Fifteen minutes later, they were joined by the 456 guns massed in the north under X and XXX Corps. Together, these 744 guns made the loudest man-made sound ever heard in Africa. Men were deafened for hours, some suffered bleeding ear-drums. No one who was there ever forgot it.[3]

The opening hurricane barrage went on until five minutes to ten, targeting German and Italian artillery positions. Then it shifted on to the Axis front line. Another five minutes and it would be time for the infantry to go in.

They had been waiting in their jump-off positions, just as their fathers had waited in trenches in the valley of the Somme and on the ridge of Passchendaele twenty five years before. Like them, they were loaded with extra ammunition and grenades. They each carried an entrenching tool and, in case the ground was too hard for digging, four empty sandbags for them to fill to form a makeshift foxhole.

They had water and rations for 24 hours. Unlike their forefathers, they were dry, but they were just as cold in the desert night. Each man was issued with a cardigan. Many still shivered. The low temperature was a blessing for it meant that your mates could not tell whether you were shivering from cold or through fear.

At ten o'clock, they hauled themselves off the shaking ground and began to do what the poor bloody infantry have always done – to close with the enemy, step by step, doing the infantry plod. No one could issue orders any more, for the guns drowned out voices. Some men had in any case been issued with white rubber ear-plugs to protect them from the sound.[4] They had to find their way by sight. The moon was shining, and searchlights pointed skywards to indirectly amplify its light. Anti-aircraft guns fired bursts of tracer ahead of them to mark the lines they had to follow. Some men had white crosses taped to the packs on their backs so that those following could see them. Out in front were the engineers and the mine-detectors, who between them carried 130 miles of white tape to mark the lanes as they cleared them. They also carried 80,000 hurricane lamps, blacked out but for a hole on one side which was pointed backwards so that the following troops could see them but the enemy could not.[5] Knowing where they were going was one of the most difficult things for everyone. The riflemen plodded behind, dropping down as they reached the minefields to prod for mines with their bayonets. Plod and prod, plod and prod.

Their job that night was to clear two corridors. In the north, 9th Australian Division under Morshead and 51st Highland Division under Wimberley were to clear a path through the positions held by 164th Light and the Trento Divisions so that Briggs' 1st Armoured Division could itself clear the mines in the middle of the corridor and pass through. To help the infantry in their task, 23rd Armoured Brigade had been assigned to XXX Corps, directly under Leese's control. It was equipped with infantry tanks, Valentines, and the regiments of the brigade were allocated to the infantry divisions. The Australians were given two regiments of tanks, the Highlanders one.

The Australians headed out into the area west of Tel el Eisa. They had taken their first objectives soon after midnight. There was little opposition at first. Then things became harder. After some stiff fighting, the northern brigade took their final objectives at 2:45. The southern brigade was still 1,000 yards short of theirs when dawn

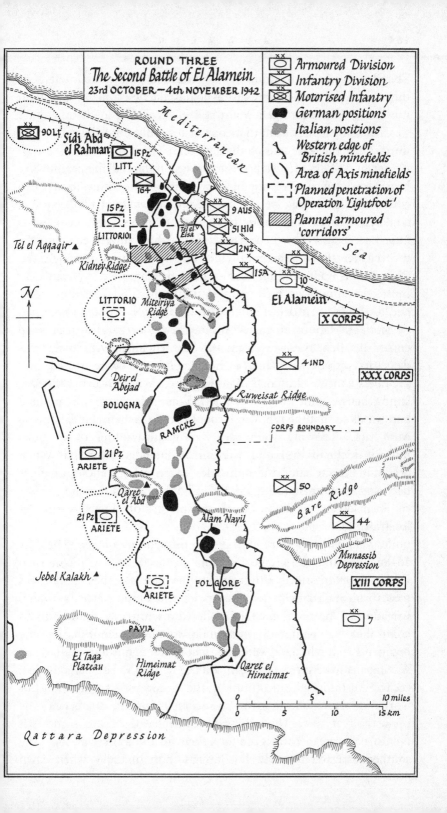

began to break, so they dug in. They had stayed in touch with each other, suffered only about 350 casualties, and secured most of their objectives. All pretty much according to plan.

The 51st Highland Division had to extend the northern corridor down from the Axis strongpoint at Kidney Ridge to the north west corner of Miteiriya Ridge. The men who advanced that night were bearing a heavy load of responsibility. In World War I, the 51st had been the most feared division in the British army. In World War II, it had been sent to France in 1940, and trapped in the town of St Valéry-en-Caux. There, on 12 June, it had surrendered to the commander of 7th Panzer Division, General Erwin Rommel. The division was built up again from scratch by General Wimberley, and most of its men were now going into action for the first time. They had to avenge their defeat and regain their honour. They felt the eyes of Scotland were on them. Wimberley had gone to great lengths to ensure that his men were from the Scottish highlands. Lowlanders were accepted on sufferance, but Englishmen were turfed out. Wimberley made a nuisance of himself at the War Office, but they got their revenge. He was given 1/7 Middlesex Regiment as a machine gun battalion, and of 175 men drafted to 5/7 Gordon Highlanders in May 1942, only 43 were Scots.[6] Notwithstanding these racial impurities, the division affirmed itself as different and special. When zero-hour came, amidst the thunder of the guns the wail of pipes droned across the desert. It was the call of home in a barren land, the call of pride and of fealty, of old unhappy far-off things and battles long ago.

Many men would need the stirring sound, for the 51st was advancing into the strongest part of the defences. Their objectives were a series of strong-points which they had named after Scottish towns or mountains. After crossing the first minefields, they met wire, and as they cut the wire, they heard machine guns as others had heard them before at Ypres and on the Somme, a sound like ripping calico. As men fell, those who were not hit crouched and pressed on, veering instinctively away from the fire. Platoons became mingled, companies bunched up, officers lost their compasses and could not work out how far they had come, and the chaos of battle began. The supporting tanks ran into mines. By the end of the night, the northern brigade had captured some of its objectives, but the southern one was short of all of them and the infantry were pinned down by fire from some of the strong-points. They had nevertheless succeeded in making contact with the New Zealanders who were clearing the next corridor. But the 51st had already taken 1,000 casualties.

The southern corridor was to be driven through positions also held by the Trento and 164th Divisions across the Miteiriya Ridge. The northern half of it was the responsibility of Freyberg's 2nd New Zealand Division, and the southern half fell to Pienaar's 1st South African Division. After the infantry had cleared the flanks, Gate-house's 10th Armoured Division was to pass through the New Zealand sector. The South Africans, like the Highlanders, were given a regiment of Valentines to help them, but the New Zealanders had the whole of 9th Armoured Brigade directly under Freyberg's command to help them punch their way through.

One battalion in Freyberg's northern brigade suffered badly after it got through the first minefield, but the brigade reached all its objectives on time at 2:45 and linked up with the Highlanders. They found more minefields, and had only just cleared them by sunrise. The southern brigade also got across the ridge by dawn, but the supporting tanks of 9th Armoured Brigade were held up by mines and gunfire, and most stayed on the eastern slope of the ridge, with the infantry out in front of them without heavy weapons. They had all got a bit lost, and bunched towards the north, leaving a gap to the south between them and the South Africans. There had been some heavy fighting, and the division had lost about 800 men.

After being delayed by some unexpectedly heavy resistance on their start lines, all three of Pienaar's brigades had got on to the ridge and captured their objectives by dawn, except to the north. Just as the New Zealanders veered north, so they veered south, and were 500 yards short of where they should have been. However, they had only had about 350 casualties.

The final infantry division of XXX Corps, 4th Indian, carried out a series of raids to distract the mixture of Italian infantry and German paratroopers on the Ruweisat Ridge in front of it. The raids helped to keep their opponents unclear about what Montgomery's real intentions were.

As the infantry of XXX Corps began their attack at 22:00, the engineers of X Corps' two armoured divisions began clearing passages of their own in the minefields. The tanks were to start moving at 2:00, and get beyond the minefields well before dawn, if necessary fighting their way through. Lumsden had warned them not to rush anti-tank guns or try to pass through bottlenecks under fire, but to organize properly co-ordinated attacks with artillery and infantry.

The delays suffered by the infantry were magnified as they filtered down the timetable, and the engineers of the armoured divisions encountered further unexpected hold-ups of their own. Some of the new mine detectors did not work, so it was back to plod and prod. The gaps were only 16 yards wide, so if even one vehicle broke down, there was a hold-up. In the swirling dust, one or two tanks ran over the poles holding up the lane tapes, and veered off into the minefields. Then nobody knew where to go. Pretty soon there was a desert traffic jam, and cases of road rage began to multiply. In the north, the leading tanks thought they had got through three minefields when in fact they had only cleared one. In the New Zealand sector, Gatehouse's leading brigade got up the Miteiriya Ridge, but found another minefield there covered by anti-tank guns, which picked off any tanks which tried to cross the top of the ridge. So it retired behind the ridge next to 9th Armoured Brigade and stayed there. Behind them were their ammunition and fuel trucks, their artillery and their ambulances, their staff cars and all the pomp and circumstance of glorious war. Behind them, the vehicles of the other armoured brigade and the infantry brigade of 10th Armoured Division stretched back several miles into their starting positions. The ammunition and fuel trucks, artillery and ambulances of 2nd New Zealand Division were trying to cut across this traffic jam to get supplies to their own battalions in exposed forward positions. The 10th Armoured and 2nd New Zealand Divisions each belonged to different corps. There was gridlock. Huge clouds of dust swirled up to greet the sun of morning. It revealed a great big mess.

The infantry of XXX Corps had broken in, and, with all the noise, dust and heat attendant upon such a task, had started the work of drilling two great holes in Rommel's dam. But not a single tank of X Corps had passed all the way through the infantry. Montgomery had said that it was imperative that they should do so on this first night. The plan was starting to go wrong.

The role of Horrocks' XIII Corps was to look threatening enough to persuade Rommel to keep 21st Panzer Division opposite it in the south. The method was similar to that employed in the north, except

that the armour would start and the infantry follow. Harding's 7th
Armoured Division was to break in to the positions of the Folgore
Parachute Division, just north of Qaret el Himeimat, supported by
44th Division's artillery. The Free French Brigade would then move
through and capture the area west of Himeimat.

The leading tanks were late, and by the time they arrived, they
found that the lamps marking the route had gone out. This caused
more delay. When they finally got to work their Scorpion flail tanks
kept on breaking down. In the end they only managed to clear one
path, and the Free French Brigade was beaten back by the defenders.
In the light of the morning, with Harding's tanks being shelled in the
open, Horrocks wondered how best to look threatening in his role of
making 'noises off'.[7]

He could in fact have done anything he liked on that first
morning, for nobody on the other side was capable of interpreting
any of his moves. No one in the Panzerarmee had any idea what was
going on because Kirkman's opening barrage had destroyed the
communication links between the army, corps and divisional
headquarters. They had to rely on runners, who told them that
tanks were everywhere, and things were pretty grim in the north,
though the defences were holding.

The shelling had been very accurate. It had shattered the Axis
artillery positions it had first targeted. For a time the Axis guns barely
responded. Stumme had ordered that ammunition was to be
conserved, and so missed the opportunity to hit the attacking troops
when they were still crowded in their assembly areas. But a lot of the
Axis guns had simply been destroyed. Prisoners reported that many
of the Axis gun positions had been wiped out in that first fifteen
minutes. When Kirkman's guns moved their fire on to the forward
lines, they caused heavy casualties and destroyed a lot of the infantry's
heavy weapons. It had the morale effect artillery always has, and one
reason the Australians did so well is that part of the Trento division
had broken and run. Most of those who stayed were dazed and
confused, which was why some resistance was sluggish. If well trained
and led, troops will recover from shelling and be able to fight back
within an hour or so. The bombardment had to be kept up.

By the end of World War I, the artillery of the British Army had
probably become the best in the field. Between the wars, it had
managed to preserve some of its skill-base, and at El Alamein really

showed what it could do. Here for the first time it used what became a stock in trade: the 'standard concentration' or 'stonk'. This simply meant concentrating the fire of multiple batteries on a single set of map co-ordinates and then moving the concentration about. It was not simple to do but, with practice, the British perfected the technique of accurately moving the fire of hundreds of guns on to different targets within minutes. It was very fast, totally flexible and utterly devastating. Writers often use the term 'a rain of shells'. British fire was less like rainfall than water from a hose – concentrated, mobile and purposeful.[8] Most of the guns were 25-pounders, which had a very high rate of fire. They could officially manage a maximum of five rounds a minute. In practice experienced crews could better that. At night, any return fire could be spotted from gun flashes, calling down a rapid response. The darkness not only obscured the infantry from enemy fire, but provided them with a protective blanket from their own guns. They had to get as far as they could before the sun rose.

With the nervous system of his army as badly affected as the nervous systems of many of his men, Stumme had gone to see for himself what was happening. His car blundered into the Australians, and as his driver swung round and raced off, Stumme, who was half in and half out of the vehicle, had a heart attack and dropped on to the desert floor, dead. He had indeed had high blood pressure. The Panzerarmee was leaderless until midday, when von Thoma took over.

Rommel had been away for some four weeks, and was now in Austria resting. At 15:00 he got a call from Rome telling him that the attack had started and Stumme was missing. A few hours later, he got a call from Hitler telling him the same thing. Rommel offered to go to Africa immediately. Hitler asked him if he was really up to it. Rommel said he was, so they agreed that he should go to the airfield at Wiener-Neustadt and wait while Hitler had a think. He was reluctant to let Rommel go. He needed good men in Russia.[9]

At Burg el Arab, Montgomery was 'getting a grip' on things, by which he meant making sure that his plans were actually being executed as intended. He controlled up to two levels down. He had a 'staff information' service which listened in to the wireless traffic of lower level formations to give him a firsthand sense of what was happening and incidentally to check what they were up to.[10] He was expecting bellyaching, and he got it. Despite early reports of objectives being captured, by 9:15 it was apparent that the armour had not got through. Montgomery noted in his diary: 'I began to form the impression at about 11:00 hours that there was a lack of "drive" and pep in the action of X Corps.' He sent for Lumsden and told him to push on through. Lumsden left to visit his divisions at 11:30. 'I can see that he will have to be bolstered up and handled firmly,' Montgomery wrote. 'This "sticky" fighting seems to be beyond him.'[11]

In the New Zealand sector on Miteiriya Ridge, Freyberg had got on the phone at 7:00 to his corps commander Leese, asking him to ask Lumsden to tell Gatehouse to get a move on. Such was the chain of command. Leese agreed with Freyberg, believing that the armour should get through come what may before Rommel got back and the Panzers got their act together. Over the phone Lumsden seemed to agree as well, but pointed out that there was a lot of congestion. Nothing happened. Gatehouse was moving his tactical HQ and could not be contacted. Lumsden was in the north with 1st Armoured Division, so did not know what was going on in the southern corridor until Gatehouse reported to him. Freyberg offered to take his own tanks of 9th Armoured Brigade over the ridge if Gatehouse would support him. At 10:40, Leese found Gatehouse, who told him that anything which moved over the ridge got shot up. Leese offered to use the whole of the XXX Corps artillery to help. At 12:25, Montgomery signalled Lumsden, telling him to use the artillery and get both his divisions moving. Lumsden met Leese and Freyberg. Freyberg suggested attacking when night fell, and Lumsden agreed. Leese protested, arguing that the delay would give the Germans time to organize their defences. They were in fact already sowing new minefields. Nothing at all happened in the northern corridor, partly because everyone was arguing about where they actually were. Then at 15:00, the 51st attacked again to clear a path for 1st Armoured. Casualties were heavy, but it seemed to have worked. By 17:20, 1st Armoured reported that it was through the minefields and on its original objective, about 12 hours late. To the south of them, one brigade of 10th Armoured Division pushed over the Miteirya Ridge ready for the night attack. No one knew where the division's other brigade was. It had got lost.

Freyberg was by no means confident that the night attack would go ahead, so he called Leese. Leese met Lumsden again, who told him that indeed he was not confident about the attack himself. The lost brigade turned up and started work clearing gaps in the mines, but abandoned it when false reports came through about an enemy counter-attack. Finally, they had made one gap by 3:45, but could not find a radio to report the fact, so nobody knew about it. The other brigade also managed to make a couple of gaps, but as they were queuing up to go through them, the Germans started shelling the ridge, setting a column of lorries on fire. As the New Zealand infantry in front waited for them in the darkness, the commander of the armoured brigade ordered his tanks to disperse to avoid the shell fire. He then called up his commander, Gatehouse, to suggest that the attack be cancelled. Meanwhile, the other brigade had found its gap and tanks were moving through it when their brigade commander, worried about the shelling, also called up Gatehouse to recommend a withdrawal. At 1:40 in the morning, Gatehouse relayed this to Lumsden. At 2:30, Lumsden relayed it to de Guingand at Eighth Army HQ, saying that he was inclined to agree. De Guingand woke Montgomery, who was sleeping peacefully despite some air raids. At 3:30, he met Lumsden and Leese in his map lorry. According to de Guingand, there was 'a certain "atmosphere" present, and careful handling was required'. Montgomery listened intently to his two corps commanders and expressed his own views in a firm but quiet voice.[12]

Lumsden told Montgomery that Gatehouse wanted to withdraw because even if he got through he would then be very exposed on the other side of the ridge and things would get very unpleasant. Lumsden had not given Gatehouse a decision, so Montgomery phoned Gatehouse directly. According to Montgomery, he applied some 'ginger' and told Gatehouse to carry on with the attack. According to Gatehouse, Montgomery agreed with him that his original orders to attack with the whole division were unworkable, and that the force should be reduced to one regiment. Whatever Montgomery actually said on the phone, when he got off it he told Lumsden that if he or Gatehouse were not inclined to break through, he would replace them with commanders who were.

Thinking his views had been endorsed, Gatehouse ordered the attack to be restricted to a single regiment from each brigade. In fact, by the time this order got through, Freyberg had already bullied the whole of one brigade through. When it got Gatehouse's order at dawn, it pulled back again. The other brigade got no orders, but by dawn had succeeded in getting through the minefields and had joined up with 1st Armoured Division to its north, which thought it was now on its first night objective. Officers of the 51st told the tankmen that they were 1,000 yards short of it, east of Kidney Ridge, which was occupied by a battery of 88s. Everything in the desert looked pretty much the same, no one was sure how far they had come, most of the movement had been done at night, there was a lot of dust everywhere and no one who wanted to stay alive could move about comparing the ground with their maps. The tankmen got rather heated. The Highlanders were new boys in the desert, so what did they know? It took everyone until 10:00 on the morning of 25 October to work out that the Highlanders were right. It turned out that Kidney Ridge was not a ridge at all, but a depression.

Rommel had spent an anxious and uncomfortable night in Austria at Wiener-Neustadt airfield, waiting for Hitler to make a decision. Finally, he got a call at 7:50 telling him to go. At 10:00 he landed in Rome to refuel and have a brief argument with von Rintelen about supplies, took off again at 10:45, arrived in Crete four hours later, and finally touched down at Qasaba at 17:30.[13]

Montgomery thought everyone was finally doing what he wanted. He was disabused at about 11:30 on 25 October at a meeting with the two corps commanders and Freyberg. 1st Armoured Division was not on its objectives and 10th Armoured had no tanks beyond the Miteiriya Ridge. The only tanks there belonged to 9th Armoured Brigade. They were in the open 1,000 yards from well dug-in Axis tanks and anti-tank guns, a situation quite as unpleasant as Gatehouse had claimed it would be. Von Thoma had worked out by now that the main thrust was being made from the Miteiriya Ridge, and was staging local counter-attacks with tanks. In the south, Horrocks was stuck. XXX Corps had suffered 4,500 casualties, almost half of them in the Highland Division, X Corps had taken 500 and XIII Corps another 1,000. Montgomery was expecting about 13,000 casualties in all, so he had used up almost half in the first 36 hours and was getting nowhere. The bits on his drill were wearing out at an alarming rate and the dam was proving to be made of very hard stuff. He had a crisis on his hands.

Freyberg did not believe the tanks would ever break out. He

suggested attacking that night with his own division to get on to the first night objectives, and Lumsden supported him. Montgomery rejected this idea and decided on a complete change of plan. He ordered Freyberg to stay where he was, and Gatehouse to withdraw. The main attack would be made in the north. First Armoured Division would push forward and shield 9th Australian Division, which would begin that night to 'crumble' the Axis forces towards the coast. Horrocks was to continue to push. Montgomery was going to widen out one of the holes his army had made by pushing the drill up through the weaker part of the dam. The long 'dogfight' was to begin.

At 23:25 that night, 25 October, the units of the Panzerarmee received a signal saying: 'I have taken over the Army again. Rommel.' As he arrived at his headquarters, the Highlanders attacked all along their front, assaulting three strong points which had been holding them up for two days, including Kidney Ridge, which they called 'Aberdeen'. They took two of them, but Kidney Ridge held out and 1st Armoured Division stayed where it was. At midnight the Australians attacked, and by morning had advanced two miles and taken a vital position called Point 29. Horrocks pushed, but resistance was strong and his casualties heavy. He decided to withdraw 7th Armoured Division and hold on to the ground he had.

On the morning of 26 October, Rommel sent a message to Rome, demanding more supplies. He then went out to look at the Australian position on Point 29. He wanted to counter-attack there, but half his armour was still in the south, and the British had moved up a lot of artillery which could break up any of his forces which tried to concentrate. Air attacks and shelling were constant. The 15th Panzer Division had been attacking all day, and was down to 31 tanks. He thought of withdrawing a few miles to the west to tempt the British into open country and defeat them in a tank battle away from their artillery. But if he moved 21st Panzer and Ariete north, Horrocks, who was established beyond the minefields, might break through. He had no choice but to react to Montgomery, to play his game, using what he had where he had it. The 164th Division was being ground away.

He decided to concentrate on Kidney Ridge. The 15th Panzer and Littorio attacked it all day. With their wretched M13s, the Italians suffered from the British anti-tanks guns in the same way that British tankmen suffered from 88s. By the end of the day, the worst hit regiment of the Littorio had had its 41 tanks reduced to 2. One junior officer of the division watched the terrible happenings, his Catholic eyes glimpsing the hereafter: 'Some of the tanks continued to advance even after they had been hit and set on fire, with only dead and dying men inside them, like huge self-propelled funeral pyres, a dead man's foot still pressing down on the accelerator. What a sight! A procession of blazing monsters, shaken by explosions and emitting coloured flashes as the shells inside went off – like something out of a terrifying ghost story. The souls of the dead men must have been trapped in their vehicle; how else could a smashed and blazing tank continue to advance towards the enemy?'[14]

Montgomery spent the morning of 26 October thinking. At midday, he issued new orders, which he amplified in the evening. Leese and Horrocks were to hold their positions, and extricate the New Zealand Division and 7th Armoured from their respective lines to form a new reserve. These moves were to be completed by the 28th. Then the Australians would continue crumbling operations to the north. Lumsden was to take over the attacks around Kidney Ridge and draw the enemy armour out. So far, the infantry had taken 90 per cent of the casualties, a situation which could not go on. In the afternoon, Montgomery spoke to Kirkman, who was worried about ammunition. He said he had enough for ten days. Montgomery told him that was all right. It would all be over by then. More worrying was the report that Lumsden was moving about without his artillery commander, so Montgomery 'ordered him up at once'. No wonder he was having difficulties. 'Lumsden', Montgomery wrote to Brooke after the battle, 'is out of his depth with a corps ... he is excitable and he loses his nerve at critical moments.' He was a good divisional commander but was 'not really a high-class professional soldier and knows very little about the co-operation of all arms on a battlefield'.[15]

On the afternoon of the 26th, Rommel decided to commit his forces. It was clear that Horrocks' demonstrations were just a bluff. He ordered 90th Light forward in the north to attack Point 29 and ordered 21st Panzer up to the north as well. He knew there was not enough petrol to move it back again if things turned bad in the south, but 15th Panzer and Littorio were getting too weak to achieve anything by themselves. By the end of the day, 15th Panzer only had 23 working tanks out of the 100 it had started with, and Littorio was down to 44 from 116, which meant 70 per cent attrition in three days.

During the day, there was some discussion about flying an infantry regiment over from Crete, but it was untrained, and the aircraft were needed for supplies. The seas had now become so dangerous for shipping that air-lifting was about the only way things could be brought in.

During the night, 1st Armoured Division confirmed Rommel's fears by finally establishing itself both north and south of Kidney Ridge to protect the Australians. Some of the tank units were ordered to take no prisoners. They did as they were told. 'The first trenches we came to were packed with Eyeties. We made short work of them, ran alongside their trenches and dropped in grenades, shouting: "Eggs for breakfast, you bastards." Then we went back, with one track on the edge, and gave them a quick burial.'[16] Surrendering in the heat of battle was always perilous. Even after the fighting had ceased, there was a lot of scope for misunderstanding. One group of British soldiers surrounded a prisoner from the Trento Division who was wearing a black armband as the Fascists did, and began threatening him until his officer explained that he was in mourning.[17]

The following day, Rommel launched his main counter-attack to try to throw back the British armour. The 21st Panzer and Ariete were delayed by air attacks. The 15th Panzer and Littorio kept up the pressure in the morning, until at 16:00 on 27 October all four divisions launched an all-out assault. The traditional roles were reversed: Axis tanks were advancing on dug-in British anti-tank guns and hull-down tanks. The results were as they always had been. The heaviest fighting was in the area held by the anti-tank gunners of 1st Armoured Division's motorized infantry. Its most exposed unit, 2nd Rifle Brigade, positioned south of Kidney Ridge, knocked out 37 tanks, a devastating loss for Rommel. Colonel Turner of the Rifle Brigade topped the list of a whole raft of decorations awarded to his unit with a Victoria Cross. Turner was wounded but survived. Second Rifle Brigade was more or less wiped out. It had had no tank or artillery support. By the end of the day, the tank strength of 15th Panzer and Littorio had been further reduced and 21st Panzer was down from 106 to 45 'runners'. The repair shops were working desperately to get broken down or damaged vehicles back into action. Montgomery's 'crumbling' was eroding parts of Rommel's dam into a thin crust, and he was running out of the material he needed to stop it from cracking.

His counter-attacks had failed, but the Desert Fox had not lost his cunning. That day, 27 October, he had got news that two tankers on whose loads of fuel he had been counting had been bombed and sunk outside Tobruk. He sent a second message to his old enemy von Rintelen in Rome, referring to his signal of the previous day. He pressed him once again to 'do everything possible to provide the Army with sufficient fuel' and demanded to know by return what steps were being taken to do so. The second need was for ammunition, and Rommel asked what measures were being initiated to deal with that. He then concluded, for the record: 'I have to point out that the Army has drawn attention again and again to the need for adequate supplies of fuel and ammunition. It is therefore those responsible for supply who are uniquely to blame for the present grave crisis.'[18] He won all those victories, and then the quartermasters got him defeated. History was his judge.

That evening, Rommel managed to compose a few lines to his wife. 'Dearest Lu', he wrote, 'Very heavy fighting! No one can imagine the fear hanging over me. Once again, everything is at stake. The circumstances we are in could not be worse. I am still hoping we can pull through. I don't need to tell you that I'll give my utmost.'[19]

At 8:00 the next morning, Wednesday 28 October, Montgomery held a conference with Leese and Lumsden in which he built on his orders of the 26th. He was going to change the bits on his drill. Now that Rommel had committed his reserves to the north, XXX Corps was to go on to the defensive to hold them, supported by the RAF. X Corps was to withdraw. They were to re-form as a reserve, augmented by 7th Armoured Division. The 2nd New Zealand Division had already been ordered to extricate itself from the front line and re-form. Freyberg was then to take his New Zealanders together with several British brigades, and exploit the successes of the Australians along the coast. In the meantime, the Australians were to keep up the pressure by crumbling away the Axis position towards the coast. The new reserve would re-balance Montgomery's forces, enable him to unbalance Rommel's and then deliver the *coup de grâce.*

During the day, 21st Panzer made continual desperate attempts to retake Kidney Ridge. The other Axis armoured units had to rest and refit. That night, the Australians attacked again around a feature called Hill 28. One of their brigades was again successful, but the other one lost touch with its supporting tanks, which took heavy casualties. They were just held by the defenders. Rommel was watching and the Australians elicited his professional admiration. The weight of the attack, he wrote, was 'quite exceptional'. 164th Division was still hanging on, but it was being destroyed. Rommel knew he would have to retreat. If he waited, there could be a breakthrough, and all could be lost. If he retreated now, he would have to abandon his immobile infantry. By dawn, he decided to have one more go at holding Montgomery, but initiated plans to withdraw 60 miles to Fuka, and fight there.[20]

Unusually, Rommel wrote to Lucie twice on 28 October. He must have needed to unburden himself to the only person with whom he was open about his emotions. His tone for the first time has a ring of despair about it, and for the first time he questioned his own survival. The first letter is one of valediction. He wrote of defeat, of North Africa falling into British hands. 'The enemy has got massive superiority,' he wrote, 'and our resources are very meagre. Whether or not I will survive the battle if it ends in defeat is in God's hands. Life is hard to bear for the defeated. My conscience tells me that I've done everything possible to win; I have not spared myself in action. If I remain here, let me thank you and our boy for all the love and joy you have brought to my life. In these few weeks I have realized how much you both mean to me. My last thoughts are with you. Mourn with pride if I should be no more. In a few years, Manfred will be a man and I hope he will always be an honour to our line.' The second letter was shorter. He held out little hope. 'I lie awake at night with my eyes open and can't sleep because of the fear lying on me. During the day I am dead tired.' He longed to be back at home with them, he said. Rommel had never written letters like this.[21]

In London that night, the British Foreign Minister, Anthony Eden, went round to 10 Downing Street to have a drink with the Prime Minister. During the day, Churchill had sent a report to the prime ministers of the Dominions, telling them that the battle had 'opened well', that Rommel was ill and short of supplies and that 'in Alexander and Montgomery we have generals determined to fight the battle out to the very end'.[22] Eden had been talking to his people in Cairo, who had got wind of the fact that X Corps and the New Zealanders were being pulled out of the line. He told Churchill that the Eighth Army was retreating.

The next morning, before Brooke had got out of bed, he was

presented with a telegram Churchill wanted to send to Alexander. 'Not a pleasant one!' he wrote. He was summoned to meet Churchill who put him on the spot, as recorded in Brooke's memoirs: 'What was *my* Monty doing now, allowing the battle to peter out.' (Monty was always 'my Monty' when he was out of favour.) 'He had done nothing now for three days, and now he was withdrawing troops from the front.' 'Why,' Churchill asked, 'had he told us he would be through in seven days if all he intended to do was to fight a half-hearted battle? Had we not got a single general who could even win one single battle?', and so on, until he ran out of breath. Brooke seized the opportunity to counter-attack and the two of them then had a little battle of their own. Churchill decided to continue the struggle at a Chiefs of Staff meeting at 12:30, but Smuts was there and supported Brooke.[23]

Churchill changed his telegram to Alexander. 'The Defence Committee', he wrote, 'congratulate you on the resolute and successful manner in which the decisive battle which is now proceeding has been launched by you and General Montgomery,' and assured him that 'whatever the cost you will be supported in all the measures which you take to shake the life out of Rommel's army'.[24] So that was all right then.

Just before midnight, Churchill sent for Brooke again. Bletchley Park had picked up Rommel's daily report to OKW, in which he described the situation as 'extremely grave'. Churchill just wanted to show Brooke the decrypt and have a chat. He thanked him for turning down the offer of the Middle East Command and remaining at his side as CIGS. Before going to bed, Brooke wrote in his diary: 'He is the most difficult man I have ever served, but thank God for having given me the opportunity of trying to serve such a man in a crisis such as the one this country is going through.'[25] Brooke had not heard directly from Montgomery. He supposed he was pulling units out to create a reserve. He did not really know. He wondered whether Montgomery knew what he was doing.

So did several other people. On the morning of 29 October, Alexander turned up at Montgomery's HQ bearing Churchill's message, and accompanied by Eden's man in Cairo, Richard Casey. Casey took de Guingand on one side and asked him how he thought things were going. He had already written a telegram for Churchill telling him that things were going badly. De Guingand was horrified.

Montgomery relates that he was too busy to bother with it, but he got the message. The 'Torch' landings were on 8 November. He needed a breakthrough fast. De Guingand and the staff had in fact been getting nervous about the location of Freyberg's planned attack. It had become clear that both 90th Light and the Trieste were now astride the coast road opposite the Australians. If the New Zealanders joined them to make the main push there, they would meet strong opposition. Montgomery was therefore persuaded to move the main point of the blow back down between Point 29 and Kidney Ridge, at what seemed to be a juncture between German and Italian troops.[26] The Australians would attack on the night of 30 October to keep attention focussed there. Then the next night, Freyberg would deliver the knock-out blow south of them and X Corps would follow through. Montgomery was going to drill at two places at once until Rommel was off-balance. It would, as he put it, be a hard right followed by a knock-out left. Montgomery called the operation 'Supercharge'.

On 29 October there was an unusual meeting in the Albert Hall in London. News had got through from intelligence sources in Switzerland that the Germans had constructed three 'death camps' at Chelmno, Belzec and Treblinka and that Jews from all over Europe were being deported to the east. The story was published in the British press. Some doubted its accuracy, but the Archbishop of Canterbury called together a meeting of Jews and Christians that night to protest about what the Nazis appeared to be doing. The soldiers in the desert knew nothing about any of this. Churchill wrote to the Zionist leader, Dr Chaim Weizmann, a few days later on the anniversary of the Balfour Declaration, to affirm the British government's pledge of a Jewish national home in Palestine, promising that 'better days will surely come'.[27] Surely, once the Axis army had been ejected from Africa, peace could come to the Middle East.

Whilst the details of 'Supercharge' were being worked out during the day, Montgomery wrote out the overall orders himself and issued them on 30 October. 'This was the master plan,' he wrote in his memoirs, 'and only the master could write it.' It did indeed bear his inimitable stamp. 'This operation, if successful', he observed, 'will result in the complete disintegration of the enemy and will lead to his final destruction.' 'It will therefore be successful,' he concluded, with a logic which would have shaken Aristotle. 'There must be no doubters,' he added, 'risks must be accepted freely; there must be no bellyaching.'[28]

In the meantime, Rommel had had a fright. Having just had news of the loss of yet another tanker, he was conferring with his staff when he was passed a report from the Commando Supremo informing him that two British divisions had slipped into the Qattara Depression, got through it, scaled the sides behind the Axis lines and were now sixty miles south of Mersa Matruh. Luftwaffe patrols were sent out, and the movement of the armoured reserves was halted. The following morning, 30 October, he discovered that it was all a chimera. Someone had made a mistake. Or made it up.

On the night of 30 October, the Australians attacked again across the railway and the coast road. They had held their new salient against counter-attacks throughout the previous day which left the ground in front of them strewn with German and Italian corpses. This new attack was supported by 360 guns and preceded by bombing. For all that, resistance was fierce and protracted, and casualties were high on both sides. By the time the night was over parts of 164th Division and a battalion of 90th Light were left with only a narrow strip of land connecting them to the rest of the Panzerarmee to the west. The top of the dam was beginning to crumble away.

While these attacks were going on Freyberg was trying to gather his forces for 'Supercharge' but found the situation chaotic. Nobody was sure which units were where, the infantry were exhausted and the artillery were confused. To add to it all, GHQ in Cairo ordered that clocks should go back an hour at midnight on 31 October. Montgomery ordered no change of time in the battle area until it was over. But the RAF was outside the battle area. In the end, all orders were issued with GMT as well. Freyberg was convinced he could not be ready on time. Montgomery reluctantly agreed to postpone 'Supercharge' by twenty-four hours to the night of 1 November.

On 31 October, 90th Light launched furious attacks on the Australians to force a way through to their lost battalion behind them. Rommel insisted, against the advice of his staff, that his men not be withdrawn, but try to eliminate the Australian position by attacking it from both sides. The Australians beat them off, drawing in the bulk of the DAK. By now, Morshead's men had suffered over 2,000 casualties.

On 1 November, Montgomery wrote a letter to Brooke to put him in the picture. It had been 'a terrific party', he wrote, carried out in 'one enormous minefield', but success was made possible by the artillery, which was 'superb'. Nevertheless, most of the artillery commanders did not know how to handle concentrated fire and had not been properly taught. (Brooke had been an artillery officer, so he would have appreciated this.) That night, Montgomery was going to put in 'a real hard blow'. If things were to go really well they might trap 90th Light and 21st Panzer, but, he added, 'battles do not go as one plans, and it may be that we shall not do this'. He was 'enjoying the battle' and keeping very fit and well. He praised Leese and Horrocks, but Lumsden had been disappointing; he was 'excitable, highly strung and easily depressed'. He would be a good divisional commander but was 'at sea in charge of a corps'. His best divisional commander was Freyberg. 'He has no great brain power,' he wrote, 'and could never command a corps. But he *leads* his division into battle.' His own great task, Montgomery concluded, was to 'keep morale high and spirits up.'

The German attacks on the Australian positions continued throughout 1 November, but at the end of the day Rommel relented and had the trapped units slip out during the night, leaving their heavy equipment behind. While they were doing so, in the middle of the night, there was terrific commotion to the south of them as the British artillery opened up and the RAF launched a series of big air raids.

Rommel could not find out what was going on. The Germans had decided to move the clocks back that night as well, staying an hour earlier than the British. This created some confusion as to the timing of some reports, but then reports from the Afrika Korps stopped. Its HQ had been hit in an air raid and communications were down until after dawn. At first it looked as if the British were attacking along the coast road, so 21st Panzer was moved north. Then there were reports of another attack further south. They finally realized that the *only* attack was in the south, north of Kidney Ridge in the direction of a hill behind the Axis lines called Tel el Aqqaqir. It was 'Supercharge'. It took until 11:00 on the morning of 2 November to organize a counter-attack, by which time, British tanks from 1st Armoured

Division were breaking through into the open desert. The dam had sprung a leak.

Creating the leak had taken enormous effort. Freyberg had opened his attack with a Brigade of the 51st Division and a Brigade of 50th Division to which he added his own Maori battalion. Both were supported by tanks of his own 9th Armoured Brigade. They met a hail of fire, but kept going. There were still mines to clear, but the tanks held off the armoured elements of 15th Panzer and Littorio facing them. By dawn, all the objectives had been reached. Despite heavy casualties, 9th Armoured Brigade hammered its way through to Tel el Aqqaqir. Though it was through, the brigade now consisted of 19 tanks out of the 94 it had started with, and 170 men out of 400. It was not only weak but also exposed. Rommel was not going to sit back and watch. X Corps had to get there before he did. There was a race on.

All the confusion at the HQ of the Panzerarmee gave X Corps some time, but they did not know that. Freyberg was frantic. The night fighting, as always, had been very confused. Come dawn, the bulk of the tanks were still grinding along narrow congested lanes in clouds of dust in which some of them got lost. At 7:35 Freyberg phoned Leese, requesting him to ask Lumsden to tell Briggs to order his lead brigadier to get a move on. Leese tried to call Lumsden to call Briggs, during which time Freyberg called him again twice, and the commander of 9th Armoured Brigade, who was out at Tel el Aqqaqir getting very angry, called Freyberg, everybody urging that fingers be pulled out, and so on. At 9:11, the radio interception service picked up an order from Rommel to 21st Panzer Division to counter-attack. By now 9th Armoured Brigade was down to 17 tanks still in action. They needed anti-tank guns and artillery support to deal with the counter-attack.

Montgomery was less worried. He knew what was going on on the other side and, to the south of Freyberg's position, some armoured cars had broken right through and were motoring about rabbit-shooting. They found a headquarters and destroyed 40 trucks in fifteen minutes. So Montgomery ordered 10th Armoured Division to head through this gap while 1st Armoured held the expected counter-attack.

The race was a draw. 1st Armoured and 21st Panzer both arrived at Tel el Aqqaqir at about 11:00. There then began the fiercest tank fight of the whole battle, a bloody, fiery battering match which lasted for two hours. Man's technology had turned the dragons of his ancient imagination into a terrifying contemporary reality. They roared and breathed fire and smoke, their engines wheezed and whined, their tracks grated and groaned, the air screamed as metal hit metal. It was Fasolt and Fafner doing each other to death, an awesome match in which human beings seemed to have no part.

Both sides' artillery and the RAF added their shells and bombs to the mayhem. Despite the aircraft, Rommel ordered every 88 to be used against the British armour. The Littorio's tanks were the most vulnerable on the field, and the division was shattered. At 13:00, the firing died down until, at 14:00, Rommel threw in the Ariete and tried again.

To the south, the remains of 15th Panzer were trying to hold up 10th Armoured Division, which was nosing forward. They slowed them down, but took heavy casualties in doing so.

By dusk, the Littorio had disintegrated, the Ariete was giving way and 15th and 21st Panzer were left with 30 to 35 tanks between them. Rommel ordered them to break off the attacks and act as a cordon to protect a retreat. The retreat was to begin in the south, and the infantry there started to move back that night heading for Fuka. But Fuka was 60 miles away, a hopeless proposition on foot. The dam had cracked.

At 19:50 on 2 November, Rommel sent a message to OKW. It was a clever piece of expectation management. His men were facing overwhelming numbers on the ground and in the air. The defence had so far been successful, but the army was now exhausted. The eight infantry divisions could not be withdrawn because of a lack of trucks, and would probably fall into enemy hands. Some of the motorized units would be able to disengage, but would not get far because of lack of petrol. The only road would be subjected to constant air attack. Therefore, despite its heroic resistance, one could expect the army to be destroyed. After that, he wrote home. 'The enemy is slowly prising us out of our position by dint of overwhelming force. That would mean the end. You can imagine how I am feeling. Air attacks and more air attacks. To you and Manfred...'[29]

Rommel's signal caused some concern at OKW, despite their preoccupation with events at Stalingrad, where progress had got maddeningly slow. There had been growing consternation in Rome for a few days, but on 1 November, Kesselring had suggested that the crisis was being mastered and sounded optimistic – but then, he always did. It was a bit unclear what Rommel was proposing to do, so at midnight someone called Rome and asked for Rommel's daily report. It arrived by teletype at 3:00 am. It was similar, except for one sentence stating that a withdrawal had been ordered, but somehow the sleepy officer on duty that night overlooked it and thought the report added nothing to the one they had already. At 9:00 am on 3 November, someone noticed the sentence and rushed the report to Hitler. He hit the roof. There was Rommel, in his hour of need, appealing to his Fatherland and his Führer, and these useless, dozy staff officers just sat on the thing. He began to suspect it was deliberate. The duty officer was demoted and sent to the front. His boss, Warlimont, was sacked. Hitler himself composed the sort of message his newest field marshal needed to bolster his resolve and see him through. At 11:05 it was sent to Rome and from there, at 11:30, passed to Egypt. During its latter passage, it was intercepted and sent to Bletchley Park as well.

Rommel was at his forward headquarters supervising the withdrawal. Despite the weakness of his forces, the enemy were not attacking in strength, but seemed to be reorganizing. He drove back to his main headquarters surprised and somewhat relieved. It was not until he arrived there at 13:30 that he became aware that his Führer was concerned about him and wanted to offer some helpful advice. He read the message.

The whole German people were watching his heroic battle, Hitler assured him, and were full of confidence in him. In such a situation, the only thing to do was to carry on and not yield one step. Air reinforcements were on their way. The enemy must be at his last gasp. It would not be the first time in history that the stronger will had triumphed over the bigger battalions. And, so, the message concluded, 'To your forces you can show no path other than to victory or death.'

Rommel panicked. What was this message? Was it an order? Was it the result of experience on the Russian front, where surrounded troops often held out for weeks and were then relieved? If so, did Hitler realize how different things were in the desert? Had Hitler misunderstood him? After all, his own message had suggested that retreat was in fact impossible. Rommel drafted replies which were left unsent. At 14:28, he passed on the message to von Thoma, interpreting it as an order, and sent for his ADC, SS Obersturmführer Berndt. Berndt had come from Goebbels' Propaganda Ministry and looked after the public relations of the Panzerarmee as well as Rommel's personal needs, so he was a good choice. Rommel told him to get on a plane, explain things to Hitler face to face, and make sure he had operational freedom – in other words, permission to retreat.[30]

In London, Sir Alan Brooke got the message about the same time as Rommel. He already knew about the ones Rommel had sent. 'Felt as if I were treading on air the rest of the day', he wrote. Churchill got hold of him in the afternoon to discuss the ringing of church bells. Brooke prevailed upon him to wait.[31]

Rommel wrote two letters to Lucie that day. Both tell of despair. He told her he was trying to save the army and racking his brains to think of a way out. 'Hard days lie ahead,' he wrote, 'perhaps the hardest a man can go through. The dead are the lucky ones, for them it is all over.' In his second note he told her that Berndt was flying off to report to Hitler, and he enclosed 25,000 lire he had saved up for her. 'Our fate is in God's hand,' he ended. 'Farewell to you and our lad. To both of you...'[32]

In the desert, Montgomery got reports of Rommel's withdrawal at 8:00 in the morning on 3 November. Explosions were heard in the south as ammunition dumps were blown up. In all, the Axis forces destroyed some 12,000 tons of ammunition during their retreat, and had never run short. The DAK was still holding the line in the north, however, so another co-ordinated night attack had to be planned in order to break it. Lumsden's armour pushed at the German tanks and anti-tank guns during the day; in the afternoon these had their resolve strengthened by the receipt from von Thoma of orders to stand firm, which they had to do anyway. They got the worst of the gun battle, but succeeded in preventing a full breakthrough.[33]

As he was making preparations for the night attack, Lumsden got news that his forward units had in fact captured Tel el Aqqaqir, so he cancelled the artillery barrage due to be made on it. Just before zero-hour, he learned that it was still in German hands after all, but by then it was too late. The 51st went in expecting to simply advance, and found that there was fierce resistance. The Gordon Highlanders rode forward on the backs of tanks, and Wimberley was sickened by

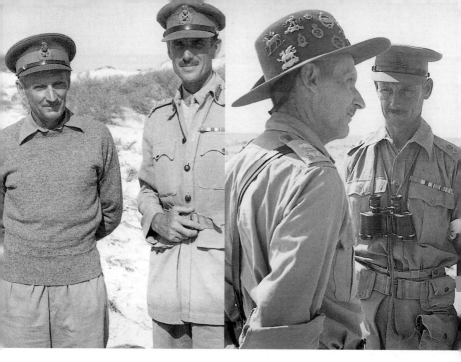

Creating the 'Monty' brand. Montgomery arrived in the desert in August 1942 as an ordinary general, seen here in regulation peaked cap with Herbert Lumsden, the troublesome commander of his armoured corps. He quickly became 'the Eighth Army Commander', with an Australian slouch hat covered in unit badges, which in October the press corps was already labelling 'famous'. The third and final stage was to give him a beret with two badges. This is the first picture of him as 'Monty', with one of the perpetrators of the deed, his ADC John Poston (who took the second photograph), behind him in the turret of a Grant tank. The picture went round the world. The 'Monty' brand stood for: 'victory' without unnecessary loss of life, achieved through 'colossal cracks' that went according to plan.

IWM E18416, E17865, E18980

LEFT: The crew of an early A10 cruiser tank eating their Christmas dinner in 1940. Their pudding was made of biscuit, prunes, marmalade and rum. Even in the early stages of the desert war, dress regulations went by the board. IWM E1500

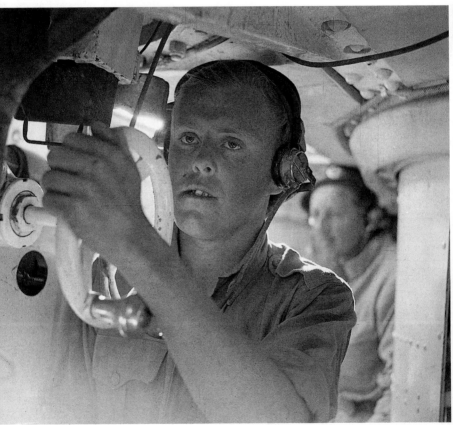

ABOVE: Cecil Beaton came to Egypt on behalf of the Ministry of Information in 1942. He captured the strange atmosphere inside a tank. It could turn from a cosy home into a claustrophobic battle station, into a trap and finally into a tomb. IWM CMB2110

RIGHT: Another of Beaton's series. Without goggles, the driver would be blinded by dust. In action, he would close down the heavy hatch and peer through a slit, relying on his commander for directions. Simply handling the machine was mentally and physically exhausting. IWM CBM1449

BELOW: Keeping in touch with home was vital for morale. These official Christmas cards had forms on which to write a short message. Santa has abandoned his reindeer for a camel – with a 'Victory V' sign on its hump. Courtesy of Madeline Weston

BELOW: Plod and prod. Mine clearance was one of the most dangerous and stressful jobs of all. At Alamein, the engineers worked in half-hour shifts, which was considered to be all a normal man could take at one stretch. IWM E16229

BELOW: Winston Churchill speaking to Lieutenant-General Sir Leslie Morshead, the able and pugnacious commander of 9th Australian Division, on 5 August 1942 during his first visit to the desert. The Australians were to play a critical role in the coming battle. IWM E15322

RIGHT: The devastating night barrage on 23 October 1942 became legendary, Churchill later claiming that it consisted of 'nearly a thousand guns' and Montgomery 'over a thousand.' Probably 744 were actually used, most of them 25-pounders like this one. They were brilliantly handled throughout. IWM E18467

ABOVE: This dramatic picture of Australians storming a strong point became one of the best known of the final battle of Alamein. The 'strong point' was their cookhouse, which Fleet Street photographer Len Chetwin and his crew had set on fire. Their editors were delighted. IWM E18908

ABOVE: A knocked-out '88'. The Krupp-designed 8.8cm Flak gun sent a larger shell over a longer distance with greater accuracy than any other anti-tank gun in the desert. Though less than a third of German anti-tank guns were 88s, they dominated the battlefield. IWM E16707

ABOVE: This time the camera does not [li]e. This portrayal of the realities of [m]echanised warfare south of [A]lamein was too much for the [c]ensors and it was not released. [G]etting close to the realities of battle [w]as dangerous. Six Allied [p]hotographers were killed in the [d]esert. E20606

RIGHT: The commander of the Afrika [K]orps, General Ritter von Thoma, was [c]aptured in one of the final tank [a]ctions on 4 November, and brought [t]o Montgomery. They discussed the [b]attle over dinner and Montgomery [t]hought von Thoma was 'a very nice [c]hap'. IWM E19130

The armies moved on, leaving a melancholy wake of waste and decay. The aftermath of battle seen through the lens of Cecil Beaton. IWM CBM2485, CBM2495

the sight of the tanks returning with the bodies of his dead men hanging from their hulls. The stock of X Corps now sank as low with Wimberley as it already was with all the other infantry commanders. The other part of the assault, conducted by a brigade of the Indian Division, did have artillery support, however, and was successful. At first light the Argylls moved through the gap and finally took Tel el Aqqaqir. As they advanced through a smokescreen, most of their casualties were caused by the Highland Division's own guns.[34]

At 6:30 on the morning of 4 November, Montgomery was able to note in his diary: 'the armour went through as the dawn was breaking'. The dam had broken. It had taken twelve days and thirteen nights.

At about the same time, Kesselring turned up to see how Rommel was getting on. He had to make his way through a mass of wrecked vehicles on the coast road next to Rommel's HQ. The RAF had been bombing and strafing all night. Rommel was not very pleased to see him. Just as Hitler imagined that the OKW staff were betraying him behind his back, so Rommel imagined that Kesselring was behind Hitler's message. Kesselring calmed him down, looked at the message and said that in his opinion it was an appeal based on Hitler's experience in Russia, and should be ignored. He sent a signal to OKW himself, saying that the message had been overtaken by events and that he had authorized a retreat. Rommel sent a similar one, and ordered a general retreat. Berndt had meanwhile arrived at the Führer's headquarters and at 20:50 that evening, Hitler and everybody else gave their reluctant blessing to Rommel's actions. It was unfortunate, but he had fallen back before and always advanced again. No doubt he would do so this time as well.[35]

After his meeting with Kesselring, Rommel set off to find von Thoma. Von Thoma was not at his HQ, but leading the remaining tanks of his two Panzer Divisions trying to hold off 1st Armoured Division about three miles north west of Tel el Aqqaqir. More and more German tanks were hit, including von Thoma's Mk III command tank. He was captured and driven to Montgomery's headquarters in a scout car. To the south of them, 7th Armoured Division had moved through the gap made by the Indians and during the afternoon engaged the Ariete which fought back stubbornly until, in the evening, it was surrounded and destroyed.

Air reconnaissance was making it clear that the remains of the

Panzerarmee were making for Fuka. Montgomery wanted to cut
them off, but there was an enormous traffic jam around Tel el
Aqqaqir, with units all mixed up together. Some had to stop to allow
others to pursue. It took quite a while to sort it all out. The dam may
have burst, but the water behind it did not pour through in the
expected torrents, but in various dribbles, which only slowly gathered
force.

That day, Alexander sent a message to Churchill, telling him that
the enemy's front had broken and that he was in full retreat.
Churchill signalled back, congratulating him on the 'splendid feat of
arms achieved by the Eighth Army under the command of your
brilliant lieutenant, Montgomery'. He was Churchill's Monty now,
and Churchill spent the day sending messages to everyone he could
think of to tell them the news. In the evening, a BBC announcer
caused national excitement by interrupting programmes to tell
people to stay tuned for 'the best news in years', to be given at
midnight. Radio listeners who stayed up heard Alexander's message
as well.

Montgomery did not stay up. He went to bed at 9:30 p.m. Before
he did so, however, he invited his captive to dinner, and so it was that
the commander of the Eighth Army and the ex-commander of the
Afrika Korps enjoyed a few pleasant hours comparing notes and
discussing the events of recent history. Montgomery felt very lucky to
be able to discuss a battle with his opponent just after it had been
fought. He thought von Thoma was 'a very nice chap'.[36]

IX

PERSPECTIVES

PROBABLY THE MOST FAMOUS TREATISE about warfare is *On War*, written by the Prussian staff officer Carl von Clausewitz and published in 1832, a year after his death. Perhaps the most famous passage in that treatise is the one which describes what he calls 'friction'. In it, Clausewitz tries to explain to those who have never experienced war why it makes doing simple things so difficult. He uses the analogy of a traveller making a simple journey, who first finds no horses, then finds the roads bad, the night dark and the accommodation miserable. Thus, 'through an infinity of petty circumstances ... things disappoint us and we fall short of the mark'.[1] No battle could better illustrate what Clausewitz meant than the third one to be fought on the land between the railway station of El Alamein and the Qattara depression, the one known during the war as The Battle of El Alamein, though it is now more generally referred to as the Second Battle of El Alamein, in recognition of the battle fought by Auchinleck in July 1942. The friction was severe all the way through it and continued after it ended. Heat continued to be generated after the war was over.

From some time on 4 November onwards, the Panzerarmee Afrika and the Eighth Army were trying to make a journey to the west.

Unlike that described by Clausewitz, both journeys were difficult to begin with, and both met, to a heightened degree, the problems he delineated.

It was a terrible journey for the Germans and Italians.

Those in the south had the worst of it. The formidable paratroopers of the Folgore who had thwarted all of Horrocks' attempts to burst through them, got the order to retreat at 2:00 in the morning on 3 November. They had no transport and only their rearguard was issued with water. At 14:35 on 6 November, they were surrounded and, out of ammunition, they surrendered. There were 306 prisoners, all that was left out of 5,000.[2]

The journey was to all intents and purposes restricted to those who had a vehicle or could hitch a ride, and they were crammed on to the single desert road. They suffered from the intermittent attentions of the Desert Air Force, but those were by no means as destructive as they could have been, for a lot of air strength was diverted to the task of protecting British troops from an almost non-existent Luftwaffe.[3] For the retreating men on the ground, it was bad enough. They travelled by night, and the rearguards fought by day.

For their would-be pursuers, the journey was a frustrating one.

Montgomery had selected Freyberg to lead part of the pursuit, not because he was best placed to do so, but because he was the man in whom Montgomery had most confidence. He was to head for Fuka to cut Rommel off. Whilst he blocked its path, Lumsden's X Corps was to crush the remains of the DAK trapped between them and the sea. It did not work. Some of Freyberg's forces were way to the rear and could not get through the mass of vehicles crowding the break-through area. He waited overnight without moving in order to give them time to move up. The tanks collected themselves together, refuelled and tried to move at night over unreconnoitred desert, something they had never done before. They had little idea where they were going, could not keep in touch and eventually stopped and waited for daylight. Then, after getting news from the RAF that the road beyond Fuka was already full of Axis vehicles, the objective was changed, which caused more confusion. Lumsden used the opportunity of the pursuit to get away from Montgomery and stayed out of radio contact with Eighth Army headquarters. Tenth Armoured Division under Gatehouse was ordered to reinforce Freyberg at Fuka, but went the wrong way. Gatehouse also distracted the Desert Air Force from doing the job he could not then do himself by ordering fighter cover for his own division. Someone at Eighth Army headquarters had a think and decided to transfer Freyberg's Division from XXX Corps to X Corps. Then de Guingand had a rethink and decided not to, which meant that two separate corps headquarters had to keep track of everyone and co-ordinate their own orders with each other. Seventh Armoured Division, now in X Corps, got clear of the congestion but ran into a minefield in the desert. It turned out to be a dummy one laid by British troops during the withdrawal in June. That cost three hours. After one more hour on the move, they had to stop for petrol. Then it was dark. So it went on.

There were some human elements to this. Montgomery himself was determined that Rommel would not come back as he always had and that the 'Benghazi handicap' would not be run again. So he insisted on an organized pursuit. Other than that, he urged his commanders on and drove hard. As Clausewitz observed, though a commander may be a man of unrelenting zeal, even one battalion consists of many men, any one of whom can occasion delay. When orders were received, not everything happened 'at once'. Conferences were held, maps were compared, features of the terrain were discussed, and waiting was enforced as the army's tail caught up with the moving body in order to provide it with food and fuel. People generally spent the nights asleep while the Germans and Italians were doing a lot of their driving. Perhaps not unnaturally, the zeal of the tired pursuers to catch the fox was surpassed by the fox's zeal to get away.

Nevertheless, these halting moves persuaded Rommel that he could not stop at Fuka, which meant abandoning the Italian infantry. He left them and headed back to Mersa Matruh.

When Montgomery got up on the morning of 5 November, he had breakfast with von Thoma and then held a press conference. He addressed the newsmen wearing a grey pullover and a black tankman's beret. He had had his own rank badge sewn on next to the badge of the Royal Tank Regiment it already bore, which was against regulations. The sight of Montgomery wearing a tankman's beret deeply offended Lumsden, who objected loudly, but no one was listening.[4] It was important, Montgomery thought, for the soldiers of the Eighth Army, who were really just 'civilians who read newspapers', to be able to recognize him. They needed not just a 'guiding mind' but also 'a point of focus', not just 'a master' but 'a mascot'. They wanted a celebrity. He was very happy to become one.[5] The beret was the idea of three men: Captain Warwick Charlton, the editor of the desert newspapers *Eighth Army News* and *Crusader*; Geoffrey Keating, the Head of the Army Film and Photographic Unit; and Montgomery's ADC, John Poston. All three had been in the desert for years, but they realized that Monty had a potential not shared by his predecessors. They thought the broad-rimmed Australian hat looked a bit silly when spread over his diminutive figure, and in any case, despite the badges, singled out one nation amongst the many in the desert. The beret identified him with the tanks, which needed friends in high places, and was more suited to his bird-like head. At the height of the battle, Keating got him to pose in the turret of a Grant tank to try out the beret. The picture went all over the world.[6]

So did the news. Alexander's message, which had arrived in London the previous night, was carried by all the papers in the morning, ascribing the victory at first to Alexander, with Montgomery as his right-hand man, though the spotlight soon shifted. In America, Wendell Willkie had not forgotten his visit to the desert. Alamein silenced American critics of the British. 'The question, can the British soldiers really fight? need never be asked again,' the International News Service announced. 'The Germans themselves are the best judges of their fighting spirit.'[7] This was music to Churchill's ears.

On the morning of 6 November, the German Embassy in Rome informed Hitler that Mussolini had had an idea. He thought that now that Stalingrad had been captured, it was just the moment to make amends to Stalin, sign a peace treaty with Russia and concentrate on the Mediterranean. Hitler also got reports that a large Allied convoy had sailed from Gibraltar. He thought it might mean an invasion of Corsica or Sardinia. The Navy thought the convoy was heading for Libya. Hitler ordered all his U-boats and torpedo boats to sink it, and decided to travel by train to Munich to sort out the Italians himself.

That afternoon, it started to rain in the desert. By the morning, the sand was a bog, providing the pursuers with a superficially plausible reason for failing to trap their quarry.[8] When the leading British tanks got to the Mersa Matruh defence line they found the remains of the

90th Light waiting for them. On the morning of 7 November Kirkman found Gatehouse's tanks parked outside Mersa Matruh with their engines running. When he asked Gatehouse what he was doing he told him his brigadier was going to fight a battle and he was not going to interfere with him. They all continued to sit there. Kirkman identified one anti-tank gun ahead, and the town could have been by-passed anyway. He had the impression that nobody wanted to get on.[9] Montgomery assumed that Mersa Matruh was already in British hands, and when he appeared at the front line himself, he was nearly captured.[10] After some sporadic fighting, the Germans withdrew, and on the morning of 8 November, the advance continued.[11]

A lot of the British troops were behind, rounding up prisoners. Keith Douglas was amongst them, trying to follow his orders to get to Mersa Matruh. His efforts were hindered by a column of vehicles four abreast and nose-to-tail on the road and Axis soldiers anxious to surrender everywhere. When he tried to speed up by leaving the road one of his tank's tracks broke, stopping him completely. He found the pursuit 'very like hunting in England, except that instead of killing the fox when we found him, we gave him a tin of bully beef and searched him for souvenirs'.[12] Whilst taking prisoners delayed him, the thought of loot spurred him on. 'The idea of loot was uppermost in everyone's mind now', he wrote, 'and what made us most impatient to catch up the regiment was the thought that the others would get to the loot first.' Douglas bagged a new Luger pistol and some Italian cutlery. [13]

During the night, while Hitler's train was in a siding in Thuringia, he picked up British radio broadcasts saying that Allied troops were disembarking in Algiers, Oran and Casablanca. The Allies were invading France's colonies. Ribbentrop suggested approaching the Russians via Sweden to send out peace feelers. Hitler told him to shut up and stick to the real issue, which was Africa. He would send forces to Tunisia and get the French to join the Axis cause. The next day, the train arrived in Munich. The French were resisting the Allied landing with varying degrees of enthusiasm. Hitler ordered that the part of France hitherto ruled by the Vichy government now be occupied by German troops, and gave orders for Operation 'Brown', the despatch of a new German army to Tunisia.[14]

The American troops who landed in Operation 'Torch' in order to fulfil their President's ambition of fighting the German Army in 1942 first found themselves fighting the French. On the morning of 9 November, however, the French commander Admiral Darlan ordered a cease-fire. Kesselring had reacted with great speed, and the same day the first German troops arrived from Sicily.

In the desert, Rommel kept moving. The lumbering pursuit was being conducted by so many units that although it did not catch him in the way that the nimble O'Connor had caught the Italians, the very size of it convinced him not to make a serious stand. On 10 November, Rommel wrote his first letter home for a week, saying that they could not go on much longer as they were being chased by greatly superior forces. At least he was falling back on his lines of supply. On 9 November, returns for 15th Panzer Division gave its strength as 1,177 officers and men, 16 guns and no tanks. As the retreat continued, men rejoined their units and tanks emerged from repair shops. On the 24 November, 15th Panzer reported that it had 4,000 men and 26 tanks.[15] But by then, they were out of Cyrenaica.

Rommel had got a bit of help on 7 November when General-leutnant Karl Buelowius arrived in the desert to take over as chief engineer. He was an expert at demolitions and booby-traps. His men set about laying mines, destroying roads, blowing bridges and turning abandoned houses into death traps. Once a few of these devices had been met, advancing troops applied caution everywhere, for nobody knew whether the places the Germans had just left were safe or not until engineers came up to clear them. Plenty of the places were not. By the end of the year, 170 British engineers had lost their lives dealing with booby-traps.[16]

Despite the efforts of Buelowius' men Rommel's decision not to fight a serious battle meant that the pursuit covered a lot of ground quite quickly. The Eighth Army had got to Benghazi on 20 November and round the bend to Agedabia by the 23rd, having covered the 780 miles in twenty days, a rate of 39 miles a day, which is a lot for an army with lengthening supply lines over an extended period. At the end of June, the DAK pursuing the Eighth Army in the other direction had taken ten days to cover the 370 miles from Tobruk to El Alamein, a rate of 37 miles a day. Going back, the Eighth Army did the same stretch in seven, which was 53 miles a day.[17] Since 1941, neither army had ever succeeded in cutting off the other in the desert during a pursuit – the laws of logistics simply would not allow it. Despite that, the desert war was over. Rommel would not be coming back.

On 19 November, Rommel's leading elements reached Mersa Brega, where he paused and got some Italian reinforcements. That same morning, two Soviet Army Groups, supported by a barrage from 3,500 guns, broke through the Rumanian Third Army holding the line along the River Don north-west of Stalingrad. The next day, another Soviet Army Group attacked the Rumanian Fourth Army to the south of the city. The attacking forces joined up at Kalach west of Stalingrad on 23 November, four days later. They had trapped something between 250,000 and 300,000 men in the Stalingrad area. They included the commander of the German Sixth Army, General Paulus, the man Halder had sent to the desert to assess Rommel eighteen months before. The Red Army in the area deployed 1,000,500 men, 13,541 guns and 894 tanks.[18]

On the 24 November, Rommel met Kesselring and the Italian commanders at Mersa Brega, and stated that the line could not be held there without substantial reinforcements of the latest tanks and guns, and a guarantee of supplies. They all knew full well that that support would never materialize. The following evening, Rommel and his staff took a break to watch some newsreels. Someone tastelessly included the one made of Rommel in Berlin. They were all very amused, apart from Rommel himself. On the 26th, he got a message from Mussolini telling him to counter-attack at once and on no circumstances to retreat further without permission from the Italian high command. That did it, and on 28 November, Rommel flew unannounced to see Hitler at his headquarters in East Prussia.

Hitler was surprised to see him. Rommel found him philosophical about things in the east. He could afford to give up ground there, and German forces had been surrounded before. They always got out. North Africa was another matter, and when Rommel told him that it could not be held, Hitler lost his equanimity, which was always a little fragile. Rommel sounded just like all the other generals and field marshals Hitler had sacked in Russia – always whinging, always wanting to retreat, always ready to give up. He got their successors to hold on, and events proved him right. Rommel would do the same. Rommel told him that of the 15,000 troops he had left only 5,000 had rifles, and he did not have enough petrol to fight a battle. Hitler told him that in that case the 10,000 without rifles should not have thrown them away to start with, and that they had not driven from Alamein to Mersa Brega on water. He packed Rommel off to Italy and gave him Reichsmarschall Göring as a chaperone to help him negotiate with the Italians. Amongst his many extraordinary powers, Göring was the Commander-in-Chief of the Luftwaffe, so at the resulting meeting Rommel felt he and Kesselring ganged up on him. Libya could be evacuated, but Tunisia would be held. General von Arnim was sent from Russia to command the newly formed Fifth Panzer Army which was already engaging the Allied invaders.[19]

On 8 December, Rommel wrote to his son Manfred to wish him many happy returns on his fourteenth birthday. The war was very hard, he told him. If things went on in the same way, the massive power of the enemy would crush them. 'For my soldiers and me, having to go through all this at the end of such a heroic and often successful campaign is a bitter pill to swallow.' He told his son that he would soon have to stand on his own two feet, for the times ahead would be very difficult. 'Like me,' he concluded, 'life will deal you a lot of hard blows. You have to take them on the chin.'[20] Rommel had taken Alamein on the chin. Now the immediate crisis was over. But the experience had shaken him like nothing else in his life.

In mid-December when Montgomery was preparing to attack him at Mersa Brega, Rommel slipped away without a fight, not stopping until he reached Buerat another 250 miles west in the middle of Tripolitania. He then abandoned Libya completely and on 23 January 1943, three months to the day after the start of Operation 'Lightfoot', the Eighth Army entered Tripoli.[21] Rommel retired to the position agreed with Kesselring, a strip of land between some hills and the coast of Tunisia called the Mareth Line. So although the desert war was over, the battle for North Africa was not. It did not end until 13 May 1943.

However one looks at it, in the third round of fighting at El Alamein Rommel was decisively defeated. His exact losses are unclear, which is hardly surprising given the rows the Panzerarmee kept having with Rome about how many men they had in the first place. The British took just over 30,000 prisoners, of whom about 8,000 were German and 22,000 Italian. Nobody knows for sure what the other Axis casualties were. If Rommel was being truthful on 28 November when he told Hitler that he only had 15,000 men left, then in addition to the prisoners, about 60,000 men were unaccounted for. This seems very high indeed, so Rommel was probably exaggerating his weakness. He was known to play fast and loose with numbers, usually inflating them to get more supplies, but here probably deflating them to get reinforcements. In mid-November, the DAK and German infantry combined were reporting a ration strength of under 5,000 men, which implies that they suffered some 37,000 casualties in addition to the 8,000 taken prisoner. That also seems very high. The survivors probably had better things to do at the time than to report to muster stations, so the reported ration strength is likely to be misleadingly low. Italian losses are even more unclear. Alexander's staff calculated that the whole of the Panzerarmee had 10,000 killed and 15,000 wounded, i.e. total losses of 55,000, including prisoners. Another contemporary estimate was 61,000 in total, i.e. 31,000 over and above those captured.[22] The Germans themselves initially reported only about 5,000 dead and wounded for the Panzerarmee as a whole, but then they were hardly in a state to make accurate reports, and most casualties would have been simply 'missing'. Over time, the losses were added up. A British intelligence report compiled later from captured documents suggested that total losses for the German contingent from November to December 1942 were just over 20,000.[23] All in all, it seems most likely that during the battle and the retreat, Rommel lost 50–60 per cent, and at the outside, perhaps as much as 70 per cent of his manpower strength. His material losses in guns and tanks were closer to 95 per cent.[24] Whatever the precise numbers, he had never suffered losses of that order of magnitude before.

One of the lessons Rommel was to take with him from Alamein to his later role as commander of the German defences in Normandy was the significance of air power. During the battle, the Allies had flown 11,586 sorties, 1,181 of them on the part of the Americans, and had lost 97 aircraft – 77 British and 20 American. The two Axis air forces had managed to put up just over 3,000 sorties divided about equally between them, and had lost about 84 aircraft – 64 German and roughly 20 Italian.[25] The slightly higher cost to the Allies was insignificant compared to the difference the two air forces made on the ground, and Allied losses were in any case swiftly made good. The 80 or so Bf 109s fielded by JG27, JG53 and JG77 (which arrived on 25 October) could do nothing to prevent the bombing and also failed to prevent their own Stukas from suffering crippling losses. Given the emergency, I./JG27 returned from Sicily on 27 October, only to have one of their remaining stars shot down two days later. For JG27 as a whole, October was an even worse month than September, with 17 aircraft losses. Ten of the pilots, mostly novices, were killed and three captured. In November, another eight pilots were killed or wounded.[26] The Desert Air Force hounded the retreat until it ran out of targets, but the Luftwaffe was unable to have any impact on the pursuers. On 11 November, 15 Stukas tried to interfere with them, but twelve were shot down by P-40s, the remaining three being despatched by American fighters marauding over their base as they tried to land.[27] As the Panzerarmee retreated, the Axis air forces were forced to abandon large numbers of unserviceable machines on their airfields. These were material losses they could not replace.

Montgomery's material losses were modest. About 100 guns and 500 tanks had been put out of action, but only 150 of the tanks had actually been destroyed. For once, the Eighth Army was in possession of the battlefield and wrecks were collected and repaired. The commonest causes of tank losses were having a track thrown by a mine and mechanical breakdown. The human losses were less modest. They were almost exactly what Montgomery had predicted – 13,560, which was about 6 per cent of the Army as a whole. Of those, 2,350 were known to have been killed and another 2,260 were registered as 'missing', but almost certainly shared their fate. The remaining 8,950 were wounded, meaning that they needed some sort of medical attention, ranging from a bandage to an amputation.[28] Alexander and Churchill have favourably compared the casualty figure of about 1,000 a day with the 60,000 casualties suffered by the British Army on the first day of the Somme offensive in 1916, about 50% of those who left their trenches in the morning.[29] Alamein was not like the Somme in its severity. It was nevertheless similar in kind, for the 6 per cent loss rate is misleading. It relates the casualties to the strength of the whole army, including its infamous 'tail'. The loss rate suffered by the front-line troops was far more severe.

Among the fighting divisions, 51st Highland had the highest number of casualties – 2,827 killed, wounded and missing, which is about 20 per cent of its ration strength. However, the bulk of those casualties were suffered by the nine infantry battalions, which numbered roughly 6,750 men. That would give a casualty rate of something like 40 per cent. The 7th Black Watch, for example, had 78 killed and 183 wounded at El Alamein, a total of 265, the highest

figure of any of its individual engagements of the war.[30] Of those, 70
were killed and 140 wounded on the first night. Before the battle, 7th
Black Watch had a strength of 781 officers and men, which means
that at Alamein it suffered a casualty rate of 34 per cent.[31] Even
within the battalions, casualties would be further concentrated
among the rifle companies rather than the men handling support
weapons. Within 7th Black Watch probably a good half of these men
at the point of the sharp end became casualties. The other divisions
suffered less than the 51st, but still severely. Ninth Australian had
2,495 casualties, the New Zealanders – with only seven rather than the
usual nine infantry battalions – 2,005, and the South Africans almost
1,000. Being issued with a rifle and told to close with the enemy was
about as dangerous during World War II as during World War I.[32]

That had been the cost of a decision in the desert. But it was a
decision, as Churchill was not slow to point out. On 10 November, he
addressed the Lord Mayor's luncheon banquet in the Mansion House
in London. He had, he said, never promised anything but blood,
tears, toil and sweat. 'Now, however,' he continued, 'we have a new
experience.' He paused. 'We have victory.' There were murmurs. 'A
remarkable and definite victory.' More murmurs. 'A bright gleam has
caught the helmets of our soldiers and warmed and cheered all our
hearts.' There was applause. Churchill started enjoying himself. He
recalled that the late M. Venizelos (the Greek prime minister who had
brought his country into World War I on the side of the Allies) had
observed that in all her wars, England always seemed to win one
battle – the last. 'We seem to have begun rather earlier this time', he
said. There was laughter. 'General Alexander' – he stopped for
applause – 'with his brilliant comrade and lieutenant General
Montgomery' – there was more applause – 'has gained a glorious
and decisive victory in what I think should be called "the Battle of
Egypt".' (It never caught on.) 'Rommel's army has been defeated. It
has been routed. It has been very largely destroyed as a fighting force.'
He went on to pay tribute to all the varied forces which played their
part, but then drove home his political message: 'But as it happened
... it has been fought throughout almost entirely by men of British
blood from home and from the Dominions on the one hand, and by
Germans on the other.' The fighting was intense, he said, but 'the
Germans have been outmatched and outfought with the very kind of
weapons with which they have beaten down so many small peoples

... The Germans have received back again that measure of fire and steel which they have so often meted out to others.' 'Now, this is not the end,' he warned, 'it is not even the beginning of the end. But it is, perhaps, the end of the beginning.' There was chuckling at this. 'Henceforward,' he went on, 'Hitler's Nazis will meet equally well-armed, and perhaps better armed troops.' He was, perhaps, thinking of the criticisms of British equipment made during the censure debate in July. The days of German air superiority were also over. Churchill conjured up the scene of the retreating Axis columns on the coastal road being bombed by the RAF and compared it with scenes from the beginning of the war, from France in 1940, when refugees were being bombed by the Luftwaffe. That was all over now, the roles were reversed. It was, he said, 'justice grimly reclaiming her rights'.[33]

Churchill gave the fourth volume of his memoirs the title 'The Hinge of Fate'. The turning of that hinge, he stated, was El Alamein. 'It may almost be said,' he then wrote, 'Before Alamein, we never had a victory. After Alamein, we never had a defeat.'[34] With that, he swept away memories of O'Connor and Auchinleck in the desert and of Wavell in Africa before Alamein, and of Cassino and Arnhem after it. The world forgot his 'almost'. And so, from a British perspective, Alamein became the 'Hinge of Fate', the turning point of the war, which from Churchill's personal perspective it was.

On 11 November 1942, the day after Churchill's lunchtime address, Buckingham Palace announced that Montgomery had been awarded a knighthood 'for distinguished service in the field'. He was also promoted to full general.[35] On 15 November, Churchill finally got his way, and bells were rung in churches throughout England.

El Alamein was a famous victory. Was it an important one?

At El Alamein, the German and Italian armies each lost perhaps 30–35,000 men at the outside. By the time the last German forces in Stalingrad surrendered to the Red Army at the beginning of February 1943, 60–100,000 German troops had died in the battle and a further 120,000 were marched into captivity, the vast majority of whom died there.[36] In the battle around Stalingrad, the Italian Eighth Army of 185,000 men was destroyed.[37] From this perspective, the Battle of Stalingrad was five to six times more important than El Alamein in weakening the fighting strength of the Axis powers.

Yet Hitler was to grant the Allies the scale of victory they needed to be able to look the Russians in the eye. Not being prepared to reinforce success, he was ready to reinforce failure. He sent Rommel more troops in Tunisia, and gave von Arnim a whole fresh Panzer Division, followed by another. So in the end, the Germans had four Panzer Divisions in Africa, the four von Thoma had said were needed in the desert from the start. They could now be supplied, as the route to Tunis was short. Hitler also sent Rommel half a dozen new Tiger tanks. The reason he did all this was the old one – to keep Italy in the war. Rommel had more tactical successes, notably when he gave the US Army its first bitter taste of combat at Kasserine in February 1943. But by then he was sick and had had enough. Shortly after an abortive and costly attack on the Eighth Army at Medenine on the Mareth line, he handed over to Italy's best field commander, the Eastern Front veteran General Messe, and on 9 March 1943 left Africa for good. Messe and von Arnim fought tenaciously, but the cause was a hopeless one and when they did surrender on 13 May 1943, the Allies counted 238,243 prisoners. Among them were over 100,000 Germans, including von Arnim. Those were losses of Stalingrad proportions and the Germans dubbed it 'Tunisgrad'. They had made their last stand close to the site of ancient Carthage, where the great general Hannibal had met his nemesis 2,000 years before.

So from the perspective of the absolute level of damage inflicted on the enemy, El Alamein was a modest success, which, in combination with 'Torch', directly paved the way to a major one.

However, from a strategic perspective, even the modest level of damage inflicted directly on the Axis at El Alamein was highly significant. It forced Hitler's attention back to the west, and began a process of serious attrition there which, combined with the relentless losses in Russia, was to lead to total defeat. Until then, his forces had been concentrated in the east, and were beginning to be stretched. With the loss of the desert, he had to divert forces to Africa. With the invasion of North Africa, he had to occupy southern France, and found a Vichy French army suddenly becoming a Free French army and fighting against him. After they had cleared North Africa, the Allies invaded Sicily. On 25 July 1943, whilst the fighting there was still going on, there was a *coup d'état* in Rome, and Mussolini was imprisoned. The Allies then invaded the Italian mainland; on 29 September Italy surrendered to the Allies and on 13 October declared war on Germany. This meant that not only did German troops have to man the lines in Russia, Italy and the Balkans to replace the Italians who had been there, but they also had a new enemy. As a result of Alamein, what had begun as an imperial war developed into a main front with broad strategic and political consequences. For Germany, the Wehrmacht's diversionary foray into Africa was turned into a significant theatre of war. Rommel's four divisions in the desert had by mid-1944 become 26 in Italy, which was not 1 per cent but 9 per cent of the total, and the Germans were forced to send another 21 to the Balkans to replace the Italian ones which had been fighting partisans there. Alamein signalled the start of the attritional stretch which enabled the western Allies and the Red Army to inflict devastating battlefield defeats on the Wehrmacht in 1944.

If the numbers involved at El Alamein do not reflect its full strategic significance, they fall even further short of reflecting its political import.

For Churchill, for Britain, and for the Army, it was vital. It silenced Churchill's critics, it kept Britain a place at the table in his Grand Alliance, and it restored faith in the Army. As it had for so long been the only front on which the Army had been fighting, the desert war had been a staple of war reporting and it loomed large in the mind of the British public. This perspective survived in Britain for many years after the war. Alamein was trumpeted not only as a great victory but as a decisive turning point. It most certainly was psychologically, because people believed it to be. In Germany, it was a huge embarrassment, kept quiet for a week. Rommel was a great hero, and his fall needed careful stage management. Reports stressed the furious fighting of the rearguard and the tenacious defence. But his star was never again to shine with the luminosity it achieved against the sky of the desert.

The blow struck at Italy at El Alamein was all but fatal, undermining Mussolini politically and leading to his fall. As in the case of Germany, Italy's losses in Russia were far greater than in the desert. The Italian Army lost an estimated 80,000 men on the eastern front, as against 20,000 on the African shores.[38] However, Africa was in many ways the vital front for Italy, at once the most visible, the closest to home and the scene of its own political ambitions. It was defeat in Africa in 1941 which had effectively made her Hitler's vassal. It was defeat in Africa which led directly to the invasion of Italian soil, and political collapse. The only thing that stopped Italy from exiting the war sooner was fear of German retribution. Italy became the first of Germany's allies to abandon and then turn on her. Hitler had gone to the desert in the first place to prevent precisely this from happening.

So how was the desert war won?

At a strategic level, it was the familiar story of the hare and the tortoise. OKW never got a proper grip on the Mediterranean as a theatre. General Jodl and a few others, including Kesselring, put forward the idea of defeating Britain by attacking it at the periphery in 1940, but the policy was never properly pursued. One person who saw the potential of the Mediterranean in the war against Britain, and argued for exploiting it in 1940, was Admiral Raeder. It is not chance that he was the head of the German Navy. But even the Navy were hares, rushing around in pursuit of one strategy after another. After becoming convinced that Italians would never take Malta, Raeder got the emphasis shifted to the Atlantic in December 1940, but gave up on that after the sinking of the *Bismarck* in May 1941, argued for the Mediterranean again, and in 1942 shifted his priority to taking Suez and Basra. Hitler paid little attention to any of this because defeating Britain had never been his priority anyway. In one of the last conversations in his bunker in 1945 he said that Britain should never have made war on him and its failure to seek peace was a great mistake.[39]

The Axis partners had totally conflicting goals. Hitler embarked on a life and death struggle. Mussolini embarked on a political adventure. His goals were ambitious but limited, designed not to eliminate his foes but to make Italy a great power. He had his eye on the post-war situation rather than the war itself, and looked for opportune moments to reach a settlement. As a result Italy grew ever more dependent on Germany, becoming a vassal state. Mussolini never fully overcame internal opposition, never fully convinced the Italian people and never understood his ally.

For OKW as a whole, the Mediterranean was a Cinderella. Resources were allocated to it, moved elsewhere, then taken away again according to fluctuating priorities. Take Malta: Fliegerkorps X arrived in January 1941 expressly to lay siege to the island, then moved to Greece after five months, allowing it to recover. Fliegerkorps II turned up in greater strength in November 1941, launched a successful bombardment in April 1942, stopped in May, did nothing to exploit the success, turned its attentions to the desert, spent July and August attacking convoys, came back to Malta in October to get a bloody nose, and then had to concentrate on getting Rommel out of a fix. Hitler's sudden decision to reinforce Tunisia after the Allies landed there falls into the same pattern. The Axis saw the Mediterranean as a series of battles and gathered their resources to fight whichever battle they thought was the most important one at the time. The Allies saw it as a long-term campaign. They fought each aspect of it with equal determination, and, despite short-term falls, steadily increased the resources they allocated to winning until they did so.

The biggest hare of all was Rommel himself. By dashing towards Alamein he put his head into a strategic noose from which Kesselring could by then no longer extricate him. He should have demanded Hercules. Had Rommel backed Kesselring, then Hitler might have been persuaded - Kesselring has described Rommel's power over Hitler as 'hypnotic'. He seduced Hitler into making opportunistic strategic moves around his tactical successes without ever addressing the real issues. That, coupled with his ambition, seduced him in turn into doubling his money in a game in which the odds were stacked against him. Rommel knew all about the realities of the supply war, but he often acted as if they were administrative inconveniences. He put his problems down to the bungling of bureaucrats rather than the strategic position he placed himself in. In seizing operational opportunities which pushed his logistics to their limits, he took calculated risks. They often paid off, at least in the short run. When they did not, he berated the quartermasters. Halder was not a popular vote-winner, but he had a point. One historian has gone so far as to upbraid OKW for putting up with Rommel. His repeated defiance of his orders was mistaken 'and should never have been tolerated'.[40]

This is a severe judgement. It was clear enough to Rommel that his problems were insoluble within the parameters he had to operate in. He wanted his masters to take the whole theatre seriously, not just the desert battlefield, and fight with consistency and determination at sea and in the air. Rommel was a man to whom everything was possible if the will were there, and he saw the solution as simply finding 'a man with real personality to deal with these questions in Rome, someone with the drive and authority to tackle the problems involved'.[41] Von Rintelen did not in his view fit the bill. Rommel could have had a great ally in Kesselring, who agreed that the Middle East was a theatre offering the Axis great opportunities, and that treating it as a distracting irritation would be a self-fulfilling prophecy. Rommel spurned him. Like many leaders who inspire devotion in their subordinates, Rommel was a difficult colleague. He did not get on with the Italian commanders or OKW or von Arnim in Tunisia. He regarded everyone else engaged in fighting the Mediterranean war, from the Italian Navy to the Luftwaffe, as servicing his needs. When they did not agree with him, he got on with what he wanted to do anyway, and then berated them for not backing him up. Kesselring has commented that he never managed to work with Rommel with the sort of trust and closeness he sought, and hints at a personality clash as the root of the problem.[42] Rommel expressed his thoughts in a letter to his wife. On 2 April 1942, he told her: 'Kesselring was over here yesterday. The news from our allies gives no cause for rejoicing. Whatever the subject, he is a total bureaucrat and has no comprehension of the demands of modern war. The pace of supplies is totally inadequate.'[43] Had Rommel been prepared to make common cause with Kesselring, then between them they might have taken on Halder, OKW and the Commando Supremo successfully and at least have got some consistency in direction.

Rommel kept going for so long because although the British had all the strategic advantages, the Germans had all the tactical ones. They generally had better equipment, better training, better battle-field communications, superior battlefield intelligence and they used a mission-based command system. The British had superior naval forces and supply ability, eventually established air superiority and, through Ultra, had decisively superior strategic intelligence. Pre-war, the British had created an army which was Rommel's dream opponent – its weaknesses, especially in command, control and battlefield intelligence, meshed perfectly with his strengths. Never-theless, closing the tactical gap was easier than closing the strategic one, and this the British did.

It was ultimately a matter of priorities. Churchill fought in order to win. Hitler fought in order not to lose. The strategic initiative therefore lay with Churchill, and in the end he, the tortoise, won, by integrating air, sea and land power across the whole theatre in a way which eluded the Axis. Rommel had plenty of daring, which is why Hitler chose him in the first place. But at the top it was a case of 'who cares wins'.

Whether Churchill did the right thing with his prize or not will probably always be debated. While he was in Moscow between his two trips to the desert he explained 'Torch' to Stalin. Frustrated by having to talk through interpreters and finding his host unresponsive, Churchill took a piece of paper, drew a crocodile on it and pointed to its belly. The crocodile was the Axis and Italy was the 'soft underbelly'. The image became a metaphor and the metaphor became a strategic principle. It was true politically, but in military terms a glance at a map of Italy will show it to be a narrow mountain range crossed by rivers, as hard and scaly a spine as any defender could wish for, looking just like the back of a crocodile. So it proved in practice.[44]

The decisive period in the desert was July 1942. It was not a turning of the tide. Until then the tide had been turning all the time, as tides do – that was the problem. July 1942 was different because then the seas crashed through the thin breakwater Rommel had provided for Axis strategy in the Mediterranean and began to submerge it. The waters Rommel got into after that were so deep that the Axis sank anyway whether the tide was high or low.

The first two victors of Alamein were Park and Auchinleck. Park stopped the bombing of Malta and Auchinleck stopped Rommel. It was no mean feat to take over command from a failing subordinate in the middle of a battle, rally a retreating army, make a semi-improvised stand and win a victory. Whatever Auchinleck's failings, the first Battle of Alamein was a great achievement which gave the Eighth Army the strategic initiative. From then on, Rommel was a condemned man. Park turned Rommel's halt at the Alamein line into a crisis. When he took over at Malta, he quickly won a decisive victory in the air which enabled him to then move on to the offensive. Park's torpedo-bombers began to throttle the Axis effort. Then it was just a matter of time. Rommel tried to punch his way through to Egypt again while he still had the strength to do so, but Montgomery held him at Alam Halfa. Kesselring tried to loosen Park's grip on Rommel's throat by blitzing Malta again in October, but by then Park was too strong. He tightened his grip on the jugular of the Panzerarmee Afrika and gave the Luftwaffe a hiding as well. When Rommel left for his cure, he knew that the clock was ticking and the odds against him were lengthening. One week after Kesselring had admitted defeat over Malta, Montgomery began the painful work of finishing off Rommel, but *his* Battle of El Alamein, which was the bloodiest, was just the final step. Auchinleck had laid out a noose which Rommel put his head into. Park tightened the rope. Montgomery's job was to kick away the trap-door beneath him.

There had to be a battle, and its outcome was not a forgone conclusion. Rommel could have got away with not losing. A stalemate at Alamein or an orderly retreat with an army still in being to Fuka, Sollum or Tobruk would have been a fine military achievement and served a strategic purpose. With Hitler's attention turned towards Africa by 'Torch', the Axis could have continued to hold out in the desert. That would have caused a crisis in London. For the British, Alamein had to be a decisive victory. Montgomery knew exactly how to deliver that decisive blow. He was the third and final victor of El Alamein.

Montgomery's was a double achievement. He fought the battle the army could win and created the army to win the battle. He had to do a lot more than Rommel, who did not have to build professional skills because the German General Staff had done that in the 1930s. Neither in fighting the battle nor in building the army was Montgomery 100 per cent successful, but he was never likely to be. He was successful enough at both to achieve his goal, which was not just to get a decision on that battlefield but to turn the army into an instrument capable of winning the battles to come.

Tobruk was Auchinleck's winter of discontent, and he was replaced by a military Thatcherite, a 'conviction' general. Montgomery had to break the desert trades union and introduce a meritocracy. A lot of battlefield failures were the result of inter-union disputes. It is common to identify the actions of armies with their generals, to imagine that the Panzerarmee was quick and clever because Rommel was, and the Eighth Army was slow and cautious because Montgomery was. In fact, those characteristics were rooted in the institutions themselves, in the behaviour of hundreds of middle ranking officers on both sides. The Eighth Army behaved the way it did long before Montgomery arrived, and German troops in every theatre of war behaved much like the Afrika Korps whoever commanded them. Both armies did what they had been told to do in the way they had been trained to do it in the 1930s. That was not going to change quickly. Montgomery was instrumental in starting to change the British Army in a lasting way which enabled it to take on both the Wehrmacht and the Waffen-SS in Normandy and, despite the faults it still displayed there, to win.

In the Eighth Army, the tanks had a demarcation line with the artillery and thought it should mind its own business, The cavalry element wanted to rid itself of infantry support as well. In analysing the failure of the attack on the Ruweisat Ridge in July, the commander of a New Zealand infantry brigade, Howard Kippenberger, concluded that the cause was a failure to co-ordinate armour and infantry, and put his finger on the problem precisely: 'That is impossible', he has written, 'without a common doctrine, a sound system of intercommunication, and training together. The attitude of the armour commanders at the time was not helpful, but I do not think we of the infantry did nearly as much as we could or should have done.' It was a matter of doctrine and attitude. Kippenberger tells a revealing story of the action on 15/16 July, when his brigade was established on the Ruweisat ridge, and being attacked in the rear by German tanks. He went to find out where his own tank support had got to, and found it sitting four miles in the rear, watching the action through binoculars. On approaching the brigadier in command of the tanks to ask him for help, he was received 'coolly' and offered a reconnaissance tank. Kippenberger thereupon asked to see the divisional commander, who was Lumsden. When Lumsden turned up, Kippenberger repeated the request. Lumsden, he wrote, got down from his tank, took a shovel off the side, killed a scorpion with several blows, and then sat on the hull with his brigadier to look at some maps and work out where they were. There was some disagreement, then Lumsden finally got down and told Kippenberger they would move 'as soon as possible'. They did arrive a bit later, drove off the German tanks quite easily, and then stopped. Whilst the incident is related through only one man's eyes, if it is even partly true it is a serious indictment of the state of the army. It certainly does not convey much urgency, initiative or a desire for good working relationships.[45]

Montgomery focussed very quickly on the problem as defined by Kippenberger. He still worked with the 'masterplan' doctrine of British Field Service Regulations, but re-interpreted it, moving it at senior levels towards the 'mission command' doctrine of the Germans. He insisted on explaining his intentions to all his commanders, and imposing his will on them. There was to be no debate about what he intended, no 'bellyaching'. But instead of trying to micro-manage and treating his commanders as automata, he picked people who as far as possible understood and bought in to his intentions and then let them get on with it. It worked with all but Lumsden, the one appointment over which he bowed to the advice of others. He sacked Lumsden on 24 November.[46] Montgomery was an autocrat, but in the middle of a war an autocrat was needed in order to impose on the whole army a unified interpretation of doctrine such as the Germans already had. Adopting a thoroughgoing mission-based system would have meant changing the culture of the army, and doing that in the middle of a war would have been well-nigh impossible.

The idea of the Montgomery 'masterplan' has had a chequered reception in part because he developed what his biographer, not mincing his words, has called 'a quasi-paranoid streak of subsequent self-justification, a noxious insistence that his battles and campaigns were fought exactly according to plan' – claims which are obviously untrue.[47] Montgomery knew full well, as he wrote in his letter to Brooke on the day of 'Supercharge', that 'battles do not go as one plans,' for that is what distinguished battles from exercises, and why armies need to be led by generals, not planners. He changed both 'Lightfoot' and 'Supercharge' as circumstances changed, and in doing so exhibited the skills of a fine general. However, he did not change his overall conception of how the battle would be fought, his broad intent, and this was a great advantage against Rommel. Rommel tended to go into action with more of an intention to seek out opportunities than a plan of battle. He was an instinctive, seat-of-the-pants entrepreneur rather than an analyst and manager. He expected Montgomery to push everywhere along his front looking for weaknesses without knowing where the decisive thrust might come. Montgomery always knew that the thrust would come in the north, but he kept changing its axis until Rommel had committed himself. That was what Montgomery meant by 'unbalancing' his opponent, and he withdrew Freyberg and X Corps in order to stay balanced himself. When it came, the final blow, though sluggishly executed, was still devastating. Rommel was flummoxed when Montgomery continued to grind away at some of the strongest parts of his defences, and he did not think much of it as a way of fighting a battle. It was, however, the one way guaranteed to make victory, when it

came, decisive, as Rommel grudgingly conceded. One member of his
intelligence staff reports that Rommel dubbed Montgomery 'the Fox'
because of 'his caution and determination not to fail as had the
"others"'.[48] Never in the history of human conflict have the
characteristics of an animal been so frequently and so capriciously
evoked as in the campaign in the desert.

Montgomery's revision of 'Lightfoot' was an attempt to *force*
infantry, armour and artillery to work together, for that was the key
to the operational effectiveness of the army as a whole. British
armoured doctrine was mired in a sterile debate between infantry
support and independent action. The whole debate was fundamentally misconceived. Tanks were much more than infantry support
weapons. They were breakthrough weapons themselves. However,
they equally could not operate effectively without artillery and
infantry which were motorized to keep up with them. Despite having
the Germans demonstrate this to them in practice for two years, the
British Army had still not caught on to the fact that both sides in the
debate it was having with itself were wrong. To get to the right
answer, it had to change the way it framed the question in the first
place.

Montgomery started to do that, but he was only partly successful,
as betrayed by his flawed notion of the *corps de chasse*. The Afrika
Korps was nothing of the kind – it was a strike weapon, not a pursuit
vehicle. Lumsden used the cavalry analogy in talking about tanks, and
so objected to the role actually given to X Corps in 'Lightfoot', which
was to break in. By the time Montgomery realized that his first idea
was not going to work, it was too late and the resulting plan added
considerably to the difficulties Eighth Army experienced during the
battle, right up to its end. Having two corps in the same area added a
tortuous chain of command to an already complex situation which
was bound to become confused anyway. It is striking that the
regiments of 23rd Armoured Brigade placed directly under the
command of the infantry divisions did their job and that 9th
Armoured Brigade performed with great courage and determination
when placed directly under Freyberg. It suffered considerably as a
result. The armour never lacked courage, it lacked skill. But even
cavalrymen could learn. The regiments of 9th Armoured Brigade
were from the cavalry, and the commanders of two of them were
masters of hounds.

The job was very difficult, perhaps too difficult, as some of the infantry commanders averred.[49] Horrocks was an infantryman who had commanded an armoured division. He had sympathy with both. He heard remarks from the infantry such as 'The only way to get them on is to put anti-tank guns behind them', and remarks from the armour such as 'How can we debouch from bottle necks formed by the lanes through minefields when these are ringed round with enemy anti-tank guns?'[50] The armour at El Alamein felt it was being asked to do what the infantry had done at the Somme, when they crowded round narrow gaps in the wire only to be massacred by machine guns. At the Somme it had been the artillery's job to cut the wire and silence the machine guns. It failed. At Alamein, the armour thought it was the infantry's job to silence the anti-tank guns. The answer was artillery.

Kirkman has observed that the armour 'didn't understand the gunners'.[51] His post-battle report was pointed. Given good use of artillery, he wrote, 'infantry, unsupported by armour, will be able to gain their objectives without undue casualties'. 'Unfortunately,' he continued, 'no occasions arose when the action of armour was supported by heavy concentrations of artillery fire.' He praised XXX Corps' use of centralized firepower, and quoted von Thoma to the effect that 50 per cent of his anti-tank guns had been destroyed by the British gunners. The armoured divisions, he added, 'rarely used pre-arranged fire plans'.[52] Without actually naming names, Kirkman was blaming Lumsden for the problems at Alamein. Montgomery cannot escape unscathed, though. The problem with his plan was that it made a difficult job more complicated, and made it harder to sort out congestion at the inevitable choke points, which is one of the main things that slowed down the start of the pursuit.[53]

There was another problem which had more far-reaching consequences. Montgomery had at last imposed what the British Army desperately needed and its most able generals like Kippenberger were calling for – a common doctrine for infantry–armour operations. However, it was flawed. After the experience of Alamein, it became established Eighth Army doctrine that in combined tank and infantry attacks, the tanks should lead and the infantry follow. When he took over command of the Allied Land Forces which were to fight the battle of Normandy, Montgomery imposed this doctrine on them. It led to some bloody reverses in the summer of 1944, and only after those reverses was the doctrine changed. The changes in doctrine went along with changes to the internal structure of armoured divisions, which reorganized themselves into brigades that mixed tanks and infantry instead of keeping them separate. One of the men to do so was Montgomery's most promising tank leader, 'Pip' Roberts, who was given command of 11th Armoured Division. It came to be generally recognized as the most effective in the British Army. In adopting these brigade groups, Roberts and his colleagues were returning to the solution first used by Auchinleck in the desert and rejected by Montgomery when he took over. It finally produced the results everyone had been hoping for.[54]

One test of a plan is how vulnerable it is to things going wrong, because if they can go wrong, they usually will. A lot of the things which mess up plans are predictable. One is the weather. This was not usually a problem in the desert, but on 6 November it rained. The rain was blamed for slowing down the pursuit, but it slowed down Rommel as well, so by and large its effect was not serious, though it was used to explain the pursuit's indecisiveness. Another is equipment. Apart from some mine-detectors and flail tanks, most of it worked, and there was the back-up system of plod and prod. The timetable should have provided for that, but the plan was not unhinged by equipment failure. A third is communications. They never broke down completely in the way they had done before, but there were plenty of instances of failure, leading to delay. A fourth is the action of the enemy. The minefields were more extensive than expected. That too caused delay. The fifth is complexity. That was an avoidable weakness. In the event, none of this was fatal. But it made everything slower and more difficult than expected. The battle lasted for twelve days against the ten predicted by Montgomery. The only solution to these causes of friction in battle is determined leadership at all levels. It was not displayed by everyone.

The battle would probably have run more smoothly, if there is such a thing as a smooth-running battle, if the armour and infantry had been integrated at a lower organizational level on the model of Freyberg and 9th Armoured Brigade, or if it had been given to XXX Corps and Leese had had an integrated force. However, that would not have eliminated the 'friction', but just made it easier to cope with. El Alamein could well be described as the battle in which almost everyone at some point got lost. There were no landmarks as in

Europe, no woods and villages, just things described on maps as ridges which sometimes turned out to be depressions. A lot of fighting was done at night. If troops are lost, or are not where they think they are, they fail to rendezvous when expected and cannot call down artillery fire, both of which were crucial. Given the environment and the way the battle was to be fought, it was predictable that a lot of this would happen. Simple as it sounds, when the battle came close to seizing up, it was through lack of traffic policemen with the authority to say where people were, where they should go, and in what order. In practice, that job was done by generals. In the end, only Montgomery could act as the head traffic policeman.

The way Rommel fought his battles appeals to the imagination in a way that Montgomery's does not. Rommel was a dashing, charismatic leader. Yet for all that, Montgomery's achievement as a leader was even greater. He was faced with a turnaround, and he fought in a way that demanded leadership at all levels, not in terms of seizing opportunities, but in terms of keeping going, of directing the traffic. He himself never lost his nerve, and helped others to keep theirs. In all the accounts of his performance in the desert, there are many critics of his manner, methods and generalship, but none of his performance as a leader. To his achievements in winning a decisive victory and starting to build an army with a battle-winning capability must come his achievement as a leader of men. Auchinleck was a man of stature who was admired by almost everyone, but the need for fresh leadership in the Eighth Army is the ultimate justification for replacing him. The decision may have been unfair on him, but it was right. He could not have achieved what Montgomery did to create faith in victory, and he could not have worked with Montgomery.

Montgomery's style of leadership is historically interesting because, unlike Wavell and Auchinleck, he was willing, indeed eager, to become a celebrity. He was the first celebrity general in the British Army, its first media personality. He deliberately decided to become one himself because Rommel was one already, and he realized that he had to fight him in men's minds as well as on the battlefield. Montgomery became the figure he did in part because of the man he fought. In that sense, Rommel made him. Whilst both of them were professional soldiers with almost no other interests in life, both are also figures who transcended the context of the war, and point to the world which was to develop, for better or worse, beyond it.

X

REPUTATIONS

TWO REPUTATIONS WERE SAVED AT El Alamein. The first was the British Army's. The second was Churchill's.

The Army showed it could win victories. It had done so before. It had won clear victories against the Italians and inflicted reverses on the Germans. But that was not enough to win the war. This was, at last, a clear victory against the Germans, or so it was perceived. In fact of course, over half the troops it defeated at El Alamein were Italian, but their commander was German and so was the famous bit of his army, the Afrika Korps, so that was good enough.

Churchill also showed he could win victories. The actual threat to his political position had not been very serious, but there was general unrest in important circles in Britain and elsewhere, and failure at Alamein could have precipitated a political crisis. Had he been removed from power, his historical reputation would still have rested securely on his extraordinary achievements in 1940. Alamein allowed him to become not just the rallier of a nation in defeat but the standard-bearer of a nation in victory. After it, there were no more motions of no confidence.

Two reputations were created at El Alamein. The first was the

Eighth Army's. The second was Montgomery's.

The Eighth Army's press corps did their job well. British and American papers gave Alamein saturation coverage, and a few very effective stills from fake footage which had been staged by a Fleet Street team led by Len Chetwin were reproduced again and again all over the world.[1] The media wanted good copy and good pictures, never mind whether they were real or not. A little later, the public got the real thing in the form of a documentary called *Desert Victory*. It was made by the Army Film and Photographic Unit and the RAF Film Production Unit, but the man behind it was the Army Unit's Head, Geoffrey Keating. Keating told an American officer in June 1943 that England had no hero, so he set out to make one and now Montgomery was 'it'. The film was all part of the plan.[2] Keating and de Guingand handled the press for Montgomery. He himself showed neither skill nor tact in dealing with the media. He was naïve, often professing surprise at some adverse reactions to his public statements. The Montgomery brand had to be carefully managed.[3]

Desert Victory used some of Chetwin's sequences, including dramatic scenes of Australian troops advancing through smoke with fixed bayonets to storm their cookhouse, which Chetwin and his chums had set on fire. However, a lot of it was film of the actual battle. One stills photographer was killed while making it. It was said that making the film cost four cameramen killed, seven wounded and another six captured. Those were the casualties suffered by film men during the whole of the desert campaign, but the suggestion that making *Desert Victory* had cost so much blood added to public interest. It was released in March 1943, and Churchill sent copies to Roosevelt and Stalin, both of whom enthused. Stalin got his copy in exchange for one of a film the Russians had made of Stalingrad. He told Churchill that it would 'stigmatize those people (there are such people also in our country) who are asserting that Britain is not fighting at all, but is merely an onlooker', which was nice to know as Stalin had been his country's leading proponent of that view when Churchill had met him the previous August. Roosevelt told Churchill that 'everybody in town is talking about it', and was pleased to note that it would soon be in the picture houses.[4] The first time the public had been shown real footage of a battle had been in 1916, when cameramen filmed the first day of the Somme offensive. Amazingly, it was shown in British cinemas. *Desert Victory*, on the other hand, was indeed about a victory, and was brilliantly done. It contained some of the jaunty commentary typical of wartime newsreels, but did not flinch from including shots of casualties, though most of the corpses were German. It became the biggest box-office success of all British war documentaries, grossing a princely £77,250 in the first twelve months, against production costs of £5,793. Its director, David MacDonald, won an Oscar. American producers were jealous, but learned well from its example.[5]

With this sort of coverage the stock of the Eighth Army rose high. The desert war had always had great prominence in the minds of the British public because it was so well reported. The Battle of the Atlantic and the bomber offensive were hard to report. They were nebulous campaigns, the one shrouded in grey, the other in darkness, their overall shape hard to grasp. The Far East was far away, the fighting mainly in jungle. The desert, on the other hand, was a reporter's dream. The events were dramatic and well-lit, the backdrop exotic and romantic, and there were star personalities. It was a 'knights' tournament in empty space'. By mid-1942 there were 92 Allied war correspondents in the desert.[6] They had excellent facilities and were free to go wherever they pleased. The Army was far more open with them than it had been in World War I. This was especially true of the most senior officers. Though Montgomery has become known for giving press briefings, he was in fact merely continuing a practice Wavell had established in 1940, and which was adopted by all his successors. Journalists were not only kept in the picture about what *had* happened but were actually told about what was *going* to happen. The morning after O'Connor launched his offensive against Graziani, Wavell summoned seven or eight journalists to his office in Cairo to tell them what he was up to. Cunningham briefed journalists about his intentions two days before launching 'Crusader'.[7] Auchinleck told journalists in June 1942 that he intended to fall back on El Alamein and defeat Rommel there. The correspondents were treated like officers and integrated into the military as part of the war effort. Despite the usual cases of silly censorship, the reporting was remarkably open by the standards of the time.

The Eighth Army's growing belief in itself was not just the product of propaganda. In the aftermath of Alamein it became clear that it had indeed beaten its old opponent once and for all. By the time it reached Tunisia, it regarded itself as an élite force which, compared with the inexperienced British, French and American troops who had landed there, it was. In Tunisia it fought more effectively than any of the newcomers, and began to lord it over them. When a friend of Alan Moorehead went up to a sergeant of the Eighth Army in Tunisia and said, 'Hello! Pleased to see you. I am from the First Army', the sergeant replied, 'Well, you can go home now. The Eighth Army's arrived.'[8] At their victory parade in Tripoli in February 1943 Churchill told them that the fame of the desert army had spread throughout the world and that when history was written their feats 'would gleam and glow and will be a source of song and story long after we who are gathered here have passed away'. This promise of epic fame has not so far been that wide of the mark. It should therefore perhaps be recorded that whilst the Eighth Army suffered 12,600 casualties in the subsequent fighting in Tunisia, the Americans suffered 18,200, the French 19,400 and the British troops in the First Army 25,700, which taken together is five times as many.[9] Small wonder that other armies resented the dusty glamour enjoyed by the veterans of the desert. It seemed as if as far as the public were concerned only the desert was cool.

There was a peculiar postscript to this. In August 1943, a campaign medal called the Africa Star was awarded to all who served at least one day in North Africa between 10 June 1940 and 12 May 1943. In addition, there were bars inscribed '1st Army' and '8th Army' to be worn on the ribbon. Anyone who served in the First Army qualified for its bar. Only those who served with the Eighth Army after 23 October 1942, over a year after that army had officially come into existence, were entitled to wear the '8th Army' bar. It looked as if in official eyes they only became the Eighth Army through fighting that third and final battle at El Alamein, Montgomery's battle. On 31 January 1944, Auchinleck wrote to the Prime Minister, saying that he felt this distinction 'would not be altogether just'. Brooke appended a minute supporting his view. The Committee on the Grant of Honours, Decorations and Medals in Time of War rejected his request to extend the wearing of the clasp to participants in other actions as it would set a precedent for numerous others. The issue did not go away. On 8 January 1961, Auchinleck wrote to the Secretary of State for Defence, John Profumo, repeating his request on behalf of 'a large body of opinion which feels strongly and bitterly that this wrong, as they consider it to be, should be righted', and asking him to see General Sir Alexander Galloway who wanted to put the case in person. Profumo did see Galloway, but stuck to the Committee's original decision. He wrote back to Auchinleck explaining that most of the 'heartburning' the matter had caused 'was due to the decision to use the figure "8" for this purpose instead of the normal silver rosette. The "8" has wrongly, but understandably, been regarded as recognizing service in the Eighth Army as such'. Auchinleck replied gracefully, but was unconvinced, adding the barbed comment that there was rightly or wrongly 'a distinct feeling' that the events of the desert war before Montgomery's breakthrough had been 'deliberately ignored and deprecated, mainly for political reasons connected chiefly with the Prime Minister's prestige and the need to display him as the architect of victory'![10]

A lot of the Eighth Army's image came from Montgomery. Nobody had heard of the First Army commander, General Anderson, and Montgomery had scant regard for him. A lot of the pride men took in being members of the Eighth Army also came from Montgomery, and he did all he could to foster it. Wounded men tried to get back to their units as soon as possible, and sickness rates fell to an all-time low. One of the reasons Montgomery refused to launch attacks before he was sure of success was to maintain the soldiers' belief in themselves as unbeatable. Others saw it as a way of insuring his own reputation as a general who was unbeatable.[11] The soldiers did not care either way. He had indeed become their 'mascot', and when Montgomery attended a special concert at the Opera House in Tripoli, the soldiers in the audience cheered when he entered his box. After the show they started chanting 'We want Monty, we want Monty'.[12] When he went back to England after the Axis surrender in May, similar scenes occurred when he went to see *Arsenic and Old Lace* in the West End.[13] There was a precedent in the public adulation of Nelson the previous century, but such things had never before happened to a British general, not even Wellington. 'Monty' had become a tabloid hero. He was the people's soldier.

Bernard Law Montgomery was not a nice man. His private life, marked by an unhappy childhood and the early loss of his wife in 1937, was sterile, and he had no close friends. In the latter decades of his life he managed in one way or another to hurt and alienate almost everyone who might have had a claim on his friendship, including his most loyal lieutenant, Freddie de Guingand. He even had a temporary rift with his son. He was vain, egocentric, self-righteous and boastful. He was insensitive to the point that one wonders whether he suffered from some undiagnosed form of autism. His desire to create an aura of success turned into a doctrine of infallibility. He developed a penchant for self-justification which was usually unsubtle and sometimes mendacious. He had a sadistic streak and was free in his criticism of others to the point of being insulting. Fame is dangerous for anyone, and was particularly bad for him. Suddenly, after Alamein, he could do no wrong. That did not do him any good.

More seriously, his reaction to his fame did not do the Allied cause any good either. The performance of large organizations is in part a function of the relationships between their leaders. This is particularly true in war. Rommel's failure to work effectively with the Italians, OKH, senior Luftwaffe staff and Kesselring contributed significantly to the Axis defeat. Though the consequences were not in the end fatal, Monty headed down the same path. His diaries are replete with unflattering comments about his colleagues. He was also free in expressing his opinions, both verbally and in letters, and often turned them into unsolicited advice. He denigrated Auchinleck to anyone willing to listen and some who were not. He told Anderson's chief intelligence officer that Anderson was 'a plain cook' and told Alexander that Anderson was 'not fit to command an army' and should be removed.[14] He told Lord Mountbatten that Alexander was 'a very dear person' but incapable of conducting 'large-scale operations in the field' on account of his 'limited brain' and lack of 'understanding of the business', and he shocked the American General Mark Clark by advising him that if Alexander told him to do anything silly, as he surely would, he should protest.[15] He commanded Canadian troops in Sicily and told Brooke that their commander, General Crerar, was 'unfit to command an army in the field' and should be replaced by one of Montgomery's British corps commanders.[16] Once the Americans arrived in Tunisia, they came in for it too. He wrote to both Alexander and Brooke to tell them that Eisenhower was good at politics but knew nothing about war or how to fight battles, a view he retained until the end of his life.[17] Patton he regarded as an ignorant sabre-rattler, who ran a hopeless headquarters and misunderstood air power, but he gave him credit as an aggressive 'thruster'.[18] He liked Clark, but observed that he did not know a great deal and needed guidance and advice, which Montgomery was sure he would welcome.[19]

As far as Montgomery was concerned, he was a plain man speaking the plain truth in plain terms. Any hurt feelings were as nothing compared to the cause of defeating Germany. Doing so meant getting the right people in the right place. Failure to do that meant that soldiers would die in battle to no purpose, as they had in World War I. Someone had to state the truth with clarity. To everyone else, this was overbearing arrogance. Many historians would agree, in broad terms, with the marks the schoolmaster assigned to his colleagues. Apart from the most sweeping of his judgements, there is something to all of them. He was more professional than most of the other Allied generals and more experienced than any of them. Eisenhower recognized that he was 'of a different calibre' from most of the others, but his ability came at a price. 'He is unquestionably able,' Eisenhower wrote to General Marshall in April 1943, 'but very conceited.' In his opinion, Montgomery was so proud of his record that he would never make a single move unless he could practically guarantee success.[20] Montgomery's plain speaking was clearly not done purely in the service of his cause, for it continued long after the war was over. Far from serving his cause, it tended to undermine it. Some of his later indiscretions actually strained international relations.

Montgomery might have thought that expressing his views as he did was a way of influencing people, but it was no way to make friends. The collection of generals sacked by Montgomery grew steadily throughout the war, and not all of them maintained perfect silence. Back in London, Lumsden had wasted no time telling everyone at the Cavalry Club what a shit Montgomery was.[21] Some other people who mattered a great deal more than Lumsden formed the same opinion.

Montgomery commanded the Eighth Army in Sicily and Italy, until it was confirmed on 23 December 1943 that he had been chosen to be Allied Ground Force Commander in Operation 'Overlord', the invasion of north-west Europe. He completely overhauled the plan for the invasion, eventually defeated Rommel once again in the Battle of Normandy, and on 1 September 1944 was made a Field Marshal. Relinquishing direct control of the American forces he continued to command the British and Canadian troops of 21st Army Group until the end of the war, when he accepted the German surrender. Despite the controversy surrounding his performance in Normandy, during which there were calls for his dismissal, and the subsequent campaign in Europe, he was clearly seen as Britain's leading soldier, and in 1946 he took over from Sir Alan Brooke as CIGS. The same year, he was created Viscount, and chose the title of 'Viscount Montgomery of Alamein'.

Churchill's 'Grand Alliance' brought together men of different abilities who needed to work together. Those needs were not best served by prima donnas. There were several in Italy and even more landed in Normandy. Montgomery was one of them. It was as well that Eisenhower was good at politics. The later criticisms of Montgomery's performance in Europe would have been far more muted had he been less provocative himself. He sowed the wind, and reaped a whirlwind.

It continued to rage after the war was over. In the late 1940s, Montgomery published an account of his campaigns in two volumes, *El Alamein to the River Sangro* and *Normandy to the Baltic*. They are spare, clear accounts based on his diary. Everything appeared to have gone according to plan. In 1958, Montgomery published his *Memoirs*. Montgomery felt that various other memoirs already published, notably those of Eisenhower, had been unfair to him. He meant to set the record straight. In his *Memoirs*, although he admitted to mistakes at Arnhem and to misjudgements over some dealings with the press, everything else clearly went according to plan, and several reputations got a bruising. Montgomery had always enjoyed a good fight. The motto of the book was a quotation from Job: 'Yet man is born unto trouble, as the sparks fly upward.' He was not to be disappointed.

Gatehouse wrote to Montgomery threatening legal action over his account of the events of 25 October 1942.[22] Auchinleck wrote a tight-lipped letter to the *Sunday Times* referring to Montgomery's allegation that when they met in August he expressed the intention of withdrawing from the Alamein line. This, he wrote, was 'incorrect and absurd'. Contingency plans for any further withdrawal had been abandoned in July when he, Auchinleck, stopped Rommel at the First Battle of Alamein. Perhaps Montgomery's memory was allowing him to make statements which were untrue.[23] Auchinleck's solicitors thought they had a 'cold hard libel suit' on their hands, but he declined to pursue it, being satisfied instead with an acknowledgement inserted into later editions. Montgomery remained unrepentant about what he had written in the main text. The *Memoirs* led to a permanent rift with Eisenhower, who was incensed at what Montgomery wrote about his abilities as a general. Having in the meantime become president of the United States he was understandably sensitive about criticism of his leadership skills. The Belgian government and the Italian press were both indignant about the denigration of their respective country's wartime performance. One Italian challenged Monty to a duel.[24]

Such was the depth of Montgomery's insensitivity that he was quite mystified by the reactions to his book. His criticisms seem to have been made quite without malice, simply as statements of fact. In the case of Eisenhower himself, for example, Montgomery expresses the greatest admiration and affection for him as a man, and there is no reason to doubt his sincerity.[25] It was precisely that, as opposed to professional respect, which was not returned.

In the first two decades after the war, the desert war was re-fought in print and became a war of reputations. In 1959, John Connell published a biography of Auchinleck, which set out to re-establish his reputation as the man who 'stopped the rot' in the Eighth Army and saved Egypt.[26] As a result, Montgomery's reputation was put in a different light. Connell added a list of guilty men of his own.[27] Ritchie was amongst them, so his reputation suffered and he was very hurt. He kept quiet, and rejected the idea of legal action out of loyalty to his former chief who told him that the opinions expressed in the book were those of its author and nothing to do with him. Ritchie himself said that one of Auchinleck's biggest mistakes had been to make him commander of the Eighth Army. He had to wait until 1986 to get a proper hearing, when Michael Carver, who had fought at Alamein himself and wrote a balanced, non-partisan and still authoritative account of the battle in 1962, published *Dilemmas of the Desert War*, designed amongst other things to make Ritchie's case.[28] John Connell also made Wavell's case in *Wavell: Scholar and Soldier* in 1964 and followed it with *Wavell: Supreme Commander* in 1969. Ronald Lewin followed up with *The Chief* in 1980. Notwithstanding his sympathetic treatment in some general histories and essays, Cunningham is still sitting in the shadows as one of Auchinleck's mistaken appointments.

Auchinleck never made out a case for himself, despite having plenty of time to do so – he died in 1981 at the age of 96. He was modest, unassuming and gave the impression that he did not greatly care about his own reputation. He thought such assessments were the task of historians, and left the job to them, a task several have taken on.[29] Some have concluded that he could have become the finest British general of the war, but, like Wavell, started too early, before the British Army had the skills and resources necessary to deliver decisive victories.[30] He also had the disadvantage of having made his career in the Indian Army. In the British Army India was regarded as a last resting place for gin-sodden majors, so Auchinleck had to overcome prejudice to make his mark at all. More seriously, it meant that when he went to the desert he met most of the men around him for the first time. Unlike Montgomery, he had no recourse to a pool of replacement officers he had already served with.

Auchinleck agreed to be interviewed for television by David Dimbleby in 1974 and again in 1976, and the BBC broadcast some of the footage in a programme entitled *The Auk at 90*.[31] He was generous in his judgements of all his contemporaries. He expressed understanding for the pressures which led Churchill to constantly goad his commanders (though he thought it wrong), and even to sack him. Montgomery established his reputation as the general who beat Rommel. Auchinleck only actually commanded the Eighth Army twice in the field, each time under the most difficult of circumstances: when he took over from Cunningham during 'Crusader' in November 1941 and again when he took over from Ritchie during Gazala in June 1942. He then fought Rommel himself on both occasions, and on both occasions he beat him. The Auk was an outstanding battlefield commander. In November 1942 Churchill spoke to some MPs about what a 'terrible thing' it had been to sack Auchinleck. 'It is difficult to remove a bad general at the height of a campaign: it is atrocious to remove a good general. We must use Auchinleck again. We cannot afford to lose such a fine man from the fighting line.'[32] But they did.

O'Connor is another general who wrote no autobiography himself, but has found recognition among historians. His defeat of Graziani was the high point of his career. After escaping from his POW camp in Italy, he went to France where both he and Ritchie served alongside Horrocks as corps commanders in the British Second Army. Both are generally regarded as having done their jobs well but without any great distinction. O'Connor had been out of it for too long. He was interviewed for the 1974 television series *The World at War*, and can be heard in the episode dealing with the desert war blaming the only person who was clearly not to blame for failing to pursue the Italians on to Tripoli in early 1941 – himself. It was just as well that he had no public relations agent, for they would have been wringing their hands in despair. O'Connor had too much integrity to be any good at marketing himself. He radiates, as his contemporaries attest, the irresistibly touching modesty and dignity of an English gentleman. His world is not our world. Nor was it Montgomery's.

It was left to the young Cambridge historian Corelli Barnett to launch the first concerted attack on the Montgomery legend. In 1960, he published *The Desert Generals* and provoked serious controversy. He covered the whole of the desert war, and in so doing produced a permanent readjustment of view. He pointed out the achievements of Montgomery's predecessors, particularly Auchinleck, and in many ways rehabilitated them. Much of what he wrote then has since become part of the mainstream. In the new edition of *The Desert Generals* published in 1983, Barnett drew on evidence from the revelation of the existence of Ultra to strengthen a lot of his conclusions, modifying only a few. The book was a remarkable achievement but, like many people challenging conventional wisdom, Barnett overstates his case. In the final part about Montgomery, which he ironically titles *Military Messiah*, the book becomes polemical. It would probably never have been written in that way had Montgomery's *Memoirs* been less self-satisfied and more magnanimous. [33]

From 1960 onwards, the desert war was re-fought between an Auchinleck camp and a Montgomery camp, with the Rommel camp generally cheering the former from the sidelines. Barnett had only devoted about a fifth of his book to dismantling the Montgomery legend, but in 1967, the former war-reporter R.W. Thompson, who had witnessed the German surrender to Montgomery at Lüneburg Heath, devoted an entire book to its destruction. [34] The figure who emerges is an eccentric whom Churchill decided to turn into a hero, and who manipulated the press to broadcast his fame and fortunes to the world. Thompson's Montgomery was a shallow, talentless soldier who did everything by the book and only won because he assembled overwhelming forces before fighting any battle. (The numbers involved at El Alamein are held to illustrate this.) Montgomery's biographer Nigel Hamilton has described Thompson's work as 'an attempted character-assassination'.[35] Perhaps as a member of the press corps he says Montgomery manipulated, Thompson felt he had been hoodwinked. However that may be, Monty and his legend continued to inspire violent and divided passions in a way that no British general has ever done. Only a remarkable man could have generated such admiration and such hatred.

Both Montgomery's successes as a general and his failings as a human being arose from the unusual way in which he thought about the world. He was brought up in a world of strict religiosity, which he accepted, and strict rules, against which he rebelled. Both were equally formative. Things were right or wrong, and there was a right and a wrong way of doing things. He was intelligent, but not an intellectual, as for example Wavell was, which meant that he could analyse situations and understand their essentials, but was not interested in subtleties and possibilities. He simplified until he arrived at a single course of action: the right one. His 'masterplans' were the result of rejecting alternatives. There were no scenarios, or options A, B and C, which is what he found when he arrived in the desert. His thinking was designed to result in action. At the end of the day, he had to do one thing, and do it with conviction. This is what distinguishes practical thinking about action from any other type of thinking. If you come to a T-junction, you have to turn right or left. If you turn right, it is no good driving for a bit and then deciding you should have turned left and going back, for the journey has moved on. So it is for a general. A general has to make choices. Situations are rarely black and white. Actions always are.

Montgomery's world view was binary. It contained no grey. Half tones and colour were absorbed into stark monochrome, devoid of gradations. People were either good or useless. 'Useless' was his favourite term in describing those he rejected – if they were not fit for the purpose envisaged, they were rejected because they were no use in accomplishing that particular task: 'useless'. They may have had many fine qualities, but as far as their purpose was concerned, those were irrelevant. As he judged people, he turned them into mental cartoons. There was no need to qualify his absolute judgements, for that could only give rise to doubt and doubt hindered action. As he told his staff on his first day in the desert: 'I don't want any doubters in this party. It can be done, and it will be done: beyond any possibility of doubt'. Doubt was banished. Once damned, sinners could not knock on the pearly gates a second time.

His orders were designed to eliminate grey, for an ambiguous order can be disastrous, as the Charge of the Light Brigade has famously demonstrated. So were his talks and briefings. They do not simply make points, but repeat and emphasize them. His desert speech was typical: 'I have no intention of launching our attack until we are completely ready ... *I will not attack until we are ready*, and you can rest assured on that point'. When he briefed Horrocks before Alam Halfa he told him above all 'not to get mauled', and, as Horrocks left, Montgomery's parting shot was: 'Remember, Jorrocks, *you are not to get mauled.*' Horrocks did indeed remember during the battle and recalled the words clearly in his memoirs nearly twenty years later. Montgomery's clarity resulted both from his saying what he did say emphatically, and from his not saying a lot of things he might have said. Before an action, this style allowed the many men who followed his orders to focus on the essentials, and gave them 'confidence'. After an action, it resulted in a tabloid view of events, which was exactly what the press and newsreels wanted. After the war, he kept it up, and it is not the way to write history. He had one way of thinking, which he could not change. In a post-war context, it became overlaid with what his biographer has called 'distasteful boastfulness and conceit'.[36] Added to his lack of magnanimity towards people he had already judged to be 'useless', he was bound to provoke a challenge.

When he came to the Eighth Army, he combined the techniques of a schoolmaster, wagging finger and all, with the convictions and moral authority of a messiah. His officers listened to the messiah. The messiah was convincing, so they allowed the schoolmaster to give them some lessons. Alam Halfa was their first exam, and they were very pleased to have passed, though a little taken aback when the schoolmaster marked their papers as well, and gave them a 'B'. As he knew, he himself was facing an exam, but at Alamein, he passed and the school governors were delighted. Historians have debated, and probably always will, whether he passed with an 'A' or just scraped through. During the war, he only got into trouble later on, when he wagged his finger at boys from other schools.

Bernard Law Montgomery was not a great man, but he was a great leader. It was bad for him, but good for his country at the time that he became a celebrity. It needed a hero then. We no longer need him to be a hero today. We have our own. His celebrity and self-regard were modern compared to the retiring modesty of a Wavell, O'Connor or Auchinleck. When the war ended, the gap between the reputation of Montgomery and those of other British generals was a distortion of their relative achievements. The extent of his fame marks a step towards the maturing of celebrity into self-sufficiency, the pure form of what might be called absolute celebrity – the person who has achieved nothing, but is famous for being famous. But only a step. Montgomery's achievements were real enough, substantial by any measure and extremely important at the time. As the figure of Montgomery passes slowly out of memory and into history, it becomes easier to acknowledge that this unpleasant personality saw certain truths with a clarity unmatched by others, and, in part because of those unpleasant characteristics in his nature, was able to win a crucial battle. Although he did not get everything right, he also became the most vigorous reformer of the British Army in a period of crisis. His greatest achievements were as a leader as much as a general, and as the builder of a weapon as much as its wielder in battle.[37]

One reputation survived defeat at El Alamein – Rommel's. On leaving Africa, he was placed briefly in command of the German army in Greece, then of an Army Group in the Alps. Then in November 1943 he was put in charge of the defences of northern Europe. His reputation also survived defeat in Normandy, but he nearly did not. On 17 July 1944, he was seriously injured when his staff car was strafed by Spitfires on a small road near the village of Sainte Foy de Montgommery. Whilst he was recovering, he was falsely implicated in the plot to kill Hitler with a bomb which exploded in his headquarters on 20 July. Rommel had become disillusioned with his Führer and had unwisely talked of deposing him and making a separate peace with the western Allies. But he had given Hitler his soldier's oath and remained loyal. Nevertheless, a few hints of suspicion were enough and on 14 October, he was forced to take poison. In exchange for his agreement to commit suicide, his wife and son Manfred were left in peace and four days later he was given a state funeral.

So it was that for the last eight months of the Third Reich,

Rommel remained a Nazi war hero. Hitler had picked him for glory, along with the now forgotten Dietl, the victor of the Norway campaign of 1940. Rommel was the warrior in the sun, gaining victories in another subsidiary theatre, while in Russia Hitler allowed his own military genius to flourish without competition. Rommel had come to his notice early on. He had commanded Hitler's personal escort at the 1936 Nuremberg rally, and was commandant of his headquarters during the occupation of Czechoslovakia and the campaign in Poland. Rommel was dashing as well as talented, and seemed to be ideologically reliable – basically a military professional with no political views of his own. Nazism filled the gap. He did well on his nine-day course in Nazi politics in 1937 and in 1938 confided to his diary that 'today's soldier must be political'.[38] At some level he believed in National Socialism, whatever he thought it was. In one of his letters in May 1942, he expressed indignation about some trouble his son Manfred was having at school and, in the style of a 'disgusted, Tunbridge Wells', he chose this way of putting it: 'The trouble is that the whole place is ridden with clerics, and can hardly be called pro-German or even National Socialist.'[39] When it came, disillusion was bitter, and eventually cost him his life.

When Rommel first arrived in the desert, not much else was going on in the war, so his impressive début formed a natural focus for German war reporting. Between April 1941 and the invasion of Russia in June, the only news competition came from the Balkans. Rommel features in far more German newsreels than any other general. Until the Russian war started, he appeared almost every week. 'Barbarossa' pushed him out of the limelight for a while, but in November 1941 he surfaced again and maintained his pre-eminence until his defeat at El Alamein.[40] He was the sort of bold, thrusting character the Nazis liked and by the time of the Tobruk siege he was getting 30 to 40 letters a day from fans in Germany, mostly girls and women, including one of mature years who signed herself 'die alte Schachtel' – 'the old maid'.[41] He told his wife in April 1942 that he had just managed to clear a backlog of 'hundreds' of letters awaiting his answer, and hoped he would get a break from the autograph-hunters.[42] His SS liaison officer, Alfred Ingemar Berndt, performed the role that Keating played for Montgomery. Rommel had ambition and was not without vanity, but unlike Montgomery, he did not consciously use the press. The only distinctive item of clothing he wore was a pair of British goggles he picked up as booty in 1941.[43]

His style of leadership marked him out as a natural small unit commander. His book, *Infanterie Greift An: Erlebnisse und Erfahrungen*, published in 1937, drew lessons from his experiences of World War I for the commanders of infantry companies and battalions.[44] He often led small units personally when a crucial attack was taking place, and consistently demonstrated great physical courage. He had developed a rare instinct for the battlefield, a sort of situational awareness allowing him to make sense out of confusion. It was a combination of an eye for the land and insight into the mind of his opponent. On the ground he could always predict where an attack was going to come from. He was always forward with the troops. Most of his men saw him at some time or another and many witnessed him performing the tasks of common soldiers, be it driving a truck or clearing mines, with great expertise and complete disregard of danger. Small wonder that he inspired respect and devotion amongst his men. He was a natural warrior, and at that level a consummate professional. On the other hand, he had never been seen as general staff material, and did not have the broad military education of many of his colleagues on the Eastern Front. With his feel for a battle and for opportunities, he was a brilliant tactician, ideally suited to command of a division or a corps, which is exactly how he started in the desert.

Like Montgomery, he was personally austere, had few friends and no interests outside soldiering. He also shared some of Montgomery's vanity, though he did not advertise it in the same way and it was more moderate. His letters hint at some jealousy of Kesselring, who was made Field Marshal in 1940, and a competitive desire to keep him off his turf. He was over the moon when Hitler promoted him. 'Being made "Field Marshal" is like a dream', he wrote to his wife. 'In fact all this business in the last few weeks is lying behind me like a dream', and he signed the letter 'Your Field Marshal'.[45] This is not very surprising in one who had made the Army his life. Yet at the margin, his desire to stand out and achieve great things impaired both his working relationships and his military judgement.

In pursuing his ambition, he was hard on himself and hard on his men, taciturn in manner, blunt in his criticisms and short tempered. His intolerance of any who in his view showed a lack of enthusiasm or initiative was such that it caused some concern in high places. In

July 1941, the then Commander-in-Chief of the Army, Field Marshal von Brauchitsch, wrote to him asking him to think again about his requests to transfer numbers of 'well-proven officers'. Rommel replied unrelentingly that his orders had been criticized in a way that came close to disobedience.[46] There was to be no 'bellyaching' in the Panzerarmee Afrika. Among his men he commanded general respect, but little love. His style left them with the impression that he was ready and willing to do their job, and would probably do it better than they could. But he was stiff and formal, with little warmth. When Heinz Werner Schmidt, a young member of Rommel's staff, met Paulus on his inspection visit in Africa, he found Paulus altogether more human and sympathetic.[47] But then, Paulus went on to command the Sixth Army at Stalingrad.

Rommel's colleagues varied in their professional judgements. He was clearly not a great innovator on the level of Guderian, but then such individuals are very rare. Halder was dismissive. Many of the others, including those like Bayerlein who served directly under him, considered that he was not a great strategist but was just right for the desert. But even that judgement was not universally endorsed. When General von Ravenstein, the commander of 21st Panzer Division, was captured in November 1941, the British cannily put him with another prisoner in a bugged cell. The conversations they recorded revealed a lot about the Afrika Korps' losses and also the 'widespread dissatisfaction with Rommel's leadership'.[48] Among the star-studded cast of the Wehrmacht's general staff, there were clearly a substantial number of Panzer generals like Hoth and Kleist, and army commanders like Bock or von Manstein, who possessed broader capabilities and greater mental resilience. Rommel fed on success like a drug and suffered withdrawal symptoms when it stopped. Alamein knocked the stuffing out of him, and in its aftermath, Kesselring thought him so depressed and moody that his judgement suffered and he was unfit for command.[49] Perhaps his was an interested view. Schmidt, who saw him close up, observes that he was 'much more unimaginative and stolid than the romanticized pictures which have been drawn of him by friend and foe'.[50] In his interview with Dimbleby, Auchinleck commented that Rommel was 'very agile' and 'very dangerous'. 'You couldn't go to sleep when he was about', he said. Then he added: 'but you could tell – more or less – what he was likely to do in certain circumstances'.[51] Indeed, Rommel's main offensives, from the first one in Libya, through Gazala, to Alam el Halfa, involved trying to turn the Eighth Army's southern flank, which was the obvious thing to do. When it was his turn, it was Montgomery who did the less obvious by attacking Rommel in the north.

Perhaps the best insight into what made him tick is a story Schmidt tells of when Rommel went hunting for gazelle south of Gazala, where they were plentiful. Rommel had his driver conduct the chase so wildly that he put all their lives in danger. He was highly competitive – he had to win, he had to gain his prize, whatever the risk, whether it was worth it or not. Schmidt observes that strategically the herd of gazelle won – Rommel ended up chasing three of the herd and only got one in the end. 'You have been misled by a succession of demonstrations into forgetting your main intention' Schmidt imagined the animals to be saying.[52]

Yet tactically, Rommel did win. He fed on venison that night, and cut off the horns as a trophy. He was a hunter and a warrior, just like Marseille. Marseille too mastered the technicalities of his job to an unprecedented degree, but lost sight of its purpose, if indeed he ever considered it. That did not prevent his star from rising at the time. During the war, fighter pilots were treated in the way footballers are today, though fighter pilots were paid a lot less and the consequences of losing were more radical. The reputations of both Marseille and Rommel have waxed further in adulatory post-war literature. They were pure professional warriors, and there will always be those who admire them on that count alone. Rommel, however, leaves a richer legacy.

What is unique about Rommel is the impact he made on his enemies. He caught their imagination in his first offensive in 1941. The sobriquet 'Desert Fox' seems to date from around the time of Wavell's unsuccessful 'Brevity' and 'Battleaxe' offensives of the early summer. He was quick, cunning and, like the fennec, was always disappearing into the sand. A lot of his opponents in the cavalry regiments in particular were fox-hunting men, and hunting metaphors pervade the language of the desert. There may have been some ambivalence about the image. After all, O'Connor announced his final victory over Graziani with the message that the fox had been killed in the open. Some fox. Calling Rommel the Desert Fox may betray the underlying belief that the hunters would get him in the end – it was just that he was difficult to catch. Be that as it may, it expresses an admiration which filtered up, and was not lost on Churchill. In a speech to a 'querulous' House of Commons on 27 January 1942, in the debate in which he asked for a vote of confidence, Churchill paid tribute to an opponent who had shown extraordinary resilience in bouncing back so soon after Auchinleck had defeated him at the end of 'Crusader'. 'We have a very daring and skilful opponent against us,' he remarked, 'and may I say across the havoc of war, a great general.' Though the remark was well taken in the Commons, others were offended. 'They could not feel that any virtue should be recognized in an enemy leader,' Churchill commented. 'This churlishness is a well-known streak of human nature, but contrary to the spirit in which a war is won, or a lasting peace established.'[53]

Rommel gained the reputation in Britain, and to some extent in America as well, as the outstanding German commander of the war. Though he was rather more than 'an ordinary German general' as Auchinleck tried in vain to persuade his own officers he was, the best ones were in Russia. After 1940, the Western Allies never encountered the likes of Hoth or von Manstein and hardly knew who they were. Rommel was the *only* German general the British fought between 1940 and 1943. He was the first one the Americans fought, and he beat them in that first encounter. The British and Americans met him again in Normandy. There is little honour to be found in being given a hard time, let alone being defeated, by a mediocre opponent, but some to be salvaged if he is an outstanding one. Rommel was clearly very good, and no comparisons were available for a long time, so there was little incentive to conduct a dispassionate appraisal of his strengths and weaknesses relative to others of his kind. Once the Allies landed in Italy and were almost defeated on the beaches at Salerno, they discovered that Kesselring was no pushover either. The top Allied commanders began to suspect that the problem was the German Army, whoever was in charge of it. Yet no one else they met who was in charge of it created the effect on them which Rommel had done in his two years in the desert. Despite the agony Kesselring inflicted on them at Cassino, the pain of Anzio and the torture of two years of bloody river-crossings up the length of Italy, the British and Americans have never hailed him as a military genius. Rommel's reputation has another quality to it which goes beyond the admiration of professional ability.

In January 1950, Collins published a book written by Desmond Young, a veteran of the desert where he had been attached to one of the Indian divisions as a public relations officer. Its title was simply: *Rommel*. It was reprinted three times that month, and became a best seller.

It is a biography with a personal touch, for it begins with a description of when Young himself was captured in June 1942, and was arguing with his captors about whether he should obey their order to ask a British artillery battery to stop shelling the position where he was held. He tells how the discussion was growing heated when a Volkswagen arrived and a short figure with 'a bright blue eye, a firm jaw and an air of command' got out and put an end to the discussion by upholding Young's refusal to comply. That was an end of the matter and Young saluted him. Young had met Rommel, on whose face, he thought, he saw 'the ghost of a smile'. It sets the tone of the book, which is well summed up in the foreword, written by Claude Auchinleck. 'Rommel,' Auchinleck wrote, 'gave me and those who served under my command many anxious moments ... He showed no mercy and expected none. Yet I could never translate my deep detestation of the régime for which he fought into personal hatred of him as an opponent.' Now that he was gone, Auchinleck continued, 'I salute him as a soldier and a man and deplore the shameful manner of his death.'[54]

It is not that unusual for historians to express admiration for some of their country's former enemies when the causes of enmity have ebbed away into distant time. It is very unusual indeed for a soldier to publish a book in tribute to the commander of the army he himself fought against just five years after the end of a cataclysmic life and death struggle.

The hero of Young's story is a simple, brave young man who scaled the heights of his profession because of his talent and courage. Halder and the High Command are given short shrift. They were jealous of him. Fortunately for the Allied cause, they let him down. From his early days in charge of Hitler's escort he defied the SS. Until his experience at El Alamein 'opened his eyes', he 'admired and respected Hitler but he had no use for Nazis'. A man of honour to the last, he became one of Hitler's victims, and to protect his family he went to a heroic death with Socratic stoicism. His virtues were physical, intellectual and moral, but Hitler turned them into pitch, and ensnared him with them. Rommel was one of 'a small company of exceptional young men', but 'on the wrong side'. He was a British hero.

Young finds a lot of 'British' characteristics in him. His native Württemberg is 'the home of common sense in Germany' where Rommel could grow up to be 'hard-headed and practical'. Whereas Germans are 'literal minded', Rommel had a sense of humour. Indeed, in Auchinleck's view, Rommel stood out as exceptional among German generals because 'he had overcome the innate rigidity of the German military mind and was a master of improvisation'. In fact, the whole German Army was a master of improvisation because it was trained to be as a core part of its doctrine. In the later stages of the war, it also had to be. It was the British Army which stuck rigidly to its orders, because that was what *it* was trained to do as part of *its* doctrine. But beliefs about national characteristics are metaphysical and largely immune to actual experience.

In saluting Rommel when he met him in the desert, Young acted as one soldier acknowledging another who has upheld the common code of their profession. In seeing, or imagining he saw, the 'ghost of a smile' on Rommel's face, Young asserted a common humanity which transcended their situation. Only politics separated them, and Rommel was not political.

In becoming the figure of 'the good German', Desmond Young's Rommel made a significant contribution to post-war reconciliation. As the world was trying to come to terms with the images of the concentration camps, a process still going on, it prompted the thought that perhaps there had been other 'good Germans'. There were, for example, the ones who fought in the desert with Rommel, including those Young interviewed for the book. There were probably others as well. In this way, Rommel made a posthumous contribution to peace as well as war.

Young's book even took Rommel to Hollywood. Twentieth Century Fox's 1951 film, *The Desert Fox*, starring James Mason as Rommel, is based on Young's book. It opens with a reconstruction of the abortive commando raid on Rommel's headquarters, followed by Young's meeting with Rommel in the desert, with Young playing himself. Mason's Rommel is stern, but chivalrous and respectful as they exchange salutes. By the end Rommel has joined the millions of others done to death by Hitler. It still gets an occasional TV screening today.

The figure of Rommel the anti-Hitler conspirator also played a role in post-war politics. In 1945 the Western Allies were all agreed that Germany should never again be allowed to raise an army. By 1948, with the ice of the cold war thickening fast, they began to have second thoughts. In December 1954, West Germany was admitted to NATO and authorized to raise an army of 500,000 men, to be called the Bundeswehr. Both it and its commanders needed to have legitimacy in the eyes of the Western powers and the German people, who were becoming increasingly pacifist. The survivors of the anti-Hitler plot, most prominently Rommel's former Chief-of-Staff in Normandy, General Hans Speidel, provided the commanders, and Rommel provided the symbol of the honour of the German Army. It is quite clear that however disillusioned he may have become with Hitler, Rommel, unlike Speidel, played no part in the plot to kill him. In 1949 Speidel nevertheless published a book in which Rommel is portrayed as a central figure in the conspiracy. Lucie Rommel took this to be a stain on her late husband's honour and vigorously denied his complicity. Most of the rest of the world saw in it confirmation that Germany's greatest general was also one of democracy's greatest heroes. Rommel represented the stern but upright ethos of the old German Army, and legitimized the Bundeswehr. Speidel became its first Commander-in-Chief. Many of the Bundeswehr's conscripts found themselves billeted in a 'Rommel' barracks, and in 1967, Lucie launched a warship bearing his name. He is the only senior figure from the darkest period of German history to have a museum devoted to him. Many of those who have visited it are Eighth Army veterans. Eighth Army veterans have also erected a permanent wreath at his graveside in the Swabian village of Herrlingen, 'as a tribute of their admiration and respect due to a gallant officer and gentleman'. There have always been codes of honour amongst warriors, the deepest significance of which is impenetrable to civilians. Soldiers have often shown respect for an honourable and courageous foe whom they will also do their utmost to try to kill. But there are few instances in the long and unrelenting history of warfare of an enemy commander being held in such profound esteem.

It does indeed seem that the desert war was fought largely without hatred. *Krieg ohne Hass*, 'War Without Hate', was the title chosen for the published version of Rommel's own memoirs. The concept of chivalry is mentioned by both Auchinleck and Young, and it was clearly important to them. Young cites examples on both sides. Bayerlein is quoted as expressing relief that the SS did not fight in the desert. There were no recorded massacres of prisoners, as there were in Normandy, and few recorded civilian casualties, though there were not many civilians there and it was not their war, just infidels fighting other infidels. It clearly mattered to the participants that they treated each other with respect. To them, there was a difference between fighting hard and fighting bestially. It allowed them to serve a cause and preserve their humanity. It was the difference between maintaining and losing self-respect. To them it was part of the spirit in which a lasting peace could be established. Perhaps they were right.

The Western Desert earned its reputation as a battlefield over two years. The armies passed beyond it at the end of 1942 and never came back. Few people have bothered with it since. It has left a melancholy legacy.

In the winter of 1942, some Bedouin moved back to loot the bodies. The remains of many men were not buried until Italian prisoners volunteered to undertake the job in the summer of 1943. They created a cemetery for the Axis dead on Hill 33 and started clearing some of the mines, but that was a very long job. The Western Desert was the first of the world's battlefields to be so thickly sown with land-mines that making it completely safe was impossible.

The Bedouin found that the pasture along the Alamein line had become very good, for the armies had fertilized the land for the first time in history. Their excrement and their bodies had provided welcome succour for the thorn bushes and desert grasses. And so, for a few seasons, Arab families camped along the battle lines to graze their goats and sheep.

One of the Italian prisoners was distracted from his work by a girl who herded her sheep on the hill of Tel el Eisa, where the Australians had fought. He had known the head of her family, Hag Latif, who had finally died in the winter after the British had moved him out of the way and made him feel like a refugee in his own country. The girl's name was Zenab, and she was five generations from Hag Latif. In 1944 she turned fourteen, and also began to turn heads. Zenab always covered her face and looked away when she saw men gazing at her lithe form, now turning into that of a woman. But from a safe distance she would glance back at her silent admirer on the hillside.

One evening that summer, the Italian heard an explosion from the direction of Tel el Eisa. When he visited the family the following day, he found the women wailing and the men feigning indifference in the name of Allah. It had probably been an MK mine which had not been properly dismantled or had corroded. It was meant for German tanks. It had got an Arab girl. 'The little fire of the Bedouin girl was extinguished,' he wrote. 'Her slim young body, her liquid eyes, the sweetness of her smile, would never be seen again.'[55]

On 24 October 1954, a memorial to the Eighth Army was unveiled at the Commonwealth War Graves Commission Cemetery in the desert near the railway station at El Alamein. At the ceremony, an address was given by Field-Marshal the Viscount Montgomery of Alamein. He summed up by saying: 'There are in this world things that are true and things that are false; there are ways that are right and ways that are wrong; there are good men and bad men. And on one side or the other we must take our stand; one or the other we must serve ... We can only secure a better world, and abolish war, by having better men and women; there is no other way and no short cut.'[56]

When he awoke one morning in late February 1976, Montgomery said he had had a very bad night. 'I can't have very long to go now,' he explained. 'I've got to go to meet God – and explain all those men I killed at Alamein'. During the night of 24 March, he died.[57]

Around that place in the desert they lie, the young men of Alamein, be they good or bad, better or worse. Nothing beside remains. All around, boundless and bare, the lone and level sands stretch far away.

Bibliography

UNPUBLISHED SOURCES
The bulk of the original German sources used can be found in the Department of Documents at the Imperial War Museum in London. They include: Halder's diary; the War Diaries of the Panzer Armee Afrika, the Deutsches Afrika Korps and subsidiary units; unpublished commentaries by Nehring and Kesselring; Rommel's correspondence; and various reports and tables of statistics.

Some of the British documents used are also from the Imperial War Museum. Others can be found at the Public Record Office at Kew. Most of the latter are catalogued as War Office (lettercode WO) or Cabinet Papers (lettercode CAB) and a few are RAF records (lettercode AIR).

The references to all individual documents are given in the footnotes, marked 'IWM' or 'PRO' with their respective catalogue references.

I am grateful to the staff at the IWM and the PRO for their help with my research, and, in addition, I am grateful to Derek Dempster for giving me access to some unpublished correspondence he conducted with Sir Keith Park in 1960.

PUBLISHED SOURCES
Works on the Campaign in North Africa and the Mediterranean
Barnett, Corelli, *The Desert Generals*, Cassell (revised edition), London 1983
Behrendt, Hans-Otto, *Rommel's Intelligence in the Desert Campaign*, William Kimber, London 1985
Carver, Field Marshal Lord, *El Alamein*, B.T. Batsford, London 1962
Carver, Field Marshal Lord, *Dilemmas of the Desert War*, B.T. Batsford, London 1986
Edwards, Jill (ed.), *Al-Alamein Revisited*, The American University of Cairo Press, Cairo 2001
Forty, George, *The Armies of Rommel*, Arms & Armour Press, London 1997
Gilbert, Adrian, *The Imperial War Museum Book of the Desert War*, Book Club Associates, Swindon 1992
Harrison, Frank, *Tobruk – The Great Siege Reassessed*, Arms & Armour Press, London 1997
Jewell, Derek (ed.), *Alamein and the Desert War*, Sphere Books, London 1967
Knox, MacGregor, *Mussolini Unleashed 1939-1941*, CUP, Cambridge 1982
Knox, MacGregor, *Hitler's Italian Allies*, CUP, Cambridge 2000
Long, Gavin, *Australia in the War of 1939-45, Series One, Army Vol. I, To Benghazi*, (Australian Offical History) Canberra 1952
Lucas, James, *War in the Desert*, Arms & Armour Press, London 1982
Martin, H. J. & Orpen, Neil, *South Africa at War – South African Forces in World War II, Vol. VII*, (South African Offical History) Purnell, London 1979
Messenger, Charles, *The Unknown Alamein*, Ian Allan, Shepperton 1982
Moorehead, Alan, *African Trilogy – The North African Campaign 1940-43*, Cassell, London 2000
Piekalkiewicz, Janusz, *Rommel and the Secret War in North Africa 1941-43*, Schiffer, USA 1992
Pitt, Barrie, *The Crucible of War Vol. III – Montgomery and Alamein*, Macmillan, London 1986
Playfair, Major General I. S. O., *History of the Second World War, UK Military Series; The Mediterranean and Middle East, Vol. III* (British Official History), HMSO, London 1960
Playfair, Major General I. S. O., *History of the Second World War, UK Military Series; The Mediterranean and Middle East, Vol. IV* (British Official History), HMSO, London 1966
Reuth, Ralf Georg, *Entscheidung im Mittlemeer*, Bernard & Graefe, Koblenz 1985
Schmidt, Heinz Werner, *With Rommel in the Desert*, Constable, London 1997

Valentin, Rolf, *Ärtze im Wüstenkrieg*,
  Bernard & Graefe, Koblenz 1984
Warner, Philip, *Alamein*, William Kimber,
  London 1979

Works on Malta and the Air War
Bekker, Cajus, *Angriffshöhe 4000*, Gerhard
  Stalling Verlag, Oldenburg 1964
Bradford, Ernle, *Siege: Malta 1940-43*,
  Penguin, Harmondsworth 1987
Hooton, E. R., *Eagle in Flames – The Fall of
  the Luftwaffe*, Arms & Armour Press,
  London 1997
Murray, Williamson, *Luftwaffe – Strategy
  for Defeat*, Allen & Unwin, London 1985
Price, Alfred, *Spitfire Mark V Aces 1941-45*,
  Osprey, London 1997
Richard, Denis & Saunders, Hilary St
  George, *Royal Air Force 1939-45, Vol. II
  – The Fight Avails*, HMSO, London 1954
Ring, Hans & Girbig, Werner,
  Jagdgeschwader 27, Motorbuch,
  Germany 1971
Shores, Christopher, Cull, Brian & Malizia,
  Nicola, *Malta: The Hurricane Years,
  1940-41*, Grub Street, London 1987
Shores, Christopher, Cull, Brian & Malizia,
  Nicola, *Malta: The Spitfire Year, 1942*,
  Grub Street, London 1991
Shores, Christopher, & Ring, Hans,
  Fighters over the Desert, Neville
  Spearman, London 1969
Spick, Mike, *Luftwaffe Fighter Aces*,
  Greenhill Books, London 1996
Spooner, Tony, *Supreme Gallantry*, John
  Murray, London 1996
Terraine, John, *The Right of the Line*,
  Sceptre, London 1988
Weal, John, *Junkers Ju 87 –
  Stukageschwader of North Africa and the
  Mediterranean*, Osprey, London 1998

**Works on General Aspects of World
War II**
Beevor, Anthony, *Stalingrad*, Penguin,
  Harmondsworth 1998
Bungay, Stephen, *The Most Dangerous
  Enemy – A History of the Battle of
  Britain*, Aurum Press, London 2000

Calvocoressi, Peter, Wint, Guy &
  Pritchard, John, *Total War – The Causes
  and Courses of the Second World War,
  Vol. I*, Penguin, Harmondsworth 1989
D'Este, Carlo, *Decision in Normandy*, Pan,
  London 1984
Ellis, John, *The World War Two Data Book*,
  Aurum Press, London 1993
Erikson, John, *The Road to Stalingrad*,
  Weidenfeld & Nicolson, London 1975
Erikson, John, *The Road to Berlin*,
  Weidenfeld & Nicolson, London 1983
Gooch, John (ed.), *Decisive Campaigns of
  the Second World War*, Frank Cass,
  Ilford 1990
Grigg, John, *1943 – The Victory that Never
  Was*, Penguin, Harmondsworth 1999
Hasting, Max, *Overlord*, Pan, London 1985
Hubatsch, Walther, *Hitlers Weisungen für
  die Kriegführung 1939-1945*, Bernard &
  Graefe, Koblenz 1983
Jacobsen, Hans-Adolf, & Rohwer, Jürgen,
  *Entscheidungsschlachten des zweiten
  Weltkrieges*, Bernard & Graefe, Frankfurt
  1960
Liddell Hart, Basil, *History of the Second
  World War*, Book Club Associates,
  Swindon 1973
Liddell Hart, Basil, *The Other Side of the
  Hill*, Pan, London 1983
Mellenthin, Major General F. W. von,
  Panzer Battles, Futura, London 1977
Montgomery, Field Marshal Viscount,
  El Alamein to the River Sangro,
  Hutchinson, London 1946
Overy, Richard, *Why the Allies Won*,
  Pimlico, London 1995
Prange, Gordon, *At Dawn We Slept*,
  Michael Joseph, London 1982
Taylor, Telford, *The Breaking Wave*,
  Weidenfeld & Nicolson, London 1967
Thompson, R. W., *Generalissimo Churchill*,
  Hodder & Stoughton, London 1973

**Works on Special Aspects of World
War II**
Anon, *War History of the 7ᵗʰ Bn, The Black
  Watch*, Markinch 1948
Addison, Paul & Calder, Angus, *A Time to*

Kill, Pimlico, London 1997

Beale, Peter, *Death by Design*, Sutton, Gloucester 1998

Cooper, Artemis, *Cairo in the War*, Penguin, Harmondsworth 2001

Delaforce, Patrick, *Monty's Highlanders*, Tom Donovan Publishing 1997

Dupuy, Colonel Trevor, *A Genius for War*, Macdonald & Jane's, London 1977

Ellis, John, *The Sharp End*, Pimlico, London 1993

Fletcher, David, *The Great Tank Scandal*, HMSO, London 1989

Fletcher, David, *The Universal Tank*, HMSO, London 1993

French, David, *Raising Churchill's Army*, OUP, Oxford 2000

Fussell, Paul, *Wartime*, OUP, Oxford 1989

Handel, Michael, *Intelligence and Military Operations*, Frank Cass, Ilford 1990

Harrison Place, Timothy, *Military Training in the British Army 1940-1944*, Frank Cass, Ilford 2000

Lewin, Ronald, *Ultra Goes to War*, Hutchinson, London 1978

Neillands, Robin, *The Desert Rats*, Weidenfeld & Nicolson, London 1991

Orgorkiewicz, R. M., *Armour*, Stevens & Sons 1960

Payton-Smith, D. J., *Oil – A Study of Wartime Policy and Administration*, HMSO, London 1971

Taylor, Philip M. (ed.), *Britain and the Cinema in the Second World War*, Macmillan, London 1988

Whiting, Charles, *The Poor Bloody Infantry 1939-45*, Book Club Associates, Swindon 1987

Winterbotham, F. W., *The Ultra Secret*, Weidenfeld & Nicolson, London 1974

Other Works of Military History

Crawford, Steve, *The SAS Encyclopaedia*, Simon & Schuster, London 1996

Holden Reid, Brian (ed.), *Military Power*, Frank Cass, Ilford 1997

Keegan, John, *A History of Warfare*, Hutchinson, London 1993

Oetting, Dirk, *Auftragstaktik – Geschichte*

und Gegenwart einer Führungskonzeption, Report Verlag, Bonn 1993

Shephard, Ben, *A War of Nerves*, Jonathan Cape, London 2000

Strachan, Hew, *The First World War, Volume I: To Arms*, OUP, Oxford 2001

Van Creveld, Martin, *Supplying War*, CUP, Cambridge 1977

Biographies, Autobiographies and Memoirs

Alanbrooke, Field Marshal Lord, *War Diaries 1939-1945*, ed. Danchev & Todman, Weidenfeld & Nicolson, London 2001

Bullock, Alan, *Hitler – A Study in Tyranny*, Book Club Associates, Swindon 1973

Bryant, Arthur, *The Turn of the Tide, 1939-43: A Study based on the Diaries and Autobiographical Notes of Field Marshal The Viscount Alanbrooke*, Collins, London 1957

Caccia-Dominioni, Paolo, *Alamein 1933-1963 – An Italian Story*, Allen & Unwin, London 1966

Charmley, John, *Churchill – The End of Glory*, Hodder & Stoughton, London 1993

Churchill, Winston S., *The Second World War, Vol. II, Their Finest Hour*, Chartwell Edition 1949

Churchill, Winston S., *The Second World War, Vol. III, The Grand Alliance*, Chartwell Edition 1950

Churchill, Winston S., *The Second World War, Vol. IV, The Hinge of Fate*, Chartwell Edition 1951

Connell, John, *Auchinleck*, Cassell, London 1959

Douglas, Keith, *Alamein to Zem-Zem*, ed. Desmond Graham, Faber & Faber, London 1992

Frankland, Noble, *History at War*, Giles de la Mare 1998

Fraser, David, *Knight's Cross – A Life of Field Marshal Erwin Rommel*, HarperCollins, London 1993

Gilbert, Martin, *Finest Hour - Winston S.*

Churchill 1939-1941(Official Biography Vol. VI), Minerva, London 1989

Gilbert, Martin, *Road to Victory - Winston S. Churchill 1941-45*(Official Biography Vol. VII), Heinemann, London 1986

Guderian, Heinz, *Panzer Leader*, Michael Joseph, London 1974

Guingand, Freddie de, *Operation Victory*, Hodder & Stoughton, London 1947

Hamilton, Nigel, *Monty - The Making of a General 1887-1942*, Hamish Hamilton, London 1981

Hamilton, Nigel, *Monty - Master of the Battlefield 1942-44*, Hamish Hamilton, London 1983

Hamilton, Nigel, *Monty – The Field Marshal 1944-76*, Hamish Hamilton, London 1986

Hamilton, Nigel, *The Full Monty*, Penguin Press, London 2001

Horrocks, Lieutenant General Sir Brian, *A Full Life*, Collins, London 1960

Irving, David, *Rommel: The Trail of the Fox*, Weidenfeld & Nicolson, London 1977

Irving, David, *Hitler's War*, Avon Books, New York 1990

Keegan, John (ed.), *Churchill's Generals*, Warner, New York 1982

Kippenberger, Major General Sir Howard, *Infantry Brigadier*, OUP, Oxford 1949

Lewin, Ronald, *The Chief*, Hutchinson, London 1980

Macksey, Kenneth, *Kesselring – The Making of the Luftwaffe*, B.T. Batsford, London 1978

Macksey, Kenneth (ed.), *The Memoirs of Field Marshal Kesselring*, Greenhill Books, London 1988

Manstein, Erich von, *Verlorene Siege*, Athenäum Verlag, Germany 1955

Milligan, Spike, *Adolf Hitler – My Part in his Downfall*, Penguin, Harmondsworth 1972

Montgomery, Field Marshal Viscount, *The Memoirs of Field Marshal Montgomery*, Collins, London 1958

North, John (ed.), *The Memoirs of Field Marshal Earl Alexander of Tunis*, Cassell, London 1962

Orange, Vincent, *Sir Keith Park*, Methuen, London 1984

Parkinson, Roger, *The Auk – Auchinleck, Victor at Alamein*, Granada, St Albans 1977

Tedder, Marshal of the Royal Air Force Lord, *With Prejudice*, Cassell, London 1966

Thompson, R. W., *The Montgomery Legend*, Allen & Unwin, London 1967

Warner, Philip, *Auchinleck, the Lonely Soldier*, Cassell, London 2001

Young, Desmond, *Rommel*, Collins, London 1950

Articles

Gruchmann, Lothar, 'Die "verpaßten strategischen Chancen" der Achsenmächte im Mittlemeerraum 1940/41' in *Vierteljahreshefte für Zeitgeschichte* 1970

Ring, Hans, Bock, Winfried & Weiß, Heinrich, 'Battle of Britain – die große Schlacht, die niemals stattfand?', *Flugzeug*, Heft 6/3 1990

Sadhovich, James 'Understanding Defeat: Reappraising Italy's Role in WWII', *Journal of Contemporary History*, Vol 24, 1989

Other Sources Referred to in Notes

Bourke, Joanna, *An Intimate History of Killing*, Granta Books, London 1999

Churchill, Winston S., *A History of the English-Speaking Peoples, Vol. IV, The Great Democracies*, Chartwell Edition, 1958

Churchill, Winston S., *The End of the Beginning*, war speeches compiled by Charles Eade, Cassell, London 1943

Clausewitz, Carl von, *On War*, trans. Graham, Penguin, Harmondsworth 1982

Douglas, Keith, *The Letters*, ed. Desmond Graham, Carcanet, Manchester 2000

James, Lawrence, *The Rise and Fall of the British Empire*, Little, Brown, London 1998

Knightley, Phillip, *The First Casualty*, Pan, London 1989

McKinley, Brian, *Australia 1942 – The End of Innocence*, Collins, London 1985

Montgomery, Field Marshal Viscount, *The Path to Leadership*, Collins, London 1961

Roberts, Andrew, *Eminent Churchillians*, Phoenix, London 1994

Rommel, Erwin, *Infantry Attacks*, Greenhill Books, London 1995

Shirer, William L., *The Rise and Fall of the Third Reich*, Book Club Associates, Swindon 1971

Notes

Chapter I: The Strategic War

1 John Keegan. *A History of Warfare*, Hutchinson, 1993, pp. 175–6.

2 There was what amounted to some skirmishing in the Western Desert between 1915 and 1918 as about 5,000 members of an Islamic sect called the Senussi made trouble for the British and their real enemies, the Italians, in eastern Cyrenaica and western Egypt. The British committed at most 40,000 men to the area, and most of the fighting was done by small columns of armoured cars and 2,000 cavalry on camels. See Hew Strachan, *The First World War, Volume I: To Arms*, OUP 2001, pp. 744–54. The Western Desert was visited by Alexander the Great, but when came in the winter of 332–331BC, it was not to conquer but to visit the shrine of the God Ammon at the Siwa oasis. He travelled out with a few companions along the coast road past el Alamein to Mersa Matruh, then called Paraetonium, and returned from Siwa south of the Qattara Depression to found the city which still bears his name. He had no army with him, and fought no battles in the desert.

3 By far the largest number from a single country, almost 40% of the total, were Italian. The figures exclude those wounded or taken prisoner. See John Ellis, *The World War Two Data Book*, Aurum Press, 1993, p. 255.

4 Lawrence James. *The Rise and Fall of the British Empire*, Little, Brown, 1998, pp. 386–94.

5 For accounts of the terms and circumstances of the 1936 'Axis' protocol and the Pact of Steel see William L. Shirer, *The Rise and Fall of the Third Reich*, Book Club Associates, 1971, pp. 297–9 and 482–3, and Alan Bullock, *Hitler – A Study in Tyranny*, Book Club Associates, 1973, pp. 350–2

and 506–511.

6 MacGregor Knox, *Mussolini Unleashed 1939–1941*, CUP, 1982, pp. 4; 102 and *Hitler's Italian Allies*, CUP, 2000, pp. 5–9.

7 Knox, *Mussolini Unleashed*, p. 89.

8 Ibid., p. 125.

9 Knox, *Hitler's Italian Allies*, p. 14.

10 See Ellis, *The World War Two Data Book*, pp. 125–7 and 155. As time progressed and British mobilization got into gear, the balance was redressed. Five further British infantry divisions took part in the Tunisian campaign of 1943.

11 Barrie Pitt, 'O'Connor', in *Churchill's Generals*, ed. John Keegan, Warner, 1992, p. 186.

12 Knox, op. cit., pp. 254–5.

13 It has often been claimed that the intervention in Greece was Churchill's pet idea and that he overruled Wavell. This is contradicted by documentary evidence. See Martin Gilbert, *Finest Hour*, Minerva, 1989, pp. 953–6, 978–80 and 1010–1014. Though Churchill strongly backed the decision, like most major decisions in the war, it was a collective one. It was also backed by Wavell, as is related by his biographer Ronald Lewin in *The Chief*, Hutchinson, 1980, pp. 79–84 and 90–91.

14 Ralf Georg Reuth, *Entscheidung im Mittelmeer*, Bernard and Graefe, 1985, p.46.

15 Walther Hubatsch, *Hitlers Weisungen für die Kriegführung 1939–1945*, Bernard and Graefe, 1983, pp. 70 and 93–4.

16 B H Liddell Hart, *The Other Side of the Hill*, Pan, 1983, p. 250.

17 Though often loosely used to refer to the German Army, 'Wehrmacht' was the name used for the armed forces as a whole. It was introduced by Hitler on 21 May 1935 to replace the term 'Reichswehr'. The Wehrmacht was run by the 'Oberkommando der Wehrmacht' or OKW, the rough

equivalent of the British Chiefs of Staff Committee, but as Hitler was its titular head, it combined some of the roles of the War Cabinet and the Defence Committee, both of which were run by Churchill. The Army ('Heer'), Navy ('Kriegsmarine') and Air Force ('Luftwaffe') all had their own high commands which were subordinate to OKW.

18 Reuth, op. cit., p. 73. On the political background in Egypt see Calvocoressi, Wint and Pritchard, *Total War*, Vol. I, Penguin,1989, pp. 179–181 and 372–4.

19 See the article by Barrie St Clair McBride in *Alamein and the Desert War*, Sphere Books, 1967, ed. Derek Jewell, pp. 182–191.

20 See D. J. Payton-Smith, *Oil – A Study of War-time Policy and Administration*, HMSO, 1971, especially the tables on pp. 103 and 207 and pp. 232–9. The shuttle policy is explained on p. 162.

21 Winston S. Churchill, *The Second World War, Vol. III, The Grand Alliance*, Chartwell Edition, 1950, p. 3.

22 Ibid., p. 237.

23 Hubatsch, op. cit., pp. 120–122.

24 His forces were then augmented by an infantry division and a parachute brigade which had been based on Crete.

25 In 1938, the British were even more pessimistic. Officers of the Imperial Army of the Nile insisted that no more than a brigade could operate in the Western Desert because of lack of water. See Field Marshal Lord Carver, *El Alamein*, Batsford, 2000, p. 20.

26 B H Liddell Hart, *The Other Side of the Hill*, pp. 233–4.

27 Knox, op. cit., p. 240.

28 Ibid., pp. 234–7.

29 Compare the table of 'military effort' calculated by John Ellis in *The World War Two Data Book*, p. 229. Multiplying the number of months by the number of divisions present in various theatres of war, Ellis shows that of a total of 9,032 'division-months' expended by the Wehrmacht in fighting the war, 91, i.e. 1%, were expended in North Africa (which includes the Tunisian campaign which followed the desert war). The total for the Eastern Front is 7,146.

30 See, for example, Telford Taylor, *The Breaking Wave*, Weidenfeld and Nicolson, 1967, pp. 64–5, which quotes an entry made in the diary kept by Franz Halder, Chief of the General Staff, on 13 July 1940. For an account of Hitler's ambivalence towards conducting a war with Britain see Stephen Bungay, *The Most Dangerous Enemy*, Aurum Press, 2000, pp. 27–34 and pp. 109–115.

31 Liddell Hart, op. cit., p. 244.

32 Further away in time, others have reached the same conclusion, describing Rommel's first lunges at Tobruk over Easter 1941, made with inadequate forces and with inadequate reconnaissance, as 'a hurried fiasco'. See Frank Harrison, *Tobruk – The Great Siege Reassessed*, Arms and Armour Press, 1997, pp. 39–63.

33 Reuth, op. cit., pp. 55–61 and 217–8.

34 IWM Dept. of Docs., EDS AL 1349/1.

35 Halder Diary, IWM Dept. of Docs., EDS A 842/G1 Bd. VIa, and Paulus, 'Bericht über die Anwesenheit beim Deutschen Afrikakorps vom 27.4 bis 8.5.41', IWM Dept. of Docs., EDS A.6. M.I.14/379/2.

36 See the slightly tongue-in-cheek article by Hans Ring, Winfried Bock and Heinrich Weiß,, 'Battle of Britain – Die große Schlacht, die niemals stattfand?' in *Flugzeug*, Heft 6/3, 1990, pp. 40–46.

37 After the air battle, he welcomed the prospect of invasion as a means of inflicting a decisive defeat on the Wehrmacht, and he was almost certainly right to do so. See Churchill, *The Second World War, Vol. II, Their*

Finest Hour, Chartwell Edition, 1949, p. 455.

Chapter II: The Tactical War

1 See Carver, *El Alamein*, pp. 22–4.
2 Reuth, op. cit., p. 93.
3 Reuth, op. cit., p. 120.
4 IWM Dept. of Docs., EDS Al 2596, 29.6.42.
5 Knox, *Hitler's Italian Allies*, p. 55.
6 R. M. Orgorkiewicz, *Armour*, Stevens and Sons, 1960, p. 241.
7 Knox, *Hitler's Italian Allies*, p. 144.
8 On all these aspects of the Italian forces in particular see Lucio Ceva, 'The North African Campaign 1940–43: A Reconsideration', in *Decisive Campaigns of the Second World War*, ed. John Gooch, Frank Cass, 1990, pp. 84–101, and Brian Sullivan, 'The Italian Soldier in Combat, June 1940–September 1943: Myths, Realities and Explanations', in *A Time to Kill*, ed. Paul Addison and Angus Calder, Pimlico, 1997, pp. 177–205.
9 Alan Moorehead, *African Trilogy – The North African Campaign 1940–43*, Cassell, 2000, p. 66.
10 Report by General Perino, 'Bericht des Verbindungstabes zur italienischen Luftwaffe, 4.11.40', IWM, Dept. of Docs., EDS AL 1061.
11 Knox, *Hitler's Italian Allies*, pp. 116–8.
12 For an excellent short account of the career of this outstanding British soldier see Barrie Pitt, 'O'Connor' in *Churchill's Generals*, edited by John Keegan, Weidenfeld and Nicolson, 1991, pp. 183–99.
13 See the comments of Colonel Norman Berry, who was the Chief Mechanical Engineer of XIII Corps from 1941–42 in Philip Warner, *Alamein*, William Kimber, 1979, pp. 178–80.
14 They were still marked enough to affect those who had to go to war in British tanks, and many were the result of neglect and incompetence. One ex-tankman, Peter Beale, has given a carefully researched but nonetheless bitter account of this sorry tale in *Death by Design*, Sutton, 1998. The title says it all.
15 Ben Shephard, *A War of Nerves*, Jonathan Cape, 2000, p. 248.
16 David French, *Raising Churchill's Army*, OUP, 2000, pp. 83–4.
17 For the technical details of these weapons see Charles Messenger, *The Unknown Alamein*, Ian Allen, 1982, pp. 28–31.
18 See Michael Handel, 'Intelligence and Military Operations' in Handel (ed.), *Intelligence and Military Operations*, Frank Cass, 1990, pp. 64–5.
19 French, op. cit., p. 96. The British also had a 3-inch AA gun. Colonel Berry, Chief Mechanical Engineer of XIII Corps and the Eighth Army recalls that it was a very effective anti-tank gun. He inspected one in use in the desert. It was fitted to a Russian gun carriage, for Britain had exported a number to Russia. However, it was being used by the Germans, along with other pieces of captured equipment. He adds that when the air defences around London replaced its 3-inch guns with 4.7-inch guns in 1941, several hundred were redundant and could, in his view, have changed the course of the fighting in the desert. See Philip Warner, *Alamein*, William Kimber, 1979, pp. 180–181.
20 Ibid., p. 166.
21 The development of these ideas into practice against indifference and some opposition within the German Army is told by Heinz Guderian himself in *Panzer Leader*, Michael Joseph, 1974, pp. 18–46.
22 See French, op. cit., pp. 17–59.
23 Hans-Otto Behrendt *Rommel's Intelligence in the Desert Campaign*, William Kimber, 1985, pp. 47–8 and 141–2.
24 Moorehead, op. cit., pp. 240–1.
25 For examples of both armies'

behaviour see Max Hastings, *Overlord*, Pan, 1985, pp. 167–80 and 217–8 and Carlo D'Este's *Decision in Normandy*, Pan, 1984, pp. 279–82, 295–7 and 374–5. The impact German officers could have on a battle by employing small numbers of superior weapons at the critical place and time is graphically illustrated by the story of how Oberst Hans von Luck of the Panzer Grenadier Regiment of 21st Panzer Division held up the main thrust of the 'Goodwood' offensive by commandeering four 88s of an AA unit of the 16th Luftwaffe Division. See D'Este, pp. 374–5.

26 Forrest's Tennessee accent camouflaged his vowels from non-Tennessee speakers so effectively that there is some doubt as to whether he said 'firstest' or 'fastest'. Accordingly, it is sometimes reported as 'furstest', which is probably closest to what he actually uttered. Whatever he said, what he meant is clear enough.

27 Examples of how Churchill was mislead by messages from Rommel which exaggerated his own weakness in order to extract supplies and reinforcements from OKH and Rome are given by Thomas Scheben in 'The German Perspective of War in North Africa 1940–42' in *Al-Alamein Revisited*, ed. Jill Edwards, The American University in Cairo Press, 2001, pp. 61–2.

28 See Janusz Piekalkiewicz, *Rommel and the Secret War in North Africa 1941–43*, Schiffer, 1992, p. 46.

29 Philip Warner, *Auchinleck – The Lonely Soldier*, Cassell, 2001 pp. 117–8.

30 Behrendt, op. cit., pp. 145–7 and 166–7.

31 Piekalkiewicz, op. cit., p. 52.

32 Keith Douglas, *Alamein to Zem Zem*, ed. Desmond Graham, Faber and Faber, 1992, pp. 108–112.

33 Moorehead, op. cit., p. 9.

34 For an account of all this, see the ground-breaking study by John Ferris, 'The British Army, Signals and Security in the Desert Campaign, 1940–42' in Handel, op. cit., pp. 255–291.

35 Conceived by Scharnhorst during the soul-searching after the Prussian Army's shattering defeat at Jena in 1806, the principles of mission command were steadily developed and refined right through to their articulation in the Wehrmacht's Field Service Regulations, a document called 'Truppenführung', of 1933. When unleashed on the French in 1870 and then on the Russians at Tannenberg in 1914, the effects of the doctrine were like a secret weapon. Because it is a doctrine and therefore invisible, and also because it was completely at odds with widespread metaphysical prejudices about 'the rigid German mind' it remained secret for a long time. It finally became embodied in the official doctrine of NATO at the end of the Cold War in the late 1980s. See Dirk Oetting's superb *Auftragstaktik – Geschichte und Gegenwart einer Führungskonzeption*, Report Verlag, 1993.

36 Warner, op. cit., p. 39.

37 Quoted in Desmond Young, *Rommel*, Collins, 1950, p. 23.

38 Young, op. cit., pp. 152–4.

39 ' ... der Mittelmeer-Kriegsschauplatz sein Gesetz vom Meere her empfing.' Walter Warlimont, 'Die Entscheidung im Mittelmeer 1942', in Jacobsen and Rohwer, *Entscheidungsschlachten des zweiten Weltkrieges*, Bernard and Graefe, 1960, p. 234.

Chapter III: The Supply War

1 John Erickson, *The Road to Berlin*, Weidenfeld and Nicolson, 1983, p. 622.

2 Colonel Trevor Dupuy, *A Genius for War*, Macdonald and Janes, 1977, pp. 253–4. Dupuy bases his claims on an

analysis of data from actual engagements in North Africa, Italy and north west Europe. This analysis has predictably been challenged, in particular its methodology, but the broad conclusions are generally accepted. See David French, *Raising Churchill's Army*, OUP, 2000, pp. 8–10.

3   What more there is to it is admirably expounded and analysed by Richard Overy in *Why the Allies Won*, Pimlico, 1995.

4   Erich von Manstein, *Verlorene Siege*, Athenäum Verlag, 1955.

5   Knox, *Hitler's Italian Allies*, p. 127.

6   Churchill, *Their Finest Hour*, pp. 533–5. In a letter to the Secretary of State for War about army organization, he pointed out that the BEF in France and the army in the Middle East had 27 divisions, each of 15,500 men. Of those 15,500, only about 6,750 were 'rifle strength' or fighting infantry. Within the divisions, therefore, 182,250 riflemen were supported by another 236,250 others, a total of 418,500 men. The actual manpower of the Army, however, was 1,015,000. In other words, a further 596,500 men were needed to support the divisions. 82% of the Army's manpower was supporting the 18% who did most of the fighting. Churchill's letter ends with an admonition to 'comb out' the 'fluff and flummery'.

7   Oberquartiermeister Rom, Zehntagesmeldung 2.10.42, Anlage 150, IWM Dept of Docs., EDS AL 1041.

8   Knox, *Hitler's Italian Allies*, pp. 96–99.

9   Panzerarmee Afrika 1a, 'Gefechtsstärke der deutschen Verbände, Stand 1.8.42.', Anlage 87, IWM Dept of Docs., EDS AL 1041.

10 See French, op. cit., pp. 110–118.

11 The issues facing the Axis powers in the supply war are laid out by Martin van Crefeld in *Supplying War*, CUP, 1977, pp. 182–201.

12 Hitler's Directive 18, covering Operation Felix, was issued on 12 November 1940. Two subsequent draft directives dealt with the operation in more detail, but on 11 December, Hitler issued Directive 19a, which cancelled Felix as 'the political pre-conditions' were no longer fulfilled, i.e. Franco had dug his heels in. See Walther Hubatsch, *Hitlers Weisungen für die Kriegführung 1939–1945*, Bernard and Graefe, 1983, pp. 67–78. Felix was due to be resurrected after the destruction of the Soviet Union, as detailed in Directive 32 which deals with 'Preparations for the Period after Barbarossa' (ibid., p. 132). Directive 32 was issued on 11 June 1941, eleven days before Barbarossa was launched. As the Soviet Union remained intact until 1990, these considerations were a little academic.

13 Churchill, *The Grand Alliance*, p.6.

14 Ernle Bradford, *Siege: Malta 1940–43*, Penguin, 1987, pp. 6–11.

15 Knox, *Mussolini Unleashed*, p. 20.

16 Gordon W. Prange, *At Dawn We Slept*, Michael Joseph, 1982, p. 320.

17 Ronald Lewin, *Ultra Goes to War*, Hutchinson, 1978, pp. 196–9.

18 Christopher Shores and Brian Cull with Nicola Malizia, *Malta: The Hurricane Years, 1940–41*, Grub Street, 1987, pp. xi and 7.

19 Bradford, op. cit., p. 27.

20 Shores and Cull, *The Hurricane Years*, pp. 1–4.

21 Ibid., p. 10.

22 Ibid., pp. 11–25.

23 PRO AIR 23/1193. An enquiry concluded that the margin of safety was 'unreasonably small, reducing the enterprise to a most hazardous undertaking'.

24 Shores and Cull, *The Hurricane Years*, pp. 47–51, 76–80 and 86–88.

25 Ibid., pp. 101 and 369–73. The legend has had some distinguished

propagators. See Churchill, *Their Finest Hour*, p. 346.

26 See John Terraine, *The Right of the Line*, Sceptre, 1988, pp. 305–6. Between September 1940 and October 1943, some 5,000 aircraft were delivered to the Middle East in this way.

27 PRO AIR 23/1200.

28 Hitler, Weisung Nr. 22, 2.), 11 January 1941, in Hubatsch, op. cit., p. 93.

29 Hitler, Weisung Nr. 29, 2.), 17 May 1941, in Hubatsch, op. cit., p. 118.

30 Bradford, op. cit., pp. 91–96.

31 See the essay by Ralph Bennett, who was a senior intelligence officer at Bletchley Park during the war, called 'Intelligence and Strategy: Some Observations on the War in the Mediterranean 1941–45' in Handel, *Intelligence and Military Operations*, p. 447.

32 Hitler, Weisung Nr. 38, 2 December 1941, in Hubatsch, op. cit., pp.169–70. The term Hitler uses in referring to Malta – 'Niederhaltung' – suggests constraining its ability to be a problem rather than eliminating it from the picture entirely.

33 See Stephen Bungay, *The Most Dangerous Enemy*, Aurum Press, 2000.

34 *The Memoirs of Field-Marshal Kesselring*, ed. Kenneth Macksey, Greenhill 1988, p. 104.

35 Ibid., p. 109.

36 See E.R. Hooton, *Eagle in Flames – The Fall of the Luftwaffe*, Arms and Armour Press, London 1997, p. 212.

37 On the problems facing the attackers see Bradford, op. cit., p. 53.

38 Knox, *Hitler's Italian Allies*, p. 139.

39 PRO AIR 23/1200.

40 Ibid.

41 Bradford, op. cit., p. 162.

42 An account of the defence of Malta from the British perspective is given by Denis Richards and Hilary St George Saunders in their official history, *Royal Air Force 1939–45*, Volume II – *The Fight Avails*, HMSO, 1954, pp. 190–216.

43 David Irving, *Hitler's War*, Avon Books, 1990, pp. 469–70.

44 Quoted by Warlimont, op. cit., p. 243.

45 IWM Dept. of Docs., EDS AL 2596, 26.6.42.

46 On the Axis decision-making process see Warlimont, op. cit., pp. 233–248. Particular insights into Kesselring's point of view, which was almost certainly correct, can be found in his own memoirs, pp. 119–136, and Kenneth Macksey, *Kesselring – The Making of the Luftwaffe*, Batsford, 1978, pp. 104–125.

47 Vincent Orange, *Sir Keith Park*, Methuen, 1984, p. 164

48 See Noble Frankland's account of a post-war interview with him in *History at War*, Giles de la Mare, 1998, p. 84.

49 For an assessment of Park's qualifications and his achievements in the Battle of Britain see Bungay, *The Most Dangerous Enemy*, pp. 130–2 and 381–3.

50 See E. R. Hooton, op. cit., pp. 210–3.

51 Unpublished letter from Park to Derek Dempster, 18 May 1960, which is part of the brief correspondence he conducted with Park during the preparation of the classic account of the Battle of Britain, *The Narrow Margin*, which he published, together with Derek Wood, in 1961. I am particularly grateful to Derek Dempster for making this document available to me.

52 For a full account of this, and the virtues of each method in practice, see Bungay, *The Most Dangerous Enemy*, passim, but especially pp. 133–6, 309–14, 328–334, 354–363 and 381–2.

53 Park's instructions, 25 July and 18 August 1942, PRO AIR 23/1201.

54 Christopher Shores and Brian Cull with Nicola Malizia, *Malta: The Spitfire Year, 1942*, Grub Street, 1991,

p. 446.

55   Hooton, op. cit., p. 213.

56   Ibid., p. 211.

57   PRO AIR 23/1201.

58   Tony Spooner, *Supreme Gallantry*, John Murray, 1996, pp. 180–2.

59   A detailed account of the 'Pedestal' drama can be found in *Malta: The Spitfire Year, 1942*, pp. 448–516.

60   Bennett, op. cit., pp. 448–9.

61   F. W. Winterbotham, *The Ultra Secret*, Weidenfeld and Nicolson, 1974, p. 80.

62   See table in Warlimont, op. cit., pp. 236–7 and p. 247.

63   See IWM Dept. of Docs., EDS AL 1041/5, Anlagen 86, 123 and 150.

64   PRO AIR 23/1201.

65   Playfair, *The Mediterranean and Middle East* Vol. III, HMSO, 1960, p. 325.

66   PRO AIR 23/1202.

67   Warlimont op. cit., p. 251.

68   Hooton, op. cit., p. 213.

69   Compare the figures given by Williamson Murray in *Luftwaffe – Strategy for Defeat*, Allen and Unwin, 1985, p. 165.

70   For what is known, see Hooton, op. cit., p. 213, Shores etc., *Malta – The Hurricane Years*, pp. 362–3 and *Malta – The Spitfire Year*, p. 646.

71   Figures from Shores etc., *Malta – The Hurricane Years*, p. 388 and *Malta – The Spitfire Year*, pp. 674–5.

72   Derived from Warlimont, op. cit, Tabelle 2, pp. 236–7.

73   Van Crefeld, *Supplying War*, p. 198.

Chapter IV: The Soldiers' War

1   Behrendt, op. cit., pp. 44–5.

2   Interning the Italians caused much distress and inconvenience in Cairo, as most of the young men were mechanics and klectricians. See Artemis Cooper, *Cairo in the War1939-1945*, Penguin 1995, p. 47.

3   Caccia-Dominioni, op. cit., pp. 25 and 27.

4   See Adrian Gilbert, *The Imperial War Museum Book of the Desert War*, pp. 40–41 and Barnett, op. cit., p. 230.

5   There is a photograph of him with it in Irving, op. cit., between pp. 86 and 87.

6   Robin Neillands, *The Desert Rats*, Weidenfeld and Nicolson, 1991, p. 37.

7   See John Ellis, *The Sharp End*, Pimlico, 1993, pp. 28–9 and 357.

8   Ellis, op. cit., pp. 285–7.

9   Rolf Valentin, *Ärzte im Wüstenkrieg*, Bernard and Graefe, 1984, pp. 33–4.

10   Heinz Werner Schmidt, *With Rommel in the Desert*, Constable, 1997, p. 150.

11   On living habits in the desert see Adrian Gilbert, op. cit., pp. 35–40 and Charles Whiting, *The Poor Bloody Infantry 1939–45*, Book Club Associates, 1987, pp. 86–90, and Knox, *Hitler's Italian Allies*, p. 155.

12   Gilbert, op. cit., p. 37.

13   In the American Civil War, the Union Army lost 7.2% of its men to disease, in World War I the US Army lost 1.3% and in World War II this had declined further to 0.6%. See Ellis, op. cit., p. 182.

14   Ellis, op. cit., p. 188.

15   See Ellis, op.cit., pp. 180–2, and Valentin, op. cit., pp. 54–61 and 134.

16   Valentin, op. cit., p. 47.

17   Whiting, op. cit., pp. 89–90.

18   See Ellis, op. cit., pp. 305–8.

19   Cooper, op. cit. p. 116.

20   Moorehead, op. cit., p. 101.

21   Gilbert, op. cit., pp. 67–77 and Knox, *Hitler's Italian Allies*, p. 56.

22   Cooper, op. cit., p. 37.

23   Moorehead, op. cit., p. 199.

24   See Ellis, op. cit., pp. 27–8 and 325–6.

25   See the article by Derek Jewell in *Alamein and the Desert War*, Sphere Books, 1967, pp. 147–154.

26   Valentin, op. cit., p. 158.

27   See Ellis, op. cit., p. 177.

28   Ben Shephard, *A War of Nerves*, Jonathan Cape, 2000, p. 33.

29   See Ellis, op. cit., pp. 68–71 and 177.

30   Shephard, op. cit., p. 184.

31 Shephard, op. cit., pp. 185–6.

32 Douglas, *Alamein to Zem Zem*, p. 49.

33 Harrison, op. cit., p. 85.

34 See Ellis, op. cit., pp. 125–154.

35 See Ellis, op. cit., pp. 118–25 and 165.

36 James Lucas, *War in the Desert*, Arms and Armour Press, 1982, p. 74.

37 Caccia-Dominioni, op. cit., p. 136.

38 See Ellis, op. cit., pp. 169–73.

39 See Gilbert, op. cit., pp. 43–51.

40 See Ellis, op. cit., pp. 103–4.

41 Ellis, op. cit., pp. 243–4.

42 See Hew Strachan, 'The Soldier's Experience in Two World Wars: Some Historiographical Comparisons', in *Time to Kill*, ed. Addison and Calder, Pimlico, 1997, p. 375.

43 Lucas, op. cit., p. 59.

44 Whiting, op. cit., p. 90.

45 Hamilton, *Monty – Master of the Battlefield*, p. 71.

46 Field-Marshal Montgomery, *The Path to Leadership*, Collins, 1961, pp. 27 and 51.

47 Valentin, op. cit., p. 44.

48 Captain Piero Santini, quoted in Caccia-Dominioni, op. cit., p. 169.

49 Ibid., pp. 58 and 77.

50 The words are those of the Italian Foreign Minister, Mussolini's son-in-law, Count Ciano. See MacGregor Knox, *Mussolini Unleashed*, pp. 108–112 and 158.

51 See Knox, *Hitler's Italian Allies*, pp. 27–31.

52 Shephard, op. cit., p. 229.

53 Gavin Long, *To Benghazi*, Australia in the War of 1939–45, Series One, Army Vol. I, Canberra, 1952, p. 57.

54 Moorehead, op. cit., p. 393.

55 Cooper, op. cit., p. 45-6.

56 Moorehead, p. 576.

57 With a population of only about 1.5 million in 1940, New Zealand raised an army of 138,000 men. There were only two infantry divisions, the 2nd, formed in 1939 and the 3rd, formed the following year. The 2nd was in constant action in Greece, Crete, North Africa and Italy, but the 3rd served only in the Pacific where it saw relatively little fighting.

58 See H. J. Martin and Neil Orpen, *South Africa at War*, South African Forces in World War II, Vol. VII, Purnell,1979, pp. 100 and 148.

59 See Gerard Douds, 'Matters of Honour: Indian Troops in the North African and Italian Theatres', in *Time to Kill*, ed. Addison and Calder, Pimlico, 1997, pp. 115–128.

60 Ellis, op. cit., p. 316. On the comparative lack of motivation in World War II see Paul Fussell, *Wartime*, OUP, 1989, pp. 129–143.

61 Shephard, op. cit., p. 233.

62 The underlying pleasure which could be derived from killing and the methods used to stimulate it are interestingly, if one-sidedly, examined by Joanna Bourke in *An Intimate History of Killing*, Granta Books, 1999.

63 See Ellis, op. cit., pp. 162 and 192–231.

64 Knox, *Hitler's Italian Allies*, p. 148.

65 See Gilbert, op. cit., pp. 129–139.

66 Ellis, op. cit., pp. 344 and 341.

67 '1st Army Soldier' by W. G. Holloway, quoted by Fussell, op. cit., p. 160.

68 Shephard, op. cit., p. 217.

Chapter V: Alamein – Round One

1 Moorehead, op. cit., p. 224.

2 Corelli Barnett, *The Desert Generals*, 2nd edition, Cassell, 1983, pp. 192–4. Auchinleck's words are taken from direct correspondence between himself and Corelli Barnett.

3 John Ellis, *The Sharp End*, p. 334.

4 In a letter to Attlee on 5 August. See *The Hinge of Fate*, p. 359. Ironically, these sentiments echo those of Scharnhorst after the catastrophic Prussian defeat at the hands of Napoleon at Jena/Auerstedt in 1806: 'Wir haben uns brav genug, aber nicht klug genug geschlagen' – 'We fought bravely enough, but not cleverly enough'. His reflections on this led

Scharnhorst to begin the long process through which the German army developed the doctrine of mission command.

5   As explained in a letter from one of the journalists, Norman Clark, to Philip Warner, June 1980, reproduced in Warner, op. cit., pp. 270–3. Clark surmises that Auchinleck deliberately kept Churchill in the dark about his intentions in order to avoid tactical interference. Indeed, after the fall of Tobruk, Churchill cabled Auchinleck to express the hope that 'earnest resistance' would be made at the frontier and that he was 'disconcerted' that further withdrawal 'may well put us back to where we were eighteen months ago and leave all the work of that period to be done over again'. (Martin Gilbert, *Road to Victory – Winston Churchill 1941–1945*, Heinemann, 1986, p. 130.)

6   Behrendt, op. cit., pp. 160–1.

7   IWM Dept. of Docs., EDS AL 2596, 4.7.42.

8   For accounts of this operation see Piekalkiewicz, op. cit., pp. 149–160 and Behrendt, op. cit., pp. 168–190. The unit was reactivated, but because of what the British learned from the captured documents and the improved signals security which resulted, it was never again as effective as it had been before 10 July.

9   IWM Dept. of Docs., EDS AL 2596, 11.7.42.

10 IWM Dept. of Docs., EDS AL 2596, 14.7.42.

11 Upham was such a difficult prisoner that he ended up in Colditz. He survived the war and died peacefully in November 1994.

12 IWM Dept. of Docs., EDS AL 2596, 18.7.42 and 2.8.42. For accounts of the First Battle of Alamein see Corelli Barnett, op. cit., pp. 195–230, Charles Messenger, *The Unknown Alamein*, passim, and from a German

viewpoint, von Mellenthin, *Panzer Battles*, Futura, 1977, pp. 163–70.

13 See Barnett op. cit., pp. 206 and 225.

14 The man who was then Auchinleck's Director of Military Intelligence and was shortly to become Montgomery's Chief of Staff, Freddie de Guingand, thought the whole of First Alamein was a mistake, and that forces should have been conserved for a future offensive. In his view, Auchinleck's battle consisted of 'one or two unsuccessful counterattacks'. See *Operation Victory*, Hodder and Stoughton, 1947, pp. 125 and 131. He passed these views on to others, including Montgomery himself.

15 John Terraine, *The Right of the Line*, Sceptre, 1988, pp. 309–318.

16 The Americans called them Warhawks and the British designated them Tomahawks. Later, improved versions of the P-40 were known in the RAF as Kittyhawks.

17 See Christopher Shores and Hans Ring, *Fighters over the Desert*, Neville Spearman, 1969, p. 217.

18 Werner Schroer quoted in Shores and Ring, op. cit., p. 231.

19 Park, unpublished letter to Derek Dempster, 18 May 1960.

20 PRO AIR 16/623.

21 See Bungay, op. cit., pp. 362–3. In the Far East, where things were truly desperate in the air, a few Spitfires could have made all the difference.

22 David Fraser, *Knight's Cross – A Life of Field Marshal Erwin Rommel*, Harper Collins, 1993, p. 330.

23 IWM Dept. of Docs., EDS AL 2596, 23.5.42.

24 601 flew in from Malta, using long-range ferry tanks, on 23 June. The personnel of 92 Squadron had arrived in the desert in April, but it took until the end of July to get them some Spitfires. A freighter carrying 42 of them to Australia was redirected to Takoradi where they were uncrated,

assembled and flown across Africa to Egypt. See Alfred Price, *Spitfire Mark V Aces 1941–45*, Osprey, 1997, pp. 55 and 62–3.

25 The memo is reproduced by Churchill in *The Hinge of Fate*, p. 684.

26 Richards and Saunders, op. cit., p. 255.

27 Ibid., p. 211.

28 For a summary of the RAF's role in the desert war see John Terraine, *The Right of the Line*, Sceptre, 1988, pp. 301–389 and for the Luftwaffe's role, Hooton, *Eagle in Flames*, pp. 77–91 and 210–218. Aircraft losses during First Alamein are from Messenger, op. cit., p. 61.

29 Richards and Saunders, op. cit., p. 219.

30 Ben Shephard, *A War of Nerves*, Jonathan Cape, 2000, p. 196.

31 Disbanded at the end of the war, the regiment was re-formed in 1950 and has now become the stuff of novels, docu-dramas and tabloid hero-worship. Data is taken from Steve Crawford, *The SAS Encyclopaedia*, Simon and Schuster, 1996.

32 Major-General Sir Howard Kippenberger, *Infantry Brigadier*, OUP, 1949, p. 180.

33 R.W. Thompson, *Generalissimo Churchill*, Hodder and Stoughton, 1973, pp. 206–7.

34 The document is reproduced by Barnett, op. cit., pp. 331–7.

35 Cooper, op. cit., p. 199.

36 Barnett, op. cit., pp. 227–30.

37 Description based on eye-witness account by Lord Tedder in *With Prejudice*, Cassell, 1966, pp. 318–9.

Chapter VI: The Political War

1 Churchill, *The Second World War, Vol. III, The Grand Alliance*, p. 474.

2 David Irving, *Hitler's War*, pp. 440–1.

3 Churchill, *The Second World War Vol. IV, The Hinge of Fate*, pp. 85–104.

4 The correspondence is reproduced in Churchill, *The Hinge of Fate*, pp. 3–15 and 120–8.

5 Churchill, *The Hinge of Fate*, pp. 291–300.

6 John Charmley, *Churchill – The End of Glory*, Hodder and Stoughton, 1993, p. 500.

7 Churchill, *The Hinge of Fate*, p. 303.

8 Gilbert op. cit., pp. 30–32, 55, 62–3, 71–2, 80–1, and *Finest Hour*, Minerva, 1989, p. 1273.

9 See the accounts by Churchill, *The Hinge of Fate*, pp. 304–317 and Charmley, op. cit., pp. 500–503.

10 Brian McKinlay, *Australia 1942 – End of Innocence*, Collins, 1985, pp. 68–9.

11 Diary of Lord Alanbrooke quoted by Arthur Bryant in *The Turn of the Tide, 1939–43*, Collins, 1957, p. 330.

12 Churchill's view exactly paralleled Abraham Lincoln's during the early years of the American Civil War, though Lincoln had far more justification for it. It is curious to note that in his *History of the English-Speaking Peoples*, in contrast with most historians, Churchill defends the Union generals, particularly McClennan, and criticizes Lincoln, writing that his appointments were 'too often made on political grounds' and that he was too ready 'to yield to the popular clamour which demanded the recall of an unsuccessful general'. Those he retained, Churchill opines, were often too nervous to fight their best 'fearing the President in the rear more than the foe in front,' and he saw Lincoln's dismissal of McClennan as a stab in the back. See *A History of the English-Speaking Peoples, Vol. IV, The Great Democracies*, Chartwell Edition, 1958, pp. 151 and 187. It is odd that Churchill should thus distance himself from a great historical parallel for his own behaviour.

13 Ibid., pp. 338–9, 380–3 and 419–20.

14 Gilbert, op. cit., p. 255.

15 Gilbert, op. cit., pp. 140–1.

16 Ibid., pp. 410n and 431–4.

17 See Barnett, op. cit., pp. 180–1 and Churchill, *The Hinge of Fate*, pp. 301–3.

18 See Lord Tedder, *With Prejudice*, Cassell, 1966, pp. 240–1.

19 See Barnett, op. cit., pp. 158–162 and Churchill, *The Hinge of Fate*, pp. 225–9 and 286–8.

20 PRO WO 106/2234, Report of Court of Enquiry Vol. I, Part II, p. 23.

21 Ibid., Vol. I, pp. 2–6.

22 Reproduced in Churchill, *The Hinge of Fate*, pp. 307–8.

23 See, for example, the remarks quoted by Nigel Hamilton in *Monty – The Making of a General 1887–1942*, Hamlyn, 1982, pp. 571–2 and 577–8.

24 Hamilton, op. cit., p. 577.

25 Brooke had written to Montgomery at the time, warning him against 'doing wild things'. See Hamilton, op. cit., p. 433. Auchinleck's view of these clashes is given in Warner, op. cit., pp. 63–7.

26 See Churchill, *Their Finest Hour*, pp. 203–4 and *The Memoirs of Field Marshal Montgomery*, Collins, 1958, pp. 69–70.

27 Churchill, *The Hinge of Fate*, p. 358.

28 Hamilton, op. cit., p. 573.

29 Ibid., p. 572.

30 Churchill, *The Hinge of Fate*, p. 359–60.

31 This account was given by the pilot concerned, Sgt Pilot H. G. James, in an interview with Nigel Hamilton on 3 November 1980. Though wounded, James trekked across the desert to get help and led a rescue party back. He was awarded the DFC. See Hamilton, op. cit., pp. 580–1.

32 Bryant, op. cit., p. 449.

33 Gilbert, op. cit., p. 168.

34 Accounts of the visit to the desert and changes in command can be found in Barnett, op. cit., pp. 231–241, Hamilton, op. cit., pp. 569–585, Churchill, *The Hinge of Fate*, pp. 353–67, Bryant, op. cit., pp. 431–53 and Tedder, op. cit., pp. 318–27.

35 Hamilton, op. cit., p. 561.

36 Churchill, *The Hinge of Fate*, p. 298.

37 Bryant, op. cit., pp. 342–3.

38 On the relationship between the two men and Montgomery's contempt for Auchinleck, see Hamilton, op. cit., pp. 398–9, 421–2, 425–9. Montgomery appears to have been the only man in the whole of the British Army to feel anything other than respect and deep personal regard for Auchinleck.

39 Hamilton, op. cit., pp. 586–7 and 596.

40 De Guingand, *Operation Victory*, p. 135.

41 Ibid., pp. 599 and 602–5.

42 The text is reproduced by Hamilton, op. cit., pp. 622–5. It is in the PRO under CAB 106/703.

43 See Hamilton, pp. 409 and 489–90.

44 Hamilton details them. See op.cit., pp. 592 and 614–5.

45 As, for example, Tedder who 'never heard a whisper of any intention after Auchinleck took over the Army on 25 June to retire eastwards; still less did I meet, or hear of, the many who were supposed to be looking over their shoulders to make sure of their seat in the lorry'. (op.cit., p. 327). Sir Brian Horrocks, who arrived on the 15th to command XIII Corps, and was a loyal lieutenant of Montgomery for the rest of the war, could make nothing of it either, despite having been 'at considerable pains to ferret out the truth'. See Horrocks, *A Full Life*, Collins, 1960, pp. 109–114. Montgomery claimed in his memoirs that Auchinleck told him in his briefing that the plan was to retreat to the Delta if Rommel attacked in strength (p. 94). It may have been what he understood. Given all the evidence, it would have strange if it had been what Auchinleck meant. Alexander claims that it was *his* idea to 'lay down the firm principle ... that no further withdrawal was contemplated'. Montgomery, he

wrote, 'concurred with this' and communicated it to the Eighth Army Staff that evening. See *The Memoirs of Field-Marshal Earl Alexander of Tunis*, ed. John North, Cassell, 1962, pp. 18–19. This reversal of roles between himself and Montgomery, with him producing the idea, would have been unique and is clearly contradicted by the recollections of John Harding, as recounted in Hamilton, op. cit., p. 590.

46 De Guingand, op. cit., p. 136.

47 There is one echo of Shakespeare, when he invites doubters to 'go at once'. The same sentiments are expressed by Henry V before Agincourt in a speech used by Churchill in 1940 and filmed by Olivier in 1944 to inspire the troops leaving for Normandy:

> 'He which hath no stomach to this fight,
> Let him depart ...
> We would not die in that man's company
> That fears his fellowship to die with us.'

Montgomery knew the play well. He pinned the line 'O God of battles! Steel my soldiers' hearts' from Act IV Scene 1 to his caravan wall. See *The Memoirs of Field Marshal Montgomery*, p. 115. At school, English had been Montgomery's weakest subject, his essay writing being particularly poor. He gradually improved until he was able to claim in 1958: 'Today I should say that my English is at least clear; people may not agree with what I say but at least they know what I am saying. I may be wrong; but I claim that I am clear.' (ibid., p. 20).

48 Hamilton, pp. 637–9.

49 Ibid., p. 653.

50 Montgomery, *Memoirs*, p. 85.

51 Horrocks, op. cit., pp.107–9.

52 David Fletcher, *The Universal Tank*, HMSO, 1993, p. 12.

53 For a range of informed and consistently damning views of Alexander, see Hamilton, op. cit., pp. 453–4, 492–5, 583–4, 590, 642 and 765–6. A more generous portrait is provided by Brian Holden Reid in *Churchill's Generals*, ed. Keegan, pp. 104–129.

54 Horrocks, op. cit., pp. 115–8 and 120–1 and de Guingand, op.cit., pp.146–8. In his account de Guingand reproduces the correct and false going maps. Rommel's real reasons for taking the route he did are explained by Behrendt, op. cit., pp. 191–2.

55 Bryant, op. cit., pp. 475–6.

56 Ibid., p. 479.

57 Churchill, *The Hinge of Fate*, pp. 399–401. So, presumably, did Alexander, despite his claim in his memoirs that he regarded the Delta as 'indefensible', and all preparations for its defence 'a misdirected effort' (op. cit., p.19). Perhaps he was not listening.

58 To this day, the background to the fiasco and Montgomery's precise role in it remains unclear, for Combined Operations kept no war diary. What is clear that Dieppe was an act of folly and that Mountbatten tried, fairly successfully at the time, to wriggle out of responsibility for its failure. See Hamilton, op. cit., pp. 546–558, and Andrew Roberts, *Eminent Churchillians*, Phoenix, 1994, pp. 64–9. Montgomery gives his own account of the tragedy in his *Memoirs*, pp. 75–7.

59 Horrocks, op. cit., pp. 118–9. Hamilton quotes an account in which Horrocks attributes the origins of this phrase to Montgomery (op. cit., p. 643).

60 Bryant, op. cit., p. 480.

61 Churchill, *The Hinge of Fate*, pp. 405–6.

62 Bryant, op. cit., p. 484.

Chapter VII: Alamein – Round Two

1   Carver, *El Alamein*, pp. 47–8.
2   Macksey, op. cit., pp. 123–4.
3   IWM Dept. of Docs., EDS AL 2596, 27.8.42.
4   IWM Dept. of Docs., EDS AL 2596, 30.8.42.
5   Hamilton, op. cit., p. 667.
6   Ibid., p. 682.
7   His technique is explained by Mike Spick in *Luftwaffe Fighter Aces*, Greenhill Books, 1996, pp. 134–140. His career is admiringly recounted by Cajus Bekker in *Angriffshöhe 4000*, Gerhard Stalling Verlag, 1964, pp. 314–325. The tone of most accounts is hagiographic, and the main concern, as with most fighter aces, is to establish who was the greatest of them all. Typical is *Jagdgeschwader 27* by Hans Ring and Werner Girbig, Motorbuch, 1971, which describes 1 September 1942 as 'the most glorious day in the history of JG27' and is very indignant that some post-war commentators questioned whether Marseille actually did shoot down 17 all by himself (p. 210). All ignore the fact that on its most glorious day, JG27 failed completely to protect the Afrika Korps from the bombers which were crippling it and that Marseille's feat had no military impact whatsoever.
8   See Shores and Ring, op. cit., pp. 168–70.
9   See Shores and Ring, op. cit., pp. 222 and 228.
10   Hamilton, op. cit., pp. 692–3.
11   See Macksey, op. cit., p. 124 and the explanation offered by Nehring, *Feldzug in Nord-Afrika, Teil IV*, p. 264, IWM dept. of Docs., EDS AL 766/3/2.
12   Hamilton, op.cit., pp. 701–6.
13   Accounts can be found in Carver, *El Alamein*, pp. 52–74, Horrocks, op. cit., pp. 122–6, Liddell Hart, op. cit., pp. 291–7 and von Mellenthin, op. cit.,

pp. 170–7. On the various names given to the action see Paolo Caccia-Dominioni, *Alamein 1933–1963 – An Italian Story*, Allen and Unwin, 1966, p. 156.
14   See Richards and St. G. Saunders, op. cit., pp. 229–231.
15   Nigel Hamilton, *Monty – Master of the Battlefield 1942–44*, Hamish Hamilton, 1983, p. 202. Montgomery was to conflict much more seriously with Tedder as well, but not until later.
16   As noted by Horrocks, op. cit., p. 125.
17   Field Marshal The Viscount Montgomery of Alamein, *El Alamein to the River Sangro*, Hutchinson, 1946, p. 8.
18   Horrocks, op. cit., p. 126.
19   They are given by Hamilton, *Monty – The Making of a General*, pp. 712–3.
20   Sir William Mather, quoted by Hamilton, op. cit., pp. 729–30.
21   Douglas, *Alamein to Zem Zem*, pp. 94–5.
22   Hamilton, op. cit., pp. 764–5.
23   David Fletcher, *The Great Tank Scandal*, HMSO, 1989, pp. 90 and107.
24   Ferris, op. cit., pp. 285–6.
25   *Notes on the Maintenance of the Eighth Army and the Supporting Royal Air Force by Land, Sea and Air from El Alamein to Tunisia*, 'Q' Staff, GHQ, MEF, 1943. IWM Dept. of Books. On 1 August, German forces in Africa had 4,117 vehicles against an establishment of 5,603. 85% of them were captured. See report from Panzerarmee Ia to Rome, Anlage 87, IWM Dept. of Docs., EDS AL 1041/5.
26   Extracts are given by Hamilton, op. cit., pp. 718–728.
27   Montgomery, *Memoirs*, p. 71.
28   Horrocks, op. cit., pp. 98–9.
29   Spike Milligan, *Adolf Hitler – My Part in his Downfall*, Penguin, 1972, pp. 65–7.
30   See Hamilton, p. 645.
31   See Hamilton, op. cit., pp. 339–44 and 487.

32 The text of the plan is reproduced in Hamilton, op. cit., pp. 732–41.

33 On this and other preparations for Alamein, see Carver, *El Alamein*, pp. 75–94.

34 Hamilton, op. cit., pp. 748 and 752.

35 See Hamilton, op. cit., pp. 755–64.

36 See Carver, *El Alamein*, pp. 79–82 and Barrie Pitt, *The Crucible of War 3 – Montgomery and Alamein*, Macmillan, 1986, pp. 34–60.

37 The report on the circumstances of Marseille's death filed by his commanding officer is reproduced in translation by Shores and Ring, op. cit., pp. 252–3.

38 Details of JG27's losses in September are taken from tables in the appendices of Ring and Girbig, *Jagdgeschwader 27*, Motorbuch, 1971. The circumstances of the losses are based on the account of the daily actions given by Shores and Ring, op. cit., pp. 168–182.

39 See Richards and St. G. Saunders, op. cit., pp. 232–4, Terraine, op. cit., pp. 383–5 and Tedder, op. cit., pp. 356–7. A greatly extended version of this use of air power came to fruition in the Gulf War of 1991.

40 Hamilton, op. cit., p. 744 and de Guingand, *Operation Victory*, p. 158.

41 Bryant, op. cit., pp. 504–5 and Churchill, *The Hinge of Fate*, p. 456.

42 Bryant, op. cit., pp. 506–510.

43 On German preparations, see Carver, *El Alamein*, pp. 95–9.

44 Rolf Valentin, *Ärzte im Wüstenkrieg*, Bernard and Graefe, 1984, p. 122.

45 'Erinnerungsprotokoll über den Empfang beim Duce in Rocca della Caminata um 11 Uhr', IWM, Dept of Docs., EDS, AL 1349/2.

46 Irving, op. cit., p. 198. Irving suggests that the film includes a shot of Rommel with his hand on the door handle. The film archive expert and historian James Barker, who has examined the newsreel, has pointed out in a conversation with the author that it does not.

47 Figures from George Forty, *The Armies of Rommel*, Arms and Armour Press, 1997, pp. 153–8 and Playfair, *History of the Second World War, The Mediterranean and Middle East Vol. IV*, HMSO, 1966, pp. 9–10 and 30. 'Battle tanks' exclude Panzer Is and IIs on the German side and the 119 Stuarts on the British side.

48 Paolo Caccia-Dominioni, *Alamein 1933–1963 – An Italian Story*, Allen and Unwin, 1966, pp. 208–210.

Chapter VIII: Alamein – Round Three

1 Keith Douglas, *The Letters*, ed. Desmond Graham, Carcanet, 2000, pp. 245–6.

2 Bryant, op. cit., p. 510.

3 The barrage fast became the stuff of legend. Churchill wrote that it was made up of 'nearly a thousand guns' (*The Hinge of Fate*, p. 458). Not to be outdone, Montgomery wrote that 'over a thousand field and medium guns were employed' (*El Alamein to the River Sangro*, p. 16). His biographer more soberly refers to 'over eight hundred guns' (*Monty – The Making of a General*, p. 774). More exact sources give different figures. The person who should have known how many guns there actually were was Kirkman. In a report written on 24 November 1942, he stated that X Corps and XXX Corps between them used 408 25-pounders and 48 medium guns on the first night, a total of 456. He also gives the number of 25-pounders available to XIII Corps as 288, but does not say how many were used. He does not mention whether or not XIII Corps had medium guns as well. Assuming all of XIII Corps' 25-pounders were used, then at its height the barrage was delivered by 744 guns. It would seem from Kirkman's figures

that not all of X and XXX Corps guns were used in the barrage, as they had a total of 546 25-pounders available (See PRO WO 201/431). The total number of field and medium guns in the Eighth Army was 882, a number sometimes quite understandably given as having taken part in the barrage, though if we believe Kirkman, it must be too high. Playfair, probably using Kirkman as his source, gives the same figure of 456 as the number used in the north, but only 136 as actually used in the south (op. cit., p. 36). It is indeed is quite possible that XIII Corps kept some of its guns in reserve, in which case the grand total used was not 744 but 592. Rounding either number up to 1,000 is applying to data the sort of licence sometimes granted to poetry. The barrage was by no means the largest since World War I, and had nothing like the concentration of those used by Haig in its later stages. It was dwarfed in size by numerous bombardments which had taken place in Russia since the German invasion in June 1941. It was nevertheless devastating – a tribute to its accuracy and the skill of the Royal Artillery.

4   Warner, op. cit., pp. 101–2.
5   Lucas, op. cit., pp. 120 and 143.
6   Patrick Delaforce, *Monty's Highlanders*, Tom Donovan Publishing, 1997, pp. 26–7.
7   Horrocks, op. cit., p. 137. For a detailed account of the first night see Carver, *El Alamein*, pp. 100–121.
8   See French, op. cit., pp. 255–258.
9   Irving, *The Trail of the Fox*, p. 199.
10 French, op. cit., p. 253, and Montgomery, *Memoirs*, pp. 137–8.
11 Hamilton, op. cit., p. 780.
12 De Guingand, op. cit., p. 200.
13 Irving op. cit., p. 200.
14 Captain Dino Campini of 4th Bersaglieri Tank Battalion, as quoted in Caccia-Dominioni, op. cit., p. 215.

15 Hamilton, *Monty – Master of the Battlefield*, p. 46.
16 Mr J. E. Delhanty, quoted in Warner, op. cit., p. 77.
17 Caccia-Dominioni, op. cit., p. 219.
18 Rommel signal Nr.124/42 g.Kdos.Chefs., IWM Dept. of Docs., EDS AL 1041/5. Author's translation.
19 IWM Dept. of Docs., EDS AL 2596, 27.10.42.
20 Accounts of the action from 24–28 can be found in Carver, *El Alamein*, pp. 122–146 and Hamilton, pp. 789–818. Further details on the German side have been derived from the unpublished account written by Nehring in 1949, *Feldzug in Nord-Afrika, Teil V*, IWM Dept. of Documents AL 766/3/2 and the *Schlachtbericht der Deutsch-Italienischen Panzerarmee* written by Oberleutnant Schmitz in 1943, IWM AL 743/1/1.
21 IWM Dept. of Docs., EDS AL 2596, 28.10.42.
22 Churchill, *The Hinge of Fate*, p. 462.
23 Bryant, op. cit., pp. 512–3.
24 Churchill, *The Hinge of Fate*, p. 463.
25 Bryant, op. cit., pp. 513–4.
26 See de Guingand, op. cit., pp. 206–7. Who precisely persuaded him is a matter of some dispute. See Hamilton, op. cit., pp. 827–30. According to Montgomery, needless to say, nobody did. He changed his plan 'at once' – at 11:00 am. See *Memoirs*, p. 132.
27 Gilbert, op. cit., p. 245.
28 Montgomery, *Memoirs*, pp. 133 and 135.
29 IWM Dept. of Docs., EDS AL 2596, 2.11.42.
30 See Irving, *The Trail of the Fox*, pp. 210–3 and *Hitler's War*, pp. 494–6.
31 Bryant, op. cit., p. 516.
32 IWM Dept. of Docs., EDS AL 2596, 3.11.42.
33 In his unpublished account, Nehring expresses amazement that the British attacks were not more vigorous,

claiming that the enemy made disengagement easy and did not follow through ('Der Feind folgt nicht', underlined in the original) (op. cit., p. 328). The reason was the past experience of the British tank commanders and the present confusion on the battlefield. Lumsden, not Montgomery, was the one unwilling to take risks at this stage.

34 Delaforce, op. cit., p. 57.

35 See Kesselring, *Memoirs*, pp. 135–6, Macksey, op. cit., pp. 130–1, Irving *The Trail of the Fox*, pp. 214–5. The idea that Hitler sent an order which brought disaster upon the Afrika Korps has had a long history in accounts of the battle. It is particularly popular in Germany, as it serves as a specious means of explaining defeat. Given the Wehrmacht's tradition of mission-based command, the notion that two German field marshals on the spot should be unable to take decisions for themselves is absurd. Rommel's reaction suggests that he was very much in awe of Hitler, but in any case he only passed on a 'stand-fast' order to the DAK which was supposed to do so anyway in its role as a rearguard. Kesselring was probably right that the message was not an order at all, and his own calm, sensible reaction attracted no retribution from Hitler.

36 Hamilton, op. cit., p. 846.

Chapter IX: Perspectives

1 Clausewitz, *On War*, translated by Colonel Graham 1908, ed. Rapoport, Penguin, 1982, pp. 164–5. In the original text, Clausewitz uses the term 'Friktion' rather than the German word 'Reibung'.

2 Caccia-Dominioni, op. cit., p. 243.

3 Nigel Hamilton, *Monty – Master of the Battlefield 1942–44*, Hamish Hamilton, 1983, pp. 30 and 56.

4 Pitt, *The Crucible of War 3*, p. 71.

5 Montgomery, *Memoirs*, p. 111.

6 Hamilton, *Monty – Master of the Battlefield*, p. 80.

7 Hamilton, *Monty – Master of the Battlefield*, pp. 3–4.

8 Notably Montgomery in *El Alamein to the River Sangro* p. 25. Carver dismisses the rain as an excuse (*El Alamein*, pp. 186–7).

9 Hamilton, *Monty – Master of the Battlefield*, pp. 41–2.

10 See *Memoirs*, p. 142.

11 Montgomery's pursuit of Rommel is described by Carver in *El Alamein*, pp. 171–8 and Hamilton *Monty – Master of the Battlefield*, pp. 11–44, criticized by Liddell Hart in his *History of the Second World War*, pp. 305–9, and lambasted by Barnett, op. cit., pp. 288–299.

12 Douglas, *The Letters*, p. 252.

13 Douglas, *Alamein to Zem Zem*, p. 69.

14 See Irving, *Hitler's War*, pp. 497–500.

15 Nehring, op. cit., pp. 345–7.

16 Pitt, op. cit., pp. 233 and 250.

17 Barnett (op. cit., p. 292) predictably concludes that Montgomery was far slower: eleven days versus nine by his reckoning. It all depends when one takes the race referees to have fired their starting guns and blown their final whistles. However one counts it, there was not a lot of difference.

18 John Erickson, *The Road to Stalingrad*, Weidenfeld and Nicolson, 1975, p. 462.

19 Irving, *Hitler's War*, pp. 509–10.

20 IWM Dept. of Docs., EDS AL 2596, 8.12.42.

21 Montgomery had originally wanted 1st Army to take it, attacking from Tunisia which was less far away. See Hamilton, *Monty – Master of the Battlefield*, pp. 64–74.

22 These two estimates are reported by Hamilton in *Monty – Master of the Battlefield*, pp. 39n and 63n.

23 IWM Dept of Docs., AL 1582.

24 For estimates of Axis losses see Carver,

El Alamein, p. 179 and Playfair, op. cit., p. 79.

25 Terraine, op. cit., p. 385.

26 Calculated from loss tables in Ring and Girbig, *Jagdgeschwader 27*.

27 John Weal, *Junkers Ju 87 – Stukageschwader of North Africa and the Mediterranean*, Osprey, 1998, p. 65.

28 Figures given by Playfair, op. cit., p. 78.

29 Alexander, op. cit., p. 28 and Churchill, *The Hinge of Fate*, p. 468.

30 *War History of the 7ᵗʰ Bn. The Black Watch*, Markinch, 1948, Appendix IV, p. 145.

31 War diary of 7ᵗʰ Battalion, The Black Watch, PRO, WO 169/4991.

32 This applied quite generally, not just in the desert, where the campaigns were in fact less intense than in Europe. See John Ellis, *The Sharp End*, Pimlico, 1993, pp. 156–169.

33 Churchill, *The End of the Beginning*, War Speeches compiled by Charles Eade, Cassell, 1943, pp. 213–4.

34 Churchill, *The Hinge of Fate*, p. 468.

35 Hamilton, *Monty – Master of the Battlefield*, p. 51.

36 Anthony Beevor discusses the various estimates of German losses in *Stalingrad*, Penguin, 1998, pp. 439–40.

37 John Erickson, *The Road to Berlin*, Weidenfeld and Nicolson, 1983, p. 63.

38 James J. Sadkovitch, 'Understanding Defeat: Reappraising Italy's Role in World War II', in Journal of Contemporary History, Vol. 24 (1989), p. 35. Italian losses in Africa were also eclipsed by the 50,000 she suffered in the Balkans campaigns of 1940–41 and the subsequent partisan war, and the 75,000 suffered in Italy itself. In all, only about 10% of the 225,000 Italian servicemen killed in the war died in Africa.

39 See Lothar Gruchmann, 'Die "verpaßten strategischen Chancen" der Achsenmächte im Mittelmeerraum 1940/41' in *Vierteljahrshefte für Zeitgeschichte*, 1970, pp. 456–75, and Reuth, op. cit., pp. 26, 50–53, 67–70 and 145.

40 Van Creveld, *Supplying War*, p. 201. For a defence of Rommel see Fraser, *Knight's Cross*, pp. 237–9 and 415 ff.

41 Young, op. cit., p. 260.

42 Kesselring, 'Final Commentaries on the Campaign in North Africa 1941– 43', 1949, IWM Dept. of Docs. AL 1077, p. 7.

43 IWM Dept. of Docs., AL 2596.

44 After the capture of North Africa, neither Montgomery nor his staff were in favour of invading Sicily let alone Italy, as they saw no point in it. They thought that the threat of invasion was sufficient to tie down German troops there and that the main thrust should be made across the Channel in 1943. See Hamilton, *Monty – Master of the Battlefield*, p. 257. In the event, they did as they were told. The controversial case for a cross-Channel invasion in 1943, the subject of heated debate at the time, has been ably made by John Grigg in *1943 – The Victory That Never Was*, Penguin, 1999.

45 Kippenberger, op. cit., pp. 173–4.

46 Hamilton, *Monty – Master of the Battlefield*, p. 69. Lumsden was knighted and sent to the Far East in 1944, where he was killed in a kamikaze attack in 1945.

47 Hamilton, op. cit., p. 606.

48 Behrendt, op. cit., p. 64.

49 Cf. Hamilton, op. cit., pp. 748 and 752–3.

50 Horrocks, op. cit., p. 138.

51 Hamilton, op. cit., p. 753.

52 S.C. Kirkman, 'RA Notes on the Offensive by Eighth Army from 23 October – 4 November on the El Alamein Position', 24 November 1942, PRO WO 201/431.

53 Something analogous happened in September 1944 when Montgomery's plan for 'Market Garden' required Horrocks' XXX Corps to advance up a single road in order to relieve the

paratroopers dropped at three bridges ahead of them. They took too long, and the final bridge at Arnhem proved to be a bridge too far.

54 See Timothy Harrison Place, *Military Training in the British Army 1940–1944*, Frank Cass, 2000, pp. 147–152 and 159–167.

Chapter X: Reputations

1 See Adrian Gilbert, *The Imperial War Museum Book of the Desert War*, BCA, 1992, pp. 184–9.

2 Hamilton, *Monty – Master of the Battlefield*, p. 339.

3 See Hamilton, *Monty – Master of the Battlefield*, p. 479. One of Montgomery's biggest *faux pas* was the press conference he gave in early 1945 after the Battle of the Ardennes. In a long address designed to counter criticisms of Eisenhower and emphasize Allied solidarity, he at one point referred to the battle, in which the US Army initially suffered a severe reverse and had 80,000 casualties, as one of the most interesting he had fought. The media, of course, ignored his message and sent the sound-bite around the world, causing a temporary rift in Anglo-American relations. See Montgomery, *Memoirs*, pp. 314–5.

4 Hamilton, *Monty – Master of the Battlefield*, pp. 172–3 and Churchill, *The Hinge of Fate*, pp. 573–4.

5 See Anthony Aldgate, 'Creative Tensions: Desert Victory, the Army Film Unit and Anglo-American Rivalry 1943–45' in *Britain and the Cinema in the Second World War*, ed. Philip M. Taylor, Macmillan, 1988, pp. 144–167.

6 Phillip Knightley, *The First Casualty*, Pan, 1989, pp. 304–5.

7 Moorehead, op. cit., pp. 59–60 and 229–30.

8 Moorehead, op. cit., p. 578.

9 Figures derived from Playfair, op. cit., p. 460.

10 PRO WO32/21668.

11 See Hamilton, *Monty – Master of the Battlefield*, pp. 93–4 and 174.

12 Horrocks, op. cit., p. 145.

13 Hamilton, *Monty – Master of the Battlefield*, p. 280.

14 Hamilton, *Monty – Master of the Battlefield*, pp. 173 and 232–3.

15 Hamilton, *Monty – Master of the Battlefield*, pp. 447–8 and 470–1.

16 Hamilton, *Monty – Master of the Battlefield*, p. 476.

17 Hamilton, *Monty – Master of the Battlefield*, p. 213.

18 Hamilton, *Monty – Master of the Battlefield*, pp. 337 and 602.

19 Hamilton, *Monty – Master of the Battlefield*, pp. 469–70.

20 Hamilton, *Monty – Master of the Battlefield*, pp. 210–211.

21 Hamilton, *Monty – Master of the Battlefield*, pp. 265.

22 Hamilton, *Monty – The FieldMarshal 1944-76*, Hamish Hamilton, 1986, p. 798.

23 John Connell, *Auchinleck*, Cassell, 1959, p. 716.

24 The reactions are detailed by Nigel Hamilton in the third volume of his magisterial biography, *Monty – The Field Marshal 1944–1976*, pp. 883–902.

25 *Memoirs*, pp. 539–41. He ranks Eisenhower alongside his father, Sir Alan Brooke (by then Lord Alanbrooke) and Churchill as the four greatest influences in his life, calling him 'a very great human being', and observing that he always found him inspiring. Montgomery expresses his devotion to him and poignantly adds that 'it is a tremendous honour to have his friendship', which he lost for good as a result of the very publication in which these words appear.

26 Connell, op. cit., p. 660.

27 Ibid., p. 703.

28 Michael Carver, *Dilemmas of the*

Desert War, Batsford, 1986, pp. 10–11.

29 Connell's biography was followed by
    Roger Parkinson's *The Auk –
    Auchinleck, Victor at Alamein*,
    Granada, 1977 and Philip Warner's
    Auchinleck – The Lonely Soldier,
    Buchan and Enright, 1981, reprinted
    by Cassell in 2001.

30 E.g. Warner, op. cit., p. 111.

31 Some of the material is reproduced by
    Warner, op. cit., esp. pp. 237–245.

32 Gilbert, op. cit., p. 166.

33 Montgomery was persuaded to invite
    Barnett to his home, where they had
    some good-natured conversation but
    hardly discussed the book. See
    Hamilton, *Monty – The Field Marshal
    1944–1976*, pp. 925–6.

34 R. W. Thompson, *The Montgomery
    Legend*, Allen and Unwin, 1967.

35 Hamilton, *Monty – Master of the
    Battlefield*, p. 225.

36 Hamilton, ibid., p. 606.

37 In September 2001, Montgomery's
    official biographer Nigel Hamilton
    published the first of two volumes
    constituting a new 'unofficial'
    biography which he entitled *The Full
    Monty* (Penguin, 2001). In it, he
    argues that the key to Montgomery's
    success as a leader was his repressed
    homosexuality which resulted in a
    mind-set and behaviour Hamilton
    describes as 'homosocial'. It enabled
    Montgomery to form a powerful bond
    with the young men he led and
    explains why he fought battles as he
    did, being careful to avoid
    unnecessary casualties. There are two
    fundamental problems with this.
    Firstly, it implies that all effective
    leaders of men must be 'homosocial',
    which, if Hamilton's neologism means
    anything beyond 'able to form bonds
    with other men', is clearly untrue. In
    the British Army in World War II, Bill
    Slim provides an example of an
    outstanding leader who inspired
    universal devotion amongst the men

of the Fourteenth Army, but was
clearly heterosexual. Turning to
Montgomery's opponent, Rommel
once wrote that he was never happier
than in the company of young men
(see Irving, *Trail of the Fox*, caption
opposite p. 83). Perhaps that makes
him 'homosocial'. There is no
evidence that he was homosexual,
repressed or otherwise. Indeed, it has
recently come to light that he had a
passionate secret love affair before the
World War I and fathered an
illegitimate daughter (as revealed in
October Films' *The Real Rommel*
screened by Channel 4 in August
2001). Almost all men, great leaders or
not, have the capacity to develop close
bonds with other men. Men without
close male friends are unusual and
generally regarded as to some extent
socially dysfunctional. Oddly enough
in the light of Hamilton's thesis,
Montgomery was one of those few.
Secondly, a repressed love of young
men does not explain Montgomery's
concern to preserve their lives. Day to
day experience suggests that it is not
necessary to feel sexually attracted to
someone in order to be repelled by the
idea of their death. Human beings –
even males – do in fact quite often
care for each other and seek to
preserve each other from harm even if
they are not sexually attracted.
Montgomery's anxiety to avoid the
waste in human lives he witnessed
during World War I was widely shared
amongst his generation of officers, not
all of whom could have been
'homosocial', or at least not
homosexual. Furthermore, any
general placed in Montgomery's
position would have been forced to
avoid casualties by the double need to
preserve his troops' morale and to
fight the war to the end in the face of a
growing manpower shortage in the
UK. By 1944, even the most

bloodthirsty of heterosexual generals would have been forced to spare his men because, even without political pressure, he would otherwise have risked running out of replacements. See the article by Stephen Hart, 'Montgomery, Morale, Casualty Conservation and "Colossal Cracks": 21st Army Group's Operational Technique in North-West Europe, 1944–45' in *Military Power*, ed. Brian Holden Reid, Frank Cass, 1997, pp. 132–153.

38 See Irving, *The Trail of the Fox*, pp. 26–37.

39 IWM Dept. of Docs., EDS, AL 2596, 17.5.42.

40 I am grateful to the film archive specialist James Barker for pointing this out.

41 Heinz Werner Schmidt, *With Rommel in the Desert*, Constable, 1997, pp. 72–4.

42 IWM Dept. of Docs., EDS, AL 2596, 23.4.42.

43 Schmidt, op. cit., p. 34.

44 Translated as *Infantry Attacks*, Greenhill Books, 1995.

45 IWM Dept. of Docs., EDS, AL 2596, 23.6.42.

46 IWM Dept of Docs., EDS AL 1349/11.

47 Schmidt, op. cit., pp. 44, 54, 85 and 197.

48 Irving, op. cit., pp. 137–8 and Piekalkiewicz, op. cit., p. 111.

49 Kesselring, op. cit., p. 141.

50 Schmidt, op. cit., p. 197.

51 Warner, op. cit., p. 239.

52 Ibid., pp. 88–90.

53 Churchill, *The Hinge of Fate*, p. 53.

54 Young, op. cit., p. 10.

55 Caccia-Dominioni, op. cit., p. 262.

56 Montgomery, *Memoirs*, p. 542.

57 Hamilton, *Monty – The Field Marshal 1944–1976*, pp. 941–2.

Index